FLOWER WISDOM

FLOWER WISDOM

THE DEFINITIVE GUIDEBOOK TO THE
MYTH, FOLKLORE AND HEALING POWER OF FLOWERS

Katherine Kear

Thorsons

While the author of this work has made every effort to ensure that the information contained in this book is as accurate and up to date as possible at the time of publication, medical and pharmaceutical knowledge is constantly changing and the application of it to particular circumstances depends on many factors. Therefore it is recommended that readers always consult a qualified medical specialist for individual advice. This book should not be used as an alternative to seeking specialist medical advice, which should be sought before any action is taken. The author and publishers cannot be held responsible for any errors and omissions that may be found in the text, or any actions that may be taken by a reader as a result of any reliance on the information contained in the text, which is taken entirely at the reader's own risk.

All references to flowers and healing in this book are general. Some cures are ancient, some yet to be substantiated. No action should be taken on any cures mentioned in this book. Qualified advice should, as with all healing, be sought.

In the Botanical sections, only a few species of each genus have been listed. Care has been taken to include popular, well-known, historic and folklore-important species. Lesser-known species have been, for the purposes of this book, omitted.

Thorsons
An Imprint of HarperCollins*Publishers*
77–85 Fulham Palace Road,
Hammersmith, London W6 8JB
The Thorsons website address is: www.thorsons.com

Published by Thorsons 2000

10 9 8 7 6 5 4 3 2 1

A catalogue record for this book
is available from the British Library

ISBN 0 7225 3996 7

Illustrations by John Spencer

Printed and bound in Great Britain by
Woolnough Bookbinding Ltd, Irthlingborough, Northamptonshire

This book is dedicated to my daughter
Claire Katherine Morgan Kear, whose
presence makes this world a beautiful garden.
And in memory of my father, Trevor George Barry Morgan.

Away before me to sweet beds of flowers.
WILLIAM SHAKESPEARE, *TWELFTH NIGHT* I.i.40

LIST OF CONTENTS

TO A LOVER OF FLOWERS

Still, gentle lady, cherish flowers —
True fairy friends are they,
On whom, of all thy cloudless hours,
Not one is thrown away;
By them, unlike man's ruder race,
No care conferr'd is spurned,
But all thy fond and fostering grace
A thousand fold return'd.
The rose repays thee all thy smiles —
The stainless lily rears
Dew in the chalice of its wiles,
As sparkling as thy tears.
The glances of thy gladden'd eyes
Not thanklessly are pour'd;
In the blue violet's tender dyes
Behold them all restored.
Yon bright carnation — once thy cheek
Bent o'er it in the bud;
And back it gives thy blushes meek
In one rejoicing flood!
That balm has treasured all thy sighs,
That snowdrop touch'd thy brow,
Thus not a charm of thine shall die,
Thy painted people vow.

ANON

PREFACE

It is sometimes very difficult to reason why a compulsion becomes a reality. Are compulsions fuelled by passions and choices, or are they subconscious actions that are part of a very deep and ancient event or way of life? *Flower Wisdom* comes from the latter: I think my genetic makeup contains too much linkage with the earth, history and a passion for flowers to deny it.

As a very young child I had two imaginary friends who lived in the hedge of a semi-wild area at the top of our garden. Hours were spent living in this wilderness with them — maybe I was responding to primitive needs to be at one with the earth and her fruits (incidentally, these 'friends' are still very present today as then!).

Many of my forebears have worked the land. I had a great-great-great-uncle who was a gardener at Windsor Castle, and a great-aunt who had a greenhouse that I thought was paradise. If I close my eyes now I can smell the atmosphere and sense the closeness of ferns, strelitzia, streptocarpus and jasmine. If only those days would stay. Sometimes doors are open long enough for us to glimpse back at what was; the secret is to be able to reopen the doors when we need a little security and reminder of our roots.

Our ancestors knew a life that consisted of trees, trees and yet more trees, separated at random intervals, as the geography of the land permitted, with meadows and grassland. Flowery meads were spotted with fragrant blooms. Maybe this fragrant area was similar to the flowery meads of medieval illustrations. The beauty of these floral visions was unsurpassed; their perfumes enlightened, uplifted, soothed and enchanted emotions. Their colours had very positive effects on behaviour; their position was revered and respected.

Today, flowers are viewed as a luxury, commercially expensive and bright, purchased on the whole for specific events. In Europe there is a slightly more positive relationship with flowers and they appear more often in homes. Occasionally a child may act spontaneously, picking a flower for his or her mother — again maybe responding to some deep-seated habit or need. I have often myself tucked a bloom in my hair, worn it with great pleasure, never knowing quite why! I'm not saying we have been here before in different guises; I think that is a subject for personal speculation. However, we are all composites of knowledge, habit and in-built intuitions from day one of creation and life as we know it, just as our actions are outcomes of a series of thoughts and messages.

There exists an ancient belief that the forests and woods of this earth are its ears, the fields its eyes. In ancient lore, it is said that a person can only feel at peace within nature if one has inner peace oneself. And how right that is today, so many centuries on. How many of us carry in our conscious secrets we refuse to unravel, and fears and emotions we fail to confront? How many of us miss the beauty and simplicity of the earth because we are too bound up with outward paraphernalia or too engrossed in our own internal baggage? Do we truly know ourselves, or do we fear what we may find? Nature never is.

I am fascinated by the beliefs and customs of life. There is an ancient area of life, saturated in traditions and ancient belief, where trees and plants have souls that work for and with us for our and the earth's benefit. How precious are our plants and trees — we have a paradise that we must look to for our salvation. She (the earth) cannot continue to support us if we fail to understand the role of plants and trees in our lives.

This use of, and affinity to plants and trees is seen in so many aspects of history, folklore and medicine. I try to instil these lores in people's lives as I work. I am inspired by a great creator, who does not fit into any man-made denomination but is an ever-present god of fields, forest, flower and folk.

There are today tribal groups on the earth who believe that to disturb the natural world is to provoke catastrophe. Is this when I say, 'I rest my case'?

How often do we view flowers and plants as time-keepers, watchful guardians of power, intrigue, mystery, healing and life? In our own misplaced ideals of human self-importance, we forget that beneath our feet lies a vital life-force that has healed, clothed, covered, protected and watched over us since time began for us, and – here comes the sobering fact – it will continue to do so long after all the calendar pages ever made have gone.

Neil Ewart wrote in his *Lore of Flowers*, 'Almost all the flowers are surrounded as if by a halo of meaning from association of the past.'

Plants are symbols of inner strength, power and growth. This symbolism is evident in the seasonal cycle of the power a root uses to survive the winter and to burst forth in the spring, rather like our own lives – or, to put it correctly, we echo nature, as we all have our own seasons. I sometimes feel mankind has an exaggerated sense of its own importance. Many of us have lost sight of our priorities, attaching too much importance to superficial images, false facades and the window dressing of life. I'd rather see a few more poppies growing by the wayside and an apple with a less than perfect shape, than nature constricted and manipulated to our plans and perfections.

That is not to say we cannot go on using the plants and trees to our delight, but we must keep our feet on the ground and not lose grip of the life-force within them. We are the guardians of nature, not its owners. Several tribal and religious cultures refuse to eat meat because they believe that animals have spirits which should not be unnaturally butchered. The Celts believed that each aspect of nature had a spirit – individual trees and plants had them, as did the seas, sky and earth. The precious plants and trees that surround us are lives and beauties to be admired and revered. Whatever our beliefs, we must understand the power of the plants and trees. Let us start to concentrate on the blooms and leaves for their own individuality, learn their history and acknowledge their importance. Let's not outshine them and become too lost in our manipulation of them. In short, let's get our priorities straight.

Plants (I include anything from a moss to the largest blooms imaginable) are inextricably linked with the science, religion and economics of the world, either by grace that they are used to further experiments and heal, provide symbols for worship and religious ritual, or used as trading commodities and status symbols. Flowers can be worn to indicate political allegiance, passions, sympathies and social class, but rarely are they acknowledged as very discreet yet immensely powerful guardians of and contributors to our well-being and safety. Flowers are more than colourings in the landscape; they are living, working and breathing powerhouses. They have individuality. To quote Gerard de Nerval, 'Each flower is a soul blossoming out to nature.'

FLORA SYMBOLICA

At the dawning of the age of mankind, the first humans saw a seed fall. It germinated, blossomed and fruit formed, which people tried and liked. The plant died back into the ground, or maybe it continued its cycle. To the first humans this process was beyond their reason. It had a mystical and supernatural power, therefore it must be sacred.

From that time to this, the life and surroundings of mankind have become more diverse, yet flowers and plants have remained constant, flowers are recognized the world over and acknowledged as things of beauty. In fact, I don't think any other form of life has been so universally accepted and carried through the ages as a symbol of beauty. As the American scientist Oliver Wendell Holmes (1809–94) said, 'The Amen of nature is always a flower.'

If we take the word 'Amen' to mean 'so be it,' then a flower is the final full stop at the end of creation. Is there anything more beautiful than a deep red rose with a pearl of dew on its petals? No one can ever improve on the beauty of a flower, no matter how priceless the container the plucked blossom is put in.

To understand the 'Flora Symbolica' it is necessary to look at the use and love of flowers by individual civilizations over the centuries.

THE PHARAOHS' FLOWERS

The Egyptian dynasties were one of the most enduring early civilizations, dating back to at least 3000 BC and flourishing up to about 332 BC.

Their religious beliefs were mainly those of an agricultural people, with fertility gods. They also believed in resurrection and eternal life. They adopted a philosophy of *Maat* (truth), and their unchanging order of life was expressed in their art and religious customs, which featured many flowers. The stylized form of the lotus/water lily, the flower of the goddess Isis, is seen time after time. This sacred flower appeared in tomb paintings, was carried in religious procession, and worn on the head or chest as a tribute. Mallow, poppies and saffron were often used in mortuary garlands, draped on mummies in preparation for the next life. Each part of the individual flower, including the seed head and leaf, were seen as part of the life and symbolism of the culture.

GRECO-ROMAN TIMES

Later on, during the Greek and Roman eras, plant material was used, on the whole, to honour gods and heroes or to create atmosphere. In fact, the Romans first introduced gardening ideas to Britain. The Roman invasion of the British isles brought with it fragrant herbs, many vegetables, flowers, trees and gardening trends.

The Greeks and Romans employed professional garland makers. Glycera was one of the most noted; she was famous throughout Greece for her wreaths and garlands. These professional garland makers were the forerunners of today's florists; their work was worn by athletes, poets, civic leaders, soldiers and sailors. Garlands were worn at weddings and also given at the birth of a son to hang upon the door. The custom of hanging a wreath on the door at the birth of a son is evident today in our tradition of the Christmas wreath.

The composition of these Greco-Roman ceremonial wreaths was varied, and they were hung around the necks, shoulders and chests of statues and humans alike. The following list shows the diversity of plant material and the varied names these wreaths went by:

FOR HONOUR:	*Corona civica* Leaves and acorns of the oak (*Quercus* sp.)
FOR GODS AND DEITIES:	*Corona radiata* A crown-like wreath
FOR A BIRTH:	*Corona natalitia* Ivy (*Hedera* sp.), Bay tree laurel (*Laurus* sp.) or Parsley (*Petroselinum crispum*)
FOR DIONYSUS/BACCHUS:	*Corymbus* A wreath of ivy berries, leaves and fruit
FOR DECORATION IN ART:	*Encarpa* A construction of fruit and flowers
FOR FESTIVALS, TEMPLES, RELIGIOUS EVENTS AND HOMES:	*Serta* A flower garland of mixed blooms

The Greeks loved strewn flowers, and it is said that the Roman Emperor Nero had a revolving ceiling to distribute petals onto the heads of his guests. The Greeks used flowers as offerings to gods to ask for favour and blessing. Roses were used to stuff mattresses.

As Rome declined, the art of flowers was eclipsed by the coming of the Dark Ages, a pause before the artists and writers of medieval Europe and the Renaissance began to record more floral customs. During this time plants were often secluded behind monastery walls, and gardens flourished in private. Feudal lords seeking battle did not need pretty gardens but drill grounds, and so the flower garden ceased to flourish in public spaces. Art of any kind tended to belong to the church or wealthy patrons.

FROM THE RENAISSANCE TO THE VICTORIAN ERA

In the 15th century, painters linked everyday life with Christian symbolism. Flowers were introduced in art to represent abstract ideas of love, purity and humility. Much of the association of flowers with religion came from a need to use pure, everyday images to symbolize a religion that had a visionary icon. 'Common' man could not read or write his vernacular language, let alone church Latin, but he understood and loved flowers and could therefore understand a painting by looking at the floral symbolism, or understand the different seasons of the church calendar – Advent, Lent, etc. – by noting what blooms were in bowls within the church.

Flowers that had associations for the gods of the ancients were adapted for use in Christianity. Many Christian martyrs and saints have their own floral symbols: Dorothea (a basket of fruit and flowers), Cecilia (a crown of roses), Dorothy (roses) and many more besides are portrayed in Christian art with flowers.

At the start of the Renaissance, flowers were used to pay homage to God; at its close they were used more for secular decoration. Children would wear garlands of miniature blooms on their heads to signify youthfulness and friendship. In England under the Tudors, floral religious symbolism was less common; flowers were used more for political symbolism: the iris was shown with the white rose of York and the red rose of Lancaster to symbolize the majesty of the Virgin Queen. The portraits of notable Tudors depicted them holding flowers: Elizabeth of York held a white rose and Lady Jane Grey a carnation. The Tudors tended to use flowers to ward off disease, and herbs as a protection against plague.

The Dutch Flemish era in art (17th century) saw a change in the emphasis of floral symbolism, as the middle classes were now becoming patrons and collectors of art. The Reformation made its mark and wonderful 'Flower Piece' paintings evolved. This was an age of scientific interest and discovery, and there was very little sympathy with floral symbolism.

By the reign of Queen Victoria, horizons had broadened. All 'well-to-do' ladies were familiar with the language of flowers and the construction of nosegays and posies. There was a sentimental interest in flowers as well as an aesthetic one. In Victorian floral symbolism all flowers had meaning. Bouquets were put together to convey messages which could be interpreted by published manuals. Love, sympathy and bereavement were all experienced in this manner.

The symbolism of the Victorian language of flowers originated in the early 1700s via a woman called Lady Mary Wortley Montague, who accompanied her husband to Istanbul where he was ambassador to the Turkish Sultan's court. Fascinated by the ideas of a language of flowers that she discovered there, she brought the idea back to England and created a book offering a code of over 800 floral meanings for men and women. Then in 1847, Thomas Miller wrote *The Poetical Life of Flowers*. This 'language of flowers' had to be used with great care – a message could be reversed by placing the flower upside down, and the material used to bind a bunch of flowers could denote a negative meaning.

William Morris, famous proponent of the Arts and Crafts Movement in 19th-century England, wrote, 'The heart of man needed to belong to nature.' Morris' floral designs brought nature to the hearts even of those trapped in the large and harsh factories which employed many men, women and children at this time, where sweet-smelling flowers and green fields were a long way away.

The European language of flowers differed slightly from that of the Americas – hardly surprising, as any culture adopted by that of another country 'loses something in translation'. In America the Puritan settlers imposed their own meanings on the language of flowers. The blooms were used to promote moral standing and decency rather than the intricacies of courtship, love and clandestine affairs. In some regions, particularly in Canada, groups met informally for 'floral chats', where posies were constructed as an aid to conversation.

The American language of flowers was influenced by the floral traditions of Europe, the Far East and, of course, the Native American peoples. Books translated for use in the Americas brought their own diversities to the mix, as inaccuracies would sometimes occur yet be retained. New traditions and lore evolved. Many early flower manuals, written primarily by women (Mrs E Washington Wirt's *Floras Dictionary* being one example), helped this lore flourish in the new world. In a land as open to immigrants as America, it was inevitable that a multi-cultural and unique language of flowers would emerge.

THE FAR EAST

Chinese Buddhism prohibited the taking of life, including plants and flowers, so in this culture cut flowers were used sparingly. In Chinese folklore all flowers were feminine and were given women's names, and each season had its own distinguishing flower. For spring this was the peony, for summer the lotus, for autumn the chrysanthemum and for winter blossoms. Fungus was viewed as a plant of long life; another plant viewed with great reverence was the tree peony. Considered to be symbolic of the king of flowers, it indicated a high position of wealth and fortune. For the Chinese, the narcissus had an association with the New Year, and was forced to bloom to bring success, good luck and fortune for the year ahead. The orchid was symbolic of love, beauty and fertility. The botanic make-up of the flower matched the reproductive organs in the female body, and thus the symbolism was formed.

In India, lotus flowers floating in bowls of water were offered to Buddha. The lotus symbolized the universe, the bowl held the water of life.

In Japan, symbolism played an important part in flower arranging, which was steeped in tradition. There were three main lines of Japanese design: Ten, Chi and Jin. These three lines indicated heaven, earth and man. The onlooker took the position of the sun looking down on these three. In Japanese folklore all small flower buds and grasses were female, the trees and more open flowers were male.

A ROSE BY ANY OTHER NAME?

It is important to remember that the flowers were here long before we were. We have imposed our own symbolism on them over the years. Similarly, we have given them names. The Latin names for flowers and plants were first drawn up by Linnaeus in 1735, as a system for categorizing plant material. This official method of naming flowers by no means detracted from the colourful vernacular names. As an example, the poisonous toadstool's official name (*Boletus satanus*) still gives us some idea of its deadly properties, and the saffron milk-cup bears the Latin name *Lactarius delicious*. The Victorians were great ones for propriety, and changed 'vulgar' names to more polite alternatives. Any name containing 'Jack' was changed, as this name was considered too close to 'jakes' (or 'jaques'), an Elizabethan water closet. But changing a plant's name often meant losing the symbolism with which it had once been associated, and makes tracing original plants difficult. When Shakespeare refers to 'the flower long purples', we cannot be sure to what he is referring: is it lords and ladies, a purple orchid, purple loostrife or something else entirely?

Perhaps without even realizing it, today we use the symbolism of flowers for personal adornment, as did our forefathers. The traditional buttonhole has its origin in 'ladies' favours': white for nightwear, red for daywear. And, of course, we wear Remembrance Day Poppies.

The 'flora symbolica' can perhaps be best summed up in a piece written in the early 1870s:

Lastly, love your flowers. By some subtle sense the dear things always detect their friends, and for them they will live longer and bloom more freely than they ever will for a stranger. And I tell you girls, the sympathy of a flower is worth winning, as you will find out when you grow older, and realize that there are such things as dull days which need cheering and comforting.

This quote serves to remind us that the language of flowers is the language of life.

Teach thee their language? Sweet, I know no tongue,
No mystic art those gentle things declare;
I ne'er could trace the school man's trick among
Created things so delicate and rare.
Their language? Prithee, why, they are themselves
But bright thoughts syllabled to shape and hue
The tongue that erst unspoken by the elves,
When tenderness as yet within the world was new.
And oh! Do not their soft and starry eyes —

Now bent to earth, to heaven now meekly pleading,
Their incense fainting as it seeks the skies
Yet still from earth with freshing hope receding
Say, do not these to every heart declare,
With all the silent eloquence of truth,
The Language that they speak is Nature's prayer
To give her back those spotless days of youth?
Such are the tenets of florigraphists, let us hope that
    such harmless
If not beneficient doctrines are destined for universal
    acceptance and that those
Bright times, foretold by Shelley, are not far distant,
    when,
'Not gold, not blood, the altar doves
But votive blooms and symbol flowers.'

ANON

INTRODUCTION TO THE FLOWERS

To create a little flower is the labour of ages.

WILLIAM BLAKE

To explore each bloom in depth, I have subdivided each chapter into different sections – Botanical, Origins, Plant Lore and History, Health and Well-being, and Observations. It must be pointed out, however, that nature does not always fit neatly into sections – much of the information pertains to several sections, so a little 'botanical' information may slip into the 'origins' section and so on.

Before mankind committed information to paper, the oral tradition was used to impart history, tales of life and famous or impressive events. Much was lost when the oral tradition faded, as poor spelling and mispronunciation led to distortions and alterations of the facts. We are perhaps poorer for the fact that some origins, histories and plant lore are lost – or maybe they are there waiting to be rediscovered!

BOTANICAL

In the section entitled 'Botanical' for each flower, its official classification (including its Latin name) is explored. Quite often the Latin gives a clue to the plant's appearance, origin, use or discoverer. The nomenclature of plants has evolved over many centuries; often a lack of or incorrect information means that a plant's name changes many times over the years.

Each plant is *binomial* – that is, it has two names. It has what could be called a surname (genus) and a first name (species).

The genus names are nouns, and their origins are often obscure. They can come from Greek, Latin or Persian origins.

Often the species name comes from a plant hunter or a botanist, for example *Wilsonii* for Wilson, a plant-hunter who 'discovered' many blooms in China. The species name might also denote the plant's country of origin (*sinensis* – from China), natural habitat (*littoralis* – seashore, *sylvatica* – woodland), colour (*rosea* – red, *aurea* – gold, *cupreus* – copper), perfume (*fragrans* – fragrant) or use (*officinalis* – medical).

ORIGINS

The sections on 'Origins' describes, as far as is possible, where the plant originated on the planet. Some flowers predate history as we know it; glacial waters brought seeds on long journeys to lands thousands of miles from their 'home', where, finding climatic conditions favourable, they set root and thrived.

Our universe carries a very varied plant life and we need this for our existence. We breathe air that has an oxygen level maintained by plants; plants are a food which sustains all forms of animal life. The product of plants' photosynthetic process is the source of all energy. Some plants which do not contain chlorophyll, such as bacteria and fungi, are vital to biological cycles. The diversity of plants is shown when one sees the varied areas of the world in which they have managed to survive – salt and fresh water areas, plains, valleys and forests. Some have adapted to live in high temperatures, others, Antarctica.

Detailed work by palaeobotonists has revealed the origins of many plants introduced to 'foreign' areas by early nomadic tribes to be used in magical rituals, as medicine or as food. Some plants were introduced to areas by natural accident, as seeds can be wind carried and on the fur of imported livestock.

PLANT LORE AND HISTORY

People have long used mythology and folklore to try to explain the unexplainable. Early communities were governed by signs and portents, their rites of passage aided by the gods, who worked through nature – falling leaves, full-bloomed flowers, wind in grasses and patterns on leaves.

The universe will only be in harmony if there is everlasting balance. Legends, myths, fables and superstitions came out of this need to keep balance where love and laughter are prominent, evil is thwarted and pure life is evident.

It is important here to make distinctions between legends, myths and fables.

The word 'legend' comes from the Latin *legee*, to read. Legends were originally narratives of the saints and martyrs, read out at Matins and in monastic refectories. There was exaggeration and a love for 'the wonderful' that predominated these renditions, thus a legend is a traditional story with embellishments.

'Myth', for its part, denotes the expression of a sacred truth. Myths help us find self-awareness and help us to understand our experiences, as superstitions give credence to the unexplainable. A myth creates a unity of experience and is totally sacred and universal, covering creation and life. A culture or civilization may change, but myths are essential to all beliefs and are the main components of culture.

'Fables', are stories told for amusement and have an overriding moral from which a lesson is to be learned.

Some of the tales in the *Mabinogion* – a Welsh saga – have fascinated historians and archaeologists alike. Most importantly to *Flower Wisdom*, the *Mabinogion* tells us the tale of 'Blodeuedd, the fairest woman in the world'. The name means 'born of flowers' or 'flower face' – she was created from the blossoms of oak, broom and meadowsweet by Math and Gwydion as a wife for Llew, whose mother had decreed he should marry no mortal. Blodeuedd betrayed Llew for Goronwy. Together she and Goronwy plotted to kill Llew – no mean feat, as his death could only be achieved if he could be struck with a spear, made over a full year, while he stood with one foot on a goat's back and the other on the edge of a bath tub!

Nevertheless the pair managed to arrange this sequence of events, but Llew did not die, instead escaping into the air as an eagle. Math and Gwydion then avenged him by turning Blodeuedd into a owl, a night bird.

HEALTH AND WELL-BEING

Flowers heal through their essences, and are used in homoeopathy, aromatherapy and herbalism.

Health is dependent on the harmony of body, mind and spirit, not just the absence of illness. Flowers and plants have for centuries been the healer of all ills. Like us, flowers and plants have energies that vibrate. This resonation enables plants to heal us on all levels, spiritual to mental.

The role of healing flowers goes back over 60,000 years, and we are still working to understand their place in our lives. We can read about how flowering plants are called angiosperms, and that the earliest to evolve, 140 million years ago, was similar to a magnolia tree. However, we have to reach a certain level of spirituality to understand their power and place in life, and to acknowledge that a flower essence that can heal the body can also heal the mind.

Asclepius was the god of healing among the Greeks; he is symbolized by a serpent. This serpent symbolized the renewal of energy. It was a creature which possessed the ability to find healing plants as it explored the undergrowth.

The Doctrine of Signatures was a theory used often in health. It was said to have been expounded by Theophrastus Bombastus von Hohenheim in the 1400s. His alchemical name was Paracelsus. It was based on the idea that the Creator had given help to humans seeking cures from plants by marking plants with outward signs – for example, walnuts look like the brain and so were said to be excellent for improving mental skills.

Most plants used by herbalists in antiquity contained chemicals still on today's drug lists. The ancient healers had no theoretical background, but they knew what worked.

OBSERVATIONS

There is always a comment or facet of information that does not sit easily into any particular slot. The 'Observations' on the flowers in this book, therefore, either complement some of the information in earlier sections or they are personal comments and perceptions that I have gained from experience of working with or studying individual blooms.

DAISY

Bellis perennis, the common daisy

BOTANICAL

The little daisy, sometimes referred to outside the British Isles as the English Daisy, has delighted people (and covered their lawns!) for centuries. Unless, that is, you are the type of gardener who insists upon a perfectly green lawn without any other plant being present. The daisy that originated in lawns has, over the centuries, been developed into a slightly more robust plant that can be used at the front of borders.

Latin name *Bellis perennis*, the daisy belongs to the *Compositae* family. The word 'compositae' describes the characteristic flower head of all the flowers in this family, a head made up of many, many smaller flowers tightly pressed together. Other flowers in the Compositae family are Chicory, Knapweed, Ox-eye Daisy and Dandelion. The word *Bellis* is thought to have come from the Latin *bellus*, meaning pretty, although there are those who suggest that the word comes from the Latin 'bello', for war. The word *perennis* indicates the fact the daisy is a perennial plant – that is, it comes back year after year. The Anglo-Saxons were said to have called the wild flower the daisy, originating from the name 'day's eye,' or in Anglo-Saxon, 'Daeges Eage'.

There are also a couple of cultivated daisies growing by the name of *Bellis rotundifolia*, indicating that the leaves have round edges, and *Bellis sylvestris*, an indication that it is a native of wooded areas.

The daisy has been found in pastureland and meadows for many centuries, although – as far as growth is concerned – it falls into the 'ground layer' group of plants (those with rosettes of foliage growing close to the ground). This immediately gives the daisy an advantage, in that its closeness to the ground means that it can be kept safe from reaping and cutting. The fact that the poor flower often loses its head is recorded in one of Robert Burns' poems entitled *To a Mountain Daisy*:

> *Ev'n thou who mourn'st the daisies' fate,*
> *That fate is thine – no distant date;*
> *Stern Ruin's plough share drives elate*
> *Full on thy bloom,*
> *'Till crush'd beneath the furrows' weight*
> *Shall be thine doom.*

The daisy is found growing in several countries of the world, although its native countries are in Europe and Asia Minor. It is a genus of perennials that contains at least seven species. They love both the sun or semi-shade and prefer quite well-drained soil. If they are bought commercially, as often they can be, they need to be tended well by being dead-headed and divided if the clump becomes too large.

The native daisy from which most of the cultivars have originated (a cultivar is an umbrella term used to describe plants that have a complex background of parentage through hybridization, where man has interfered with natural reproduction) grows in a clump with a basal rosette of leaves. It is a plant that flowers prolifically and, quite often, the little flowers can be touched with pink instead of the usual white. Several of the more popular cultivars are 'Pomponette', 'Goliath' and 'White carpet'.

'Pomponette' also has a nickname, 'Bachelors Buttons', and is a good plant for putting in the garden in the spring in rock gardens. Its flowers are double and come in pink, cerise and white.

The natural flowering time for any daisy is between March and October. Sadly, many of the old cultivars have disappeared. A glance through old gardening books shows us such delightful names as 'The Bride' and 'The Bridegroom', 'Alisa', 'Glory of Frankfurt', 'Rubens', 'Crown', 'Rose Conspicua', 'Venus Snowflake' and 'Snowball', most of which were either white or pink, yet none of which is still with us in any great number, though it would be wrong to say that all these varieties have died out. It may be that a couple of the seeds are still contained in packaged mixtures that can be grown and bought today.

There is also a miniature cultivated daisy called 'Dresden China'. It is about the same size as the native daisy, but the flowers are a lighter pink, and are as delicate as the china it is named after.

A cultivated daisy found commonly in many cottage gardens is called 'Rob Roy'. It is much brighter and stronger than its native counterpart.

The very ancient daisy *Bellis perennis* 'Prolifera' was nicknamed the 'Hen and Chicken's daisy' (many blooms with tiny or additional flowers and leaves were given this nickname); the Elizabethans called it 'Childing daisy'. This name was actually in direct response to the way the flower head was composed: double white, but sometimes with flecked pink flowers that had smaller flowers growing from the main flower head, almost like a star. It really is a very ancient plant and prefers to grow in damper, richer soil than the common daisy, and prefers the shade, which is possibly why it is rarely found in lawns.

Gardeners throughout the centuries have sought to provide different varieties of daisies, all of which have originated from the common daisy, *Bellis perennis*. One very distinctive cultivated daisy was a quilled daisy; historical garden books give reference to this daisy as being included in border planting combinations. The plant was named the quilled daisy because the flower heads were small and the petals, often from double heads, were quilled (that is, the petals were fused in tube shapes).

ORIGINS

The daisy must be one of
the most well-known flowers
on earth. That is to say, *Bellis
perennis*, the wild daisy, the
flower used in daisy chains
throughout the centuries. It is
very much a flower associated
with the light and sun – and
like a lot of other flowers with
these associations, daisies were
considered by our forebears as suitable

Bellis perennis, 'Prolifera'
the hen and chicken's daisy

time pieces and weather guards. Linnaeus thought up the idea of a floral
clock, where flowers could actually plot the time throughout the day
depending on when they opened. Unfortunately, the little daisy would
have not taken its place in the floral clock, as it does not open at all on
very overcast cloudy days.

Because of children's love of making daisy chains, the flower is always
linked with children, symbolizing their innocence. There is one very sobering rule to making a daisy chain: it should always, when finished, be joined
at the ends to make a circle. As a circle has no conceivable beginning or end,
the finished daisy chain represents the sun, the earth and the cycle of life.

The flower also has origins in the Celtic world, where it was believed
that daisies were really the spirits of children who died at birth – today
this tale lingers in the superstition about it being unlucky to step on a
daisy or even to uproot the plant.

The association of the flower with children was carried through into
Scotland, where the flower was called 'Bairnwort' (bairn, or course, being
a Gaelic word for children). Along with the Latin generic name *Quercus*
for oak and *Hedera* for ivy, *Bellis* was one of the first names brought into
use by classical writers such as Virgil and Pliny. Centuries later another
famous writer, Chaucer, put pen to paper to praise the English daisy:
'English rhyme or prose/Suffisant this floure to praise I write.'

9

Chaucer also said:

> *And whan that hit [it] is eve, I renne blyve [truly*
> *believe]*
> *As sone [soon] as ever the sonne ginneth weste*
> *To seen this flour, how it wol go to reste,*
> *For fere of night, so hateth she derknesse.*

During the Middle Ages the daisy again finds a link with innocence and simplicity, when it comes to symbolize humility. Again, Chaucer uses it in his legend of 'Good Women', where he says:

> *Of all the flowers in the mead*
> *Then love I most those flowers white and redde,*
> *Such that men call daisies in our town*

The daisy was also a very popular flower in medieval times, where many gardens were divided into small square sections, each of which contained plants of one type set out in a knot pattern. The slow-growing, closely clumped daisy was a popular flower for this sort of knot design. The fashion for knot designs spread all over Europe and to the New World – sadly, however, climatic conditions did not allow the English daisy to thrive in American gardens.

Back in the medieval period, lawns were referred to as 'flowery meads' and were completely different to our idea of a lawn today. Of course there were no man-made pesticides, no mowing machines, so the medieval lawn was less like a carpet and more like a fragrant meadow. These meads were long and full of aromatic flowers, herbs and grasses – in fact they were made to be walked upon, lain upon, sat and danced in. No particular flower dominated, but there was a mixture of all sorts of wild flowers. *Bellis perennis* was a frequent plant in this collection, symbolizing purity and charm.

Nor did the Victorians overlook the beauty of the daisy, and it was at this time that the name 'Daisy' became very popular for girls. A young woman with this name was thought to aspire to modesty as a reflection of the flower's humble growing habitat, quietly tucked away and very unassuming. Many Victorian gardening periodicals praise the daisy as a perennial bedding plant to be used at the front of herbaceous borders, where the best double pink varieties were used in large quantities, while the wild daisy was considered a pest to be removed.

Some of the tales of daisies have their origin in spring traditions, and spring was often personified as a very beautiful woman. In a poem by Winifred Sutcliffe we are given some idea about how the daisy actually originated upon this earth. The poem *Daisies* quotes:

> Spring wore a chaplet in her hair
> Of milky pearls, so frail and fair,
> Young love perused her one March day
> While she, shy maiden, fled away.
> But when at last he held her tight
> And pressed sweet kisses on her brow,
> They broke, those pearls so milky white,
> And scattered on her homeward flight,
> And mortals call them daisies now.

Because the daisy appears just as winter ends and spring begins (early March in the northern hemisphere), it is very much identified as a spring flower – thus one finds the origin of the saying that it is not spring until you can put your foot on 12 daisies (although the number here is open to debate: some people say nine, some seven, and so the debate goes on. It would certainly depend on the size of the treading foot!). There is certainly no debate to the beauty of the daisy and the inspiration that it gives to all. Poets, playwrights and other writers have praised it widely over the centuries. Shakespeare, who was very fond of including in his plays the plants he saw around him says in *Love's Labours Lost* (V.ii.902):

When daisies pied and violets blue/and lady-smocks all silver-white/and cuckoo-buds of yellow hue/do paint the meadows with delight,/the cuckoo then, on every tree,/mocks married men; for thus

11

sings he,/Cuckoo,/cuckoo, cuckoo; Oh, word of fear,/unpleasing to a married ear!'

PLANT LORE AND HISTORY

Most women, whether city-bred or country-dwellers, will have at some point in their lives plucked the petals from a daisy while chanting 'he loves me, he loves me not'. This may make the daisy one of the earliest 'divination flowers'. The tradition of using the daisy to 'foretell' one's true love is mentioned in Goethe's *Faust* of 1808, where Marguerite pulls a daisy to pieces to discover if her true love loves her back. Goethe's choice of the name Marguerite was possibly less random that it may at first appear. *Bellis perennis* was once known as 'Herb Margaret' or 'Marguerite' and, as well as being named after St Margaret of Cortona, was possibly named after the very virtuous St Margaret of Antioch.

It is important to note here that although the daisy is sometimes still referred to as 'Herb Margaret' or 'Marguerite', it should not be confused with other garden flowers which are always referred to as 'Marguerites' and are nothing to do with the daisy family. Nevertheless, 'Daisy' continues to be a nickname for those christened Margaret – an example, perhaps, of how a misinterpretation can take on a life of its own.

Another link with the daisy and the name Margaret comes very much in a lost language with ancient roots, possibly originating in Druidic circles. In a tradition where many stories were oral and where spelling had no continuity, a lot of discrepancies cropped up. The English translation of Marguerite is Margaret, or Peggy (via the nickname 'Meg') for short. In the Persian language, Peggy can sometimes mean 'pearl' or 'child of light'; in England, pearls were once referred to as 'Margarets'. In the poem quoted earlier linking the daisy to a personification of Spring, who wore around her head a circlet (or chaplet, as it is called in the poem) of pearls which fell and became daisies, we see that the oral tradition can offer explanations for the many names attached to a given plant. It is important to realize that facts passed down through the oral tradition which are presumed to be 'wrong' are not necessarily so, they just hearken back to important linguistic and symbolic links from the past.

There are a lot of traditions to do with daisies. In medieval times knights going into battle wore daisies as a symbol of their fidelity; wearing a double daisy (a common occurrence in many wild daisies) would be an emblem of a knight's love for his lady, and confirmation that she loved him back. Conversely to this, quite often a woman who could not decide whom she loved would wear a wreath of daisies upon her head. Maybe she would then have plucked the petals from the flower saying, 'he loves me, he loves me not', letting the flower decide. It was said that the proper way to use a daisy for this kind of divination was to stand facing the sun and only pluck the petals at midday. If plucking the petals of the daisy did not work to find your true love, there was a belief that if you wanted to dream of your lover you should put daisy roots under the pillow. This motif of laying a flower under your pillow is associated with many different varieties of flowers. Some people say that dreaming of a daisy in spring and summer brings luck, while dreaming of it at other times of year foretells bad fortune.

It is quite common in plant lore for a flower to have both negative and positive meanings. A variation on the power of the daisy to bring good luck to those who wear it is the belief that picking daisies and putting them in a vase in the home will actually protect the house from external dangers and threats. There was also once a belief that dressing children in daisy chains protected them from being stolen by fairies. Again, this hearkens back to the association of daisies with the sun, which is all powerful and all protective.

On the other hand, in some parts of the world it was considered unlucky, as mentioned earlier, even to step upon the bloom, and it was said that any child who touched the plant before he or she had been weaned would become stunted. Interestingly enough, this belief is echoed in the tale of the fairy Milkeh, who, having a royal foster child, fed the child daisy roots so that he would never grow beyond and above the height of a daisy. Through this practice, Milkeh created a beautiful miniature man. And while it was unlikely anyone would attempt to feed a child daisy roots, in some areas it was common practice to feed them to unweaned puppies, thus ensuring that they did not thrive, as a way of dealing with the problem of large and unwanted litters.

The Victorians loved the daisy, in fact it was once considered to be Queen Victoria's favourite flower. In the Victorian language of flowers it symbolized innocence and the sharing of sentiments. In Norfolk, England, young ladies believed that if they walked into a field where daisies grew aplenty, if they closed their eyes and picked a handful of flowers, the number they picked would indicate how many years they would have to wait to be married.

Country folk used the flower to foretell the weather, but of course there was no great skill attached to this because everybody knew that the petals opened when the sun was out, so obviously if the petals were open then good weather was the order of the day.

In 16th-century France, there existed an 'Order of the Daisy'. In Britain, too, the daisy was associated with importance, belonging and patriotism. Empire Day on the 24th of May was celebrated by many folk and it was said that schoolgirls wore daisies on that day, which with their compact and single flower symbolized a united empire.

For a flower so linked with history and symbolism, the daisy has a simplicity about it. Growing low and humble, one of the most delightful and endearing beliefs about the daisy is that its seeds were sown by the spirits of the babies that had died at birth, and that the flowers were sown in plenty to bring cheer and delight to grieving parents.

This link between the daisy and innocence was explored by the Renaissance painter Botticelli. It is said he was the first to use the daisy as a symbolic representation of the innocence of the baby Jesus. Maybe he was aware of the legend that the pink-tipped varieties came to be that way when they were splashed with drops of Christ's blood as he hung on the cross, as the white daisy flowers gently grew beneath him. Another tale recounts that the bloom grew from the tears of Mary Magdalene at Christ's death.

HEALTH AND WELL-BEING

Throughout the world there are many tales about flowers growing on the site of ancient battles, as a way of healing the soil. During the Middle Ages, the daisy was often used to treat battle wounds. Hence the theory that the daisy's Latin name comes from the word for 'war' rather than 'pretty'. It was said that the plant could stop bleeding and relieve bruising and shock – one of its vernacular names was 'bruise wort'. Limbs and wounds were dressed with bandages containing crushed daisies to give relief and effect a cure.

Folklore and plant lore have given us many varied cures using this humble flower. The leaves can actually be eaten, and it was said that anyone eating the leaves of the 'hen and chicken' daisy would be gratefully blessed. If a pregnant woman ate the leaves of this daisy, her unborn child would be blessed. The daisy was also used to make a wine; the saying 'to be pie-eyed' comes from over-indulging in daisy wine. It was said that if insane people drank a concoction of daisy juice for 15 days, they would either be cured or would die!

The juice of a daisy put into running eyes was said to cure the problem, and the flower was used as a charm to relieve gout, ulcers, remove warts and turn grey hair back to black.

Ancient healing also indicated that daisy juice could cure migraines. As the juice that was used by the Elizabethans tasted very acrid, the juice would actually be sniffed up the nose. Animals and insects, perhaps a bit more discerning than their human counterparts, avoided eating the plant completely!

Gerard's *Herbal* gives quite a lot of interesting information about the plant for healing. He refers to the plant once being called 'bone flower', and claims that the daisy keeps at bay all sorts of pains, especially those in the joint, and gout: 'If they be stamped with new butter unsalted, and applied on the pained place: but they worke more effectualy if Mallowes be added there to.'

Gerard also offers the fascinating piece of information that if daisies are given to young dogs in milk, it stops them from growing too large (again, this refers back to the belief that eating daisy root could stunt the growth). Culpeper, in his own famous *Herbal*, reminds us that the plant is dominated by the zodiac sign Cancer and under the rule of Venus, so is therefore good for wounds on the breast and is a good plant to be put into oils, ointments and syrups. He tells us that daisy juice can refresh the liver and other internal organs, and helps 'ulcers and pustules' in the mouth and tongue. Culpeper gently reminds us also that the leaves from the daisy, when bruised and applied to swollen areas, bring instant relief and lower a fever. He intimates delicately that this cure works for all parts of the body, however private.

Today it is the leaves and the flowers of *Bellis perennis*, the common daisy, that are used in healing. It is an astringent and can relax spasms. The younger leaves, flowerbuds and petals are added to salads; their flavour is delightful. The plant can be used to cure coughs and catarrh internally, and externally is used on varicose veins, wounds and watery eyes. It is a homoeopathic remedy for bruises. It is still being used to treat the complaints mentioned many centuries ago by Gerard and Culpeper. As a herbal remedy Pliny and the Romans used it for 'Scroflous tumours'; it was also, as we have discovered, used to treat battle wounds. A final ancient daisy cure was to eat three daisies to relieve toothache.

The daisy has diuretic abilities and can be used for arthritis, gout treatment and skin problems such as acne. It is also a popular remedy for problems such as engorgement of the breasts and uterus after injury, surgery or childbirth, and for abnormal heat in the reproductive organs – both homoeopathic and herbal remedies incorporate the daisy for treating these problems. The Doctrine of Signatures dictates that as a daisy looks like an eye, it can be used for eye problems. The plant's properties certainly help irritated eyes. Daisies will stop bleeding from cuts and wounds and, if taken internally, are thought to reduce bruising and shock. Perhaps the daisy's greatest virtue is that it helps people recover from the bruising and batterings of life.

In homoeopathic healing, the daisy is referred to as a poor-man's substitute for arnica. It is used to cure skin problems, gout, rheumatic pains and women's problems. The flower essence treats both children and adults alike, encouraging better concentration and helping the person become slightly more focused. It also gives enhanced stamina to those who are having reoccurring problems. On a very simple beneficial level, a daisy will provide a very beautiful bath: if the flowers are allowed to steep in water for 30 minutes, they can then be added to a warm bath for a very healing and relaxing soak.

OBSERVATIONS

To most people the daisy is a symbol of childhood, simplicity and pleasure. Yet the daisy has many detractors, who will remove it from wherever it grows, and view it as a weed.

In the 14th century weeds were viewed as 'an abundance that grew at God's command' and it was considered wrong and against creation to remove any plant completely, so all gardeners who respected nature and the Creator would leave at least a few of each variety, just in case. They were of the opinion that there was no one worthy of judging above the Creator which plants stayed and which were rooted out.

Many of today's gardeners spend hours trying to oust the little plant from lawns and boarders. I ask myself what soul is it that feels a lawn bereft of its 'guests' is a better place? Though I must admit it is almost impossible to sit on grass surrounded by daisies and not pick them, pluck their petals or make a daisy chain. But perhaps this urge speaks to a deeper need. The daisy reminds us of innocent pleasures, and taking time to communicate with nature and to share time with children, encouraging in them a love of flowers. And what better way to be part of an ancient and multi-cultural tradition of peoples and healers than by picking, plucking and loving the humble daisy?

BLUEBELL

Hyacinthoides non-scripta

BOTANICAL

They say that nature always puts the right thing in the right place at the right time. So what better place to find a magical blue carpet than in the shelter of soft green woodland? What magic makes us catch our breath and linger on the sweet scent when we find a mass of bluebells bathed in spring sun, growing amid hazel, beech or oak trees?

The term 'bluebell' is somewhat misleading, in that it refers to different flowers in different parts of the world. *Endymion* is the correct name for a genus of 10 species that were at one time included in the *Scilla* genus. Sometimes the *Endymion* genus is referred to as the *Hyacinthoides* genus. These synonyms can be confusing, but whichever genus name is used, the plant actually belongs to the *Liliaceae* family. What then do we call this pride of the woodlands? In England, the bluebell lives under the name *Hyacinthoides non-scripta*. It is important to remember its Latin name because the vernacular term 'bluebell' does not always conjure up the same image across the continents. In Scotland *Hyacinthoides non-scripta* is nicknamed 'the harebell' or 'campanula', yet further south the harebell and campanula bear it no resemblance. Sometimes *Hyacinthoides non-scripta* is referred to as 'wild hyacinth' – it is easy to trace this link, as the *Hyacinthus orientalis* grown in many homes and gardens is all but a larger similarly designed flower to the bluebell.

A few more names can also be added to the list: the Spanish bluebell (*Hyacinthoides hispanica, Scilla campanulata* or *Scilla hispanica*), which looks very similar to the English bluebell, and the 'Virginian Bluebell' (*Mertensia virginica*, also known as the American bluebell).

Whatever the name, this flower turns woodland into a mystical sea of blue. The English bluebell has at the bottom of its stem two small pointed leaflets. It has tripartite flowers shaped like a bell, housing six stamens and yellow anthers. Nature, being as ever wonderful, prevents the rain from damaging the pollen by making sure the flower heads droop. That is until after fertilization, when the fruit becomes erect.

The very similar *Hyacinthoides hispanica* differs very little from the English bluebell. It has a loose spike of pendant-like bell-shaped flowers and grows to a height of approximately 12 inches.

Both the Spanish and English bluebell hybridize easily. The bulbs have no outer skin to protect them from drying and damage. They shrivel and go mouldy if stored in a domestic environment where the atmosphere may be too dry or damp. In a domestic garden the genus offers flowering bulbs suitable for borders and naturalizing in grass under trees and shrubs. It is hardy, preferring semi-shade, moisture and a heavy soil.

But what of the growing preferences for *Hyacinthoides non-scripta*, the English bluebell? It is in England and Scotland a prolific grower, less so in Ireland, and not at all in the Orkneys or Shetland Isles. Contrary to popular belief, picking them does very little damage – that is, no damage to the plant, but once picked the flower head, which can grow to 16 inches, becomes lifeless and limp. Their beautiful blue colour always makes them popular to pick, even though people doing so know they will last but a short time once picked. The worst problem as far as survival goes is damage to the leaves; many a careful picker can inadvertently and irreversibly damage the plant by treading on its leaves.

The English bluebell is a native to woodland edges and copses, and it flowers after the primroses and lemon brimstone butterflies are out.

Throughout the winter the plant stores energy in its bulbs and tuberous root system. Interestingly, the plant has contractile roots and, as new bulbs form on top of the soil, they are drawn down into the earth for safety. The plant continues to survive in arable landscapes, in woods that are felled and beaten about with frightening frequency. Today an old undisturbed wood is a unique environment absorbing changes to its history and yet outwardly never changing. Out of choice the bluebell prefers old woods. In early spring the small bulbs project leaves throughout the leaf mould to greet the early spring sun. Nature's timing is perfect: the flowers and leaves develop as the leaf canopy above awakes from its winter rest. The blue flowers are more often that not found under beech, oak and other deciduous trees. The blooms mature in late April and early May; once out, the wood or copse becomes an enchanted world with the most powerful and distinctive perfume. Because the leaves need light it is important that they flower and develop before the woodland canopy is fully out, as once this happens the light source to the leaves is shut off and the plant will fail. The bluebell grows better in strong sun, however it cannot always maintain rapid growth and so seeks to be a shade-lover for most of the year.

Britain hosts over 20 per cent of the world's bluebell population. Their profusion is attributed to their preference for undisturbed woodland, helped by the fact that a great deal of British woodland is impenetrable to feet that will trample the leaves. Sadly, as is always the case with nature's beauty, people do try and dig up this magical flower, but to no avail – exposed gardens are too sunny and the plants die. In Britain it is illegal to dig the plant up. Far better to leave it to thrive in the dappled woods amongst the wild garlic, spurges and other woodland plants.

ORIGINS

Bluebells have been growing in woods for longer than we have been keeping records about the flora that inhabit the earth. In fact, the bluebell was one of the first plants to arrive on the Atlantic coast of Europe, spreading from Holland in the north to Portugal in the south. This arrival was post-glacial. There are in fact about 85 different species that are linked geographically. It is very difficult to be exact as to which were the first arrivals. It is thought that with the bluebells came wild cabbages, some Ericas, some orchids, gorse, the Welsh poppy (*Mechonopsis cambrica*) and the autumnal crocus.

Because the bluebell is an angiosperm – that is, a flowering plant that produces a seed in an ovary – it is possible that this protective seed survived the journey through glacial waters. *Endymion non-scriptus* is a plant found in Great Britain and Western Europe, more specifically in an area covering Western France, Belgium and Portugal. It is also naturalized further east in the Mediterranean and in the leafy soil near the Atlantic coast of Europe. The Spanish bluebell, *Hyacinthoides hispanica*, is more native to Spain, Portugal and North Africa, with a concentration in Morocco and Algeria. It is easily distinguished from the English bluebell by its taller racemes, erect and more open flowers, and broader leaves.

The origins of the name of this plant are myriad. The name *Scilla* is thought to originate from the Greek word 'skilla' meaning a 'sea onion', perhaps a reference to the fact that the bulb resembles an onion some-what. Another thought on the name scilla was that it originated from the Greek word 'schidzoo' meaning 'to split' – this may well refer to the bulb scales. *Endymion* comes from the Greek word for 'sunset personified' and 'with whom the moon is in love'. *Hyacinthus* comes from the story of a Greek boy who was the son of the King of Sparta. He was an amazingly handsome young man and, along with his friend, the god Apollo, he hunted in the forests and participated in sports on the plains. One day they decided to put their skills to the test by throwing a heavy quoit. Apollo's flew as high as the stars, but jealous Zephyr, who was watching, made the quoit suddenly fall back to earth, hitting Hyacinthus and killing him. His blood flowed from his head wound, soaking the earth. Apollo, unable to help his friend, formed a flower out of the blood and earth and named it 'hyacinth'. Ancient Greeks believed they could see the syllables *ai, ai,* meaning 'woe, woe', marked upon the petals and leaves, as it was said that these were Hyacinthus' last words as he lay dying. Virgil records this: 'still on its bloom the mournful flower retains/The lovely blue that dyed the stripling's veins.'

The myth of Hyacinthus is also found in the *Metamorphoses* written by the great poet Ovid (43 BC–AD 17). The story has also been kept alive by sculptors, composers, artists and writers alike, especially in the 17th and 18th centuries, when the story was used by Wolfgang Amadeus Mozart who used it as the subject for his first opera *Apollo and Hyacinthus* written in 1767.

The species part of the *Endymion* name, *non-scriptus*, means 'unwritten' – that is, without any marking on the petals. This is in reference to the 'ai' found on the petals of the hyacinth – the bluebell is distinguished thus because it has no such markings.

So far we have concerned ourselves with *Endymion non-scriptus* as the English bluebell, but in fact the Americans have a very similar flower. Both types bloom in the spring in woodlands, but they are not related botanically. The American bluebell is in fact *Mertensia virginica* (referred to in Britain as the Virginian cowslip). It is as blue as English bluebells, and named after a German botanist, Franz Karl Mertens. It exists in Europe because it was brought there via the hand of a young cleric, John Banister, who had been sent to Virginia to serve the spiritual needs of the American colonists by his Bishop, Henry Compton. As was often the case in those days, many clerics were keen amateur botanists.

PLANT LORE AND HISTORY

The bluebell can delight the eyes, but it also served other very important needs over the course of history. During the Elizabethan era the bulbs would be ground down in a pestle and mortar; the resulting mucilage or simple gum and starch would be used to stiffen the fluted ruffs worn by the Elizabethans, and to help bind books.

Nor were the stems of the bluebell overlooked. These would also be ground down for glue to fix feathers into the ends of arrow shafts.

The popularity of the bluebell has always owed a great deal to its special colour. Blue carries a vast folklore with it. Blue or azure is a colour very much linked with divinity. In the Christian world, blue is the colour of the Virgin Mary. It also symbolizes the blessed waters of baptism. Blue was said to be the colour of divine eternity and immortality, traditionally a mortuary colour and often used as a covering for the coffins of young people. In artistic representations we find angels in blue costumes, to signify faith and fidelity; it can also be the colour of peace, contemplation and intellect. In the pre-Christian era it was the colour of Venus, Greco-Roman goddess of love. Of course it is also the colour of water and coolness, the sky, infinity, an infinity from which life begins and returns.

Over the ages the colour has been used to ward off gout, and women would wear a blue ribbon or woollen threads around their necks until their children were weaned. This tradition continued even up until the early 1800s, the idea being that the blue ribbon would somehow prevent fever. Doctors in the early 19th century were advising patients to wear blue ribbons and live on onions to avoid rheumatic fevers, abscesses and anaemia. This advice had a long history: the Old Testament Book of Numbers 15:38 says, 'speak unto the children of Israel, and bid them that they make them fringes in the boarders of their garments throughout their generations, and that they put upon their fringe of the boarders a ribband of blue'. A visit to any school in Britain in the early 1900s would reveal up to a third of children wearing blue bead necklaces as a guard against colds and quinsys. Their parents and other adults would also wear such necklaces, to avoid bronchitis and other chest infections. More often than not they were worn beneath the outer costumes and were never removed, not even at death.

If blue could protect, it also could be lucky. In the south of Britain it was said regarding love and weddings, 'Those dressed in blue have lovers true, in green and white forsaken quite, blue is true, yellow is jealous, green's forsaken, red's brazen, white is love and black is death.' Blue is universally known and recognized as a popular colour and the saying 'true blue' has become synonymous with fidelity. In Spanish the phrase 'true blue' indicates the belief that aristocratic families have veins that are more blue than those of peasants – and of course the term 'blue-blood' is common throughout the English-speaking world. In the Far East blue was said to be the colour that averted the evil eye; and for that reason many good-luck charms were blue.

Blue has always been the colour of lovers;

'If you love me, love me true, send me a ribbon and let it be blue.'

And of course what better quotation about love than the tradition still current for a new bride's wedding outfit: 'something old, something new, something borrowed and something blue'?

With so much diversity and imagery attached to blue and the bluebell itself, it is no surprise that it was the inspiration of many poets. The French referred to it as 'Jacinthes des bois' and it is also known as the 'Sapphire queen,' particularly by John Keats, as in his poem *The Lovely Daughters*:

> A filbert hedge with wild briar overtwined,
> And clumps of woodbine taking the soft wind
> Upon their summer thrones; there too should be
> The frequent chequer of a young tree,
> That with a score of light green brethren shoots
> From the quaint mossiness of aged roots:
> Round which is heard a spring-head of clear waters
> Babbling so wildly of its lovely daughters
> The spreading blue-bells: it may haply mourn
> That such fair clusters should be rudely torn
> From their fresh beds, and scattered thoughtlessly
> By infant hands, left on the path to die.

Keats also reminds us of the poor youth Hyacinthus in his poem appropriately entitled *Endymion*:

> Or they might watch the quoit-pitchers, intent
> On either side, pitying the sad death
> Of Hyacinthus, when the cruel breath
> Of Zephyr slew him; Zephyr penitent,

Who now ere Phoebus mounts the firmament,
Fondles the flower amid the sobbing rain.

Because of its colour, the bluebell was once considered to be the Virgin's flower; its mystical association is spoken of in a book entitled *Equinox*, published in Edwardian times: 'Oh though mighty God, make me as a fair virgin that is clad in the fair bluebells of the fragrant hillside.'

Legends grew, too, around the ill-advised picking of the bluebell. Very often country folk would leave the flowers un-pulled, considering the bluebell as a flower of dread (the reasoning behind this was the hanging head of the flower). The fear of flowers with hanging heads was common centuries ago, when people believed that the flowers hung their heads in sorrow either at Christ's crucifixion or man's fall from grace in the garden of Eden. Bringing such flowers indoors would bring in sorrow. The snowdrop is another flower associated with this belief.

Bluebells are considered as unlucky indoors as hawthorn blossom, and should only go as far as a scullery or wash house. Again an irrational fear, but many a woman being proffered a gift of bluebells from a child found herself most disturbed about bringing the blooms indoors. In some parts of the world it was believed that a bluebell indoors would bring a dreadful depression upon the whole family, whereas left in its natural surroundings it would bring only happiness and delight to those who gazed upon them. Maybe the ancient superstitions are right and these beautiful blooms are best left to delight outdoors.

In the Victorian language of flowers the bluebell symbolized constancy – a tribute, perhaps, to its never-ending struggle to be left to grow in its native habitat.

HEALTH AND WELL-BEING

The bluebell is not a flower widely used as a healing agent. To some extent its greatest healing properties lie in its beauty in the wild, as something to relax in and to wonder at. In the 19th century, Western

European families would take excursions into the countryside to escape the dirt of the industrial cities and enjoy the natural world. They started the trend of picking the wild flowers, bluebells amongst them. This pastime may have been relaxing, and was certainly popular, but sadly led to the clearing of many areas from which nature had to retreat. Burgeoning roadsides had to be sprayed and kept neat; many large areas of flowers were lost.

Bluebells can present a hazard to wildlife. The soft green leaves are a tempting treat to hungry cattle, but if a cow grazes on bluebells in preference to grass she will dry up, as the toxins in the leaves will effect her milk. These toxins are called glycosides and are similar to those in the foxglove.

During the medieval period when flowers were so well used in healing, the bluebell was not viewed as medicinally important, however in past ages it was said that a concoction distilled from the bulb could prevent a young boy's voice breaking too soon; many a singing master gave his pupils the mixture. No scientific evidence exists to substantiate this, and it is wise to remember that the bulbs, when fresh, are poisonous.

OBSERVATIONS

The bluebell is one of a very few true blue flowers that exist. It is the colour of the sky on a perfect cloudless summer's day, or the blue of the ocean that laps the shores – it is the blue dreams are made of, cooling, tranquil, deep, protective.

As for the Elizabethan discovery of the starch and glue within the bulbs, what idle journey into the glades produced this revelation? Respect and credit must be given to the wise 'plant women' who were the nerve centre of healing and survival in the early ages. Many were persecuted and even killed as witches. They can indeed be said to have performed magic – nature's magic. So it was with those who discovered soap wart (*Saponaria officinalis*) and the ability to work the sap of this plant into a lather.

An ancient undisturbed wood will host far more bluebells, and the blooms in multitude are nature's way of saying the area is just as it was centuries ago. What better place to wander and try and find an essence of ourselves in the quiet? Today one of the greatest fears man has is to be on his own, to find himself in his own company. Why? Because we are never given time to find ourselves and be at peace and one with ourselves, and so facing ourselves and inner thoughts when alone is no welcome prospect. A profusion of bluebells in a wood makes the area timeless and converts the undergrowth to a tranquil sea. Sitting amid them carries one's thoughts and dreams on its crest. Over the centuries many a hope, dream or ideal has been borne on such a tide. The perfection of nature yet again has to be acknowledged, and we must stand in awe of it.

The Greek youth Endymion, so the mythology goes, was a shepherd whom Selene, the moon, fell in love with and would often watch in the fields. She became smitten by his beauty and, with a magic spell, made him sleep forever. This then enabled her to shine over his body and kiss him with her moonbeams as he slumbered. He still slumbers and she still kisses him, as the bluebells lie peacefully asleep under the moon's tender watch.

ANEMONE

Anemone nemorosa, the wood anemone

BOTANICAL

The Anemones likewise, or winde flowers, are so full of variety and so dainty, so pleasant and so delight-some flowers that the sight of them doth enforce an earnest longing desire to be the possessour of some of them at least.

JOHN PARKINSON, *PARADISUS TERRESTRIS*

The anemone belongs to the *Ranunculaceae* family; a popular name for the anemone is 'wind flower'. The word 'anemone' comes from the Greek *anemos*, meaning 'wind', and *mone*, meaning 'habitation', indicating the sort of area in which a lot of these species grew.

The anemone genus has over 150 species, most of which are hardy herbaceous perennials. Many of this very large genus have unprotected flower heads, growing high on stalks above the leaves, as a great deal grow in barren places and need to push their flower heads above rocky crevices to attract insects for pollination. Their flowering time begins in early spring, though there are some autumn-flowering species. The later-flowering plants are mostly fibrous-rooted, the earlier spring flowers are tuberous and better for naturalizing if planted in gardens. The flowers are usually cupped or bowl-shaped, made up from between 5 and 20 petaloid sepals which, when fully mature, open flat. The leaves are usually three- or five-lobed, deeply cut and often carried in whorls of three on the stems.

The anemone genus once included the *Pulsatilla*, which is now classified as a separate genus. Within the anemone genus, the species name often gives an indication of the plant's growing habitat:

ANEMONE ANGULOSA	angular
A. APENNINA	from the Apennines
A. BALDENSIS	from Mount Baldo
A. BLANDA	pleasing, delightful, enchanting
A. CORONARIA	crown, wreath-like
A. FULGENS	glowing
A. HALLERI	named after the botanist Haller
A. HEPATICA	liver-like
A. HORTENSIS	of gardens
A. JAPONICA	of Japan
A. NARCISSIFLORA	narcissus-flowering
A. NEMOROSA	of open glades (the wood anemone)
A. PATENS	spreading open
A. PULSATILLA	to shake (or move in the wind)
A. RANUNCULOIDES	similar to a buttercup
A. RIVULARIS	of streams
A. RUPICOLA	living amongst rocks
A. SULPHUREA	coloured like sulphur
A. SYLVESTRIS	belonging to the Woods
A. VERNALIS	belonging to Spring

Many of the smaller anemones are alpine growers, such as *A. tryfolia*, the three-leaved anemone, found in the southern Alps. The narcissus-flowering anemone (*A. narcissiflora*) is similarly found in the Alps between France and Switzerland, in the lower altitudes on the Jura and Chasseron. These Alps

Anemone pulsatilla, sometimes called *Pulsatilla vulgaris*

also host the *Anemone alpina* and many more. Despite the size of this very large genus, only a few of the more popular and ancient anemones come to mind when one thinks of the anemone: the wood anemone (*A. nemorosa*), the pasque flower (*A. pulsatilla*, sometimes called Prairie smoke) and the bright and vibrant colours of *A. coronaria*, from which species come the two very popular florists' anemones: 'De Caen' and 'St Brigid'.

The wood anemone (*A. nemorosa*) flowers in open woodland from about March through to May. Given a choice, it seems to favour rich soils beneath sycamore trees, however it is common to all woodland over 5,000 feet. It makes the woods alive with its brilliant white petals, occasionally tinged with purple. It carries on its stalk three irregularly yet finely cut leaves of dark green that are halfway up the stem. The stems grow from about 4 to 12 inches.

A. pulsatilla, the pasque flower, is very different from the wood anemone. It is a very hairy plant and moves in the slightest breeze – its species name of pulsatilla indicates this characteristic. It is very popular as a decorative plant, growing happily in the wild or gardens alike. In its native habitat this perennial prefers calcareous grassy slopes and old earthworks; it is rare and is only found growing in central England during April and May, although throughout the world there exist 30 species of this clump-forming plant.

A. coronaria takes its name from the change of colour at the base of the petals and stamens, giving the appearance of a wreath at the base. This anemone grows much taller than any of the others, to about 24 inches in height. The colour varies, as does the shape of the leaves, and the flowers, which are carried at the top of hairy stalks. The leaves are divided into small lobes; each stem carries one flower, below which there is a whorl of leaves. Usually there are between five and eight petals, many many stamens and a colour range from blue to red and white. *A. coronaria* is found wild in fields, orchards and vineyards in Mediterranean areas and eastwards to Asia Minor. The 'De Caen' and 'St Brigid' varieties have a similar colour range but a much longer flowering season and stronger, straighter stems. *A. coronaria* was a popular flower with the Victorians, who called it 'the poppy anemone' and used it in borders and as a cut flower; its bright, vibrant reds would often feature at the front of a large herbaceous border.

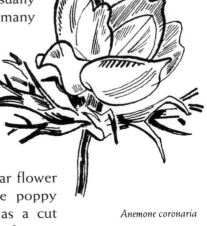
Anemone coronaria

ORIGINS

All anemones, irrespective of their species, are referred to as wind flowers. Anemone was a beautiful nymph of Greek mythology, beloved by Zephyr, the god of the west wind. His wife Flora was jealous of this love, and so turned Anemone into a small flower. Zephyr deserted her, but Boreas, god of the north wind, wooed Anemone in the spring when she would open to his north winds.

The origins of the anemone go further back than the time of the Greeks, however. There is evidence of cultivated anemone blooms having been present in the new kingdom of Egypt (circa 1570–1085 BC), though the precise species is unknown. In artwork the anemone took pride of place along with other Egyptian favourites such as the cornflower, poppy and chrysanthemum.

In spite of their nickname, wood anemones are not always found growing in woods and may sometimes be in evidence in meadows or hedges. This is not because they have chosen to grow elsewhere, nor because the wind has blown the seeds far from their natural habitat – their presence indicates the site of long-vanished woodlands.

The positioning of the pasque flower (*A. pulsatilla*) tells us something about the history of the land around it. Quite often in Britain it is found growing around sites where ancient warriors have fallen, as in Cambridgeshire and Suffolk, which saw their share of battle between natives and Danes. Indeed, the pasque flower is occasionally called 'Dane's flower'. The flower also appears on the border areas between Berkshire and Hampshire, where there were battle sites from the days of King Alfred.

A. pulsatilla is the adopted flower of the US state of South Dakota. Popular during the Renaissance, it is thought that it was introduced to Britain from Europe in the 16th and 17th centuries. In High Renaissance society ballrooms and dining rooms, the anemone – along with hyacinths, crocuses and primroses – was a featured flower for court decorations during the month of January. Up until this point new varieties of flowers had been the prerogative and indulgence of the rich. It was in the 1600s that the turning point came, as more and more people had access to land and rural folk began to rear flowers for pleasure. During the 16th century in England, wonderfully illustrated floral books were beginning to appear. In the 1500s, Britain had up to 200 cultivated plants in its gardens; by 1839 this figure had risen to 18,000, and the anemone was one of the most vivid and exciting.

Gerard in his *Herbal* has much to say about anemones. He mentioned their variety of colours and says he has at least 12 different sorts growing in his garden, while elaborating that he has heard of many different sorts growing elsewhere. He says that every new year brings different and strange sorts of anemones from far-off countries, and expresses the hope that they will yield well in this 'land of England'.

Several anemones are native to Northern Europe. *A. nemorosa* originated towards Turkey and northwest Asia, where it was found in woodland and shady places. Once it began to be cultivated, several varieties were named for Victorian gardeners – such as *robinsoniana*, named after William Robinson, who found the plant, which originated in Ireland, in a botanical garden in Oxford. *Alenii* is named after one Mr James Allen of Somerset, who produced it in the mid-Victorian era.

The origins of *Anemone coronaria* are fascinating and very much linked with biblical lands. It is a native of the Mediterranean regions of Spain and Greece, Turkey and Algeria; it is also found in Central Asia. Some people say that the seeds of this plant were brought to Europe by Crusaders returning from the Holy Wars; it was said that the flowers sprung up mysteriously in Pisa's Campo Sancto cemetery at about the same time that a Crusader ship had returned with earth from the Holy Land to be used for graves. Legend had it that the red petals of these anemones originated from the blood of Christ crucified. This may be a pointer towards the association of the *A. coronaria* and the biblical 'lilies of the field': 'Consider the lilies of the field, and how they grow: they toil not, neither do they spin. And yet I say unto you, that even Solomon in all his glory was not arrayed like one of these' (Luke 12:27). There is much debate about the flowers indicated in this passage of the bible, in a time where botanical identification was unknown and all plants had colloquial or vernacular names. So it is possible that the 'lilies of the field' were not in fact lilies at all. (This problem continues today, in the popular names of flowers such as the primrose, which does not belong to the rose family, or the lily of the valley, which bears no relation to the lily family.) There are many possible flowers that could have been the inspiration for the 'lilies of the field' passage in the Bible, ranging from white lilies, red tulips, gladiolus and so on. However, the majority of thought considers *A. coronaria* to be the flower in question. Certainly at the height of its season in the spring it covers the landscape with brilliant scarlet, a reminder of the splendour of the East. Maybe the brilliance of this flower was in Christ's mind as he spoke these words.

Despite the belief that Crusaders brought the plant back in seed form, it is usually thought that *A. coronaria* came into English gardens in about 1596. There is even a possibility that this bright and colourful flower was brought into the country by wandering clerics and friars. Whichever means the flower took to get to England, by the middle of the 17th century there were at least 30 different varieties.

Meanwhile there were even more varieties on the Continent. It is reputed that a Parisian called Maître Bachelieu grew an excellent strain, but would not give seed or plant away. The Burgomaster of Antwerp, who had for years requested seeds and been constantly rejected, resorted to underhand means. He took a servant with him to visit Bachelieu at the time when the fluffy seeds would be ripe. As usual he was shown the garden, and as he passed the anemone bed he slipped his fur coat off his shoulders, letting it fall onto the flower beds. The servant grabbed the cloak, seeds attached, and ran to a waiting carriage before the plan was discovered. Next year, the captured seeds, now plants, were shared with the Burgomaster's friends and then scattered throughout Europe. For a long time afterwards the flowers were called French anemones. Interestingly enough now, the connection with France still exists in that many of the commercially produced anemones for florists' shops come from France.

A. coronaria was one of two species cultivated as 'florists' flowers'. These florists' flowers were a result of the late 16th-century craze for gardening for beauty instead of utility. Herbalists became florists and there were eight main florists' flowers. Apart from the anemone, there was the auricula, polyanthus, hyacinth, ranunculus, tulip, pink and carnation. Catalogues from the time mention numerous varieties, with at least 30 single narrow-leaved anemones (according to Parkinson, 1629). A later catalogue from Mason in 1820 notes 75 varieties. As was the practice in those days, florists did not usually name varieties they had cultivated; they were more interested in clear and distinctive colours, a strong erect stem no less than 9 inches high and a blossom, or corolla, of at least 2½ inches in diameter surrounded by large well-rounded petals forming a broad shallow cup. As well as *A. coronaria*, the second florists' anemone was *Anemone pavonina*, the star anemone. It is thought that the red *A. fulgens* is a variety of this species.

As with so many plants and flowers, *A. coronaria* was known before the Linnean style of naming as *Anemone tenuifolia* (meaning narrow leaves); *A. pavonina* was known as *Anemone latifolia* (broad-leaved). These two anemones are thought to have come into Western horticulture from the gardens of Turkey. Whilst they were known to 16th-century botanists, they were first distinguished between and illustrated by Venetian P A Michiel. The bright flowers, both single-coloured and striped, feature prominently in early Flemish and Dutch paintings by artists such as Breughel and Bosschaert the Elder. The popularity for these two anemones knew no bounds at that time: in 1601 the *Historia Rariorum* lists 20 tenuifolias and 18 latifolias. So popular were these flowers that it is said that many rich people had as many as 28,000 of them planted in their parterres. As the decades passed, *A. coronaria* became more popular than *A. pavonina*; by 1676, there existed 75 varieties of the former and only eight of the latter. Towards the end of the 1600s, roots of the plants were being imported from France and Flanders to sell in London. By 1730 many continued to appear in catalogues, though fewer plants were being grown in gardens. By the middle of the 19th century people were trying to make the anemone more popular again, and horticulturists such as Carey Tyso were writing articles in magazines praising the flower. In the years between 1856 and 1871 prizes were offered for people growing anemones. It would take several decades more, however, for *A. coronaria* to become a popular cut flower. The variety 'De Caen' dates from the middle of the 19th century – a certain Madame Quetel of Caen showed magnificent blooms and offered at least 500 cultivars in horticultural catalogues. These strong blooms were adopted by nursery men and the name 'De Caen' became synonymous with the single-flowering anemone. The strain 'St Brigid', the semi-double (more petals than the single, though not so many as the double), followed in the 1880s from Ireland under the auspices of a grower named Mrs Lawrenson.

The importance of the anemone as a florists' flower is not to be underestimated; in the 19th century a garden containing several florists' flowers could be worth, at today's prices, several million pounds. These showpiece flowers displayed in a fret (a geometric pattern) of small beds would receive thousands of visitors a year.

PLANT LORE AND HISTORY

Anemones understandably have an important place in plant lore, and there are many legends about them. The flower is associated with Adonis, with whom Venus fell desperately in love. Her love was so great for him that she tried to protect him by hiding him in the underworld, but to no avail – Zeus made her share Adonis with the underworld goddess Persephone. Venus lived in fear of the youth being hurt. One day whilst out hunting he was indeed killed by a wild boar; he died in Venus' arms. Some legends say that the red anemone grew up from the ground where her tears fell; other tales report that the flowers sprang up from where Adonis' blood fell. This goes some way towards explaining the name sometimes used for the anemone, 'naamam', which is Persian for 'the Adonis' – and of course the anemone is dedicated to Venus.

The death of Adonis is also immortalized in the traditional Greek pot garden, which is called the garden of Adonis and is with great ritual annually planted in the spring in memory of the young man's violent death. The Adonis cult had a rather shadowy origin in the East before it was adopted by Athenian women, who put a likeness of the god on roof terraces to welcome the arrival of spring. Earthen pots were planted with fennel, lettuce, wheat or barley to grow quickly and then die in the hot sun, a ritualistic reminder of nature's cycle, spring to winter and to death.

The anemone's association with death is also evident in Chinese folk-lore where, along with roses, anemones were planted over graves.

In the medieval era the pasque flower (A. pulsatilla), was a prolific grower, blooming at Easter time. The plant produced a rich green dye that was very popular in medieval times. The flowers, which were vivid and beautiful, were used in medieval posies and decorations during Easter rituals. Sometimes the green dye was used to decorate eggs for the celebrations.

In folklore the flower has a special place, although it can serve very contrary ends. It was believed to bring luck, to guard against evil and to keep the powers of the night and darkness at bay. Yet in some regions it was believed that picking the wood anemone brought on thunderstorms – among country folk it was often referred to as 'thunderbolt', and would certainly *not* be a flower to tuck in one's buttonhole while out walking.

Yet the anemone was said to foretell rain by closing its petals up tight, so indeed might have been quite a useful flower to have to hand. The flower also closes its petals at sundown, and so the legend grew that woodland fairies would shelter beneath the petals at night.

HEALTH AND WELL-BEING

The scentless yet beautiful anemone has long been treasured by early healers and herbalists for its medicinal properties. It was said that tying the flower to one's arm with a red cloth would cure many ills.

As with many flowers and healing in ancient times, the first flower of the year or the season was deemed very important. The Romans would gather up the first anemone of the year while chanting, 'I gather thee for a remedy against disease.' They regarded the anemone as capable of dispelling fever. This belief prevails in the British Isles (perhaps a legacy of the Roman invasion?), evident in the following rhyme: 'The first spring-blown anemone she in his doublet wove/to keep him safe from pestilence where 'ere he should rove.'

Strangely enough, in other countries there is a belief that the wild anemone is to blame for polluting the air. It was thought that any person smelling the plant's aroma would suffer from a severe malady. It was also believed that anyone eating more than 30 plants would die! The wood anemone does indeed contain poison in the sap; when fresh it can blister susceptible skins, and anyone picking it and then rubbing their eyes will suffer itching and discomfort. However, it is used in herbal medicine to kill bacteria and other microscopic fungus. To protect itself from being eaten by grazing animals, the plant carries a very bitter taste, but this disappears once the plant is dried out.

In general terms, if the root of the plant is boiled it will produce a drink which, when taken, will cure fevers, relieve coughs and other chest problems.

The pasque flower (A. pulsatilla) is used more often in modern healing than any other member of the anemone family. It falls into the category of traditional European herb. Herbalism in Europe, albeit eclectic, came from ancient Greek and Roman practices which had themselves already been altered by ideas from ancient Egypt, Assyria, India and the Arab world.

In general terms, A. *pulsatilla* was used in European herbalism as a pick-me-up for the nervous system; it healed through its ability to impart relaxation and sleep. It was also an analgesic and a respiratory aid. The fresh pasque flower contains glycoside ranunculin, which changes to anemonine when dried. It is most important to remember that the plant fresh is poisonous; it should only be used dried. The dried parts that grow above ground can be used for headaches, earaches, skin problems and nervous disorders, not forgetting gynaecological problems, where it will give relief from pain and tension and produce rest.

It seems incredible that such a small flower can be so important in healing. The key lies in its affinity to mucus membranes, which is why it is so useful in healing respiratory and digestive problems. To induce sweating and fevers it brings blood to the surface.

In homoeopathic healing the anemone is used on people who, like the plant's common name, 'wind flower' are changeable, gentle and easily blown around. In today's herbal healing A. *pulsatilla* is used; while homoeopathic healing makes use of the A. *pratensis* variety. Pulsatilla-type people are changeable, like the weather: happy one minute, sad the next; one moment sunshine, the next storm. Perhaps, like the nymph Anemone of mythology, they fear being forsaken – thus the flower with a sad drooping head can be used to heal those who hang their head in sorrow.

A. *pratensis* will help varicose veins, nose bleeds, lethargy and sleep that is peppered with restless dreams. The flower essence helps people establish the gentle side of themselves whilst strengthening security and stability.

OBSERVATIONS

As a commercial bloom the anemone has to fight hard to compete with all the other blooms resplendent in florists' shops. It has neither the length of stem of the gladioli, the wealth of blooms of the multi-headed flowers nor the heady perfume of the lily, so it is sometimes overlooked – until, that is, its beauty is perceived. To look at it is to see geometric perfection: its black centre is made up of thousands of perfectly placed individual elements, all necessary for the bloom's growth. In contrast, the vibrant coloured petals fascinate the viewer with the deepest reds and blues.

In the wild, *A. nemorosa* and *A. pulsatilla* are very different to their cultivated brethren; their heads are daintier and almost humble in character, and they lack the vibrant eye-catching colours of the florists' blooms. However, nature is subtle enough not to need 'blatant advertising'. She is balanced perfectly and each element is coloured or shaped to appeal or respond to its pollinator. Unlike mortals, nature looks beyond what is obvious and finds the heart of what is necessary and important. Thus the little wood anemone works its own magic in the woods, the pasque flower exerts her medicinal magic and the lily of the field carries its own symbolism, as nature intended. While designers uses the florists' bloom to add the finishing touches to interior design, others will always prefer to think on the tales of Anemone, Zephyr and Boreas, and cherish the anemone in its native, wild state.

POPPY

Papaver rhoeas

BOTANICAL

The poppy carries on its stem much more that just four overlapping petals that taper towards a stem, creating the characteristic cup shape. It carries for the onlooker reminiscences of lost childhood, nostalgia and the fallen dead. As if to echo this, the budded flowers bow their heads and the paper-thin, delicate petals last but a short while.

The *Papaveraceae* genus is made up of a mixture of annuals, biennials and perennials which readily make and sow seeds in profusion. In fact Linnaeus, the 18th-century Swedish botanist, once counted 32,000 seeds in one head!

The Latin name *Papaver* has several origins, none of which can be either proved or disproved. One thought is that the word originates from the word 'Pap' (a word used for nipple or breast, and thus for any semi-liquid infant food), as Celtic mothers used to give their children opium to lull them into quietness when they needed to hide in silence and safety from their enemies. A further rather strange origin of the name is said to have derived from the noise made when the poppy seeds are chewed in the mouth. In the genus name, the word *aceae* comes from *aceous*, meaning 'like'.

Some of the species names also have varied and interesting origins. *Somniferum* comes from *somnus*, meaning 'sleep', and *fero*, 'I bring'. There is sparse information to endorse the species name *rhoeas*, but a common belief is that it stems from *rheo*, meaning 'I flow' – a reference to the milky juice released when the stems are cut. The other species names have slightly stronger elements of definition:

PAPAVER NUDICAULE	naked stem
P. ORIENTALE	eastern
P. PAVONINUM	peacock
P. RUPIFRAGUM	rock-breaking
P. UMBROSUM	growing in the shade

From a genus of at least 100 species, the word 'poppy' for most of us is synonymous with *Papaver rhoeas*, the wild countryside flower, and *P. somniferum*, the fast-growing annual opium bloom.

Poppies are very much dependent on contemporary agricultural trends, as the powerful chemical fight against weeds means the bloom is not so often found growing proudly in cornfields. Weed killer, combine-harvester cutting and post-harvest burning are hardly conducive to a plethora of poppies. For some while the poppy was left to strive on road-sides and field edges, and the harmony of poppies and corn that had lasted for thousands of years was threatened. The flower was part and parcel of the corn fields for so long that its true geographical origins have been lost. The flower, as with all weeds, is only germinated when the soil is torn up and broken, as in the case of road development, new housing estates, battle fields and ground that has seen conflict. These soils play happy hosts to this colourful invader.

Poppies remain especially prolific in less intensely farmed arable areas. Just before the beginning of the 19th century, corn fields were vastly different in appearance than those we see today. Old, established, natu-rally growing corn varieties stood more than 3 feet high, giving cover for birds and animals as well as providing a natural habitat for the poppy.

Science, religion and politics have always changed the lifestyle of flowers. During the Middle East crisis, oil-based weed killers increased in price beyond the pocket of smaller farmers, and even those more affluent farmers chose not to spray outlying fields. City councils short of funds no longer, thankfully, spray roadsides in some areas. Poppies take advantage of all these opportunities. With up to about 17,000 seeds in its seed head (despite Linnaeus' earlier estimation), the poppy began once again to predominate the countryside. An average field can carry thousands of millions of seeds. It is possible that many seeds will lie dormant for decades until conditions are right for germination.

P. rhoeas is a prolific producer of seeds because its ovary contains many ovules. The seeds are dispersed as the heads are shaken in a process similar to shaking pepper from a pot. A ring of small valves below the shield of stigmas operate the ovate capsule; as the valves open, the seeds escape.

The flower itself is neither fragrant nor produces nectar, however bees and flies still visit the blooms, attracted by the red petals which emit ultraviolet rays, and so the reproductive process continues.

P. rhoeas, the field poppy, has poisonous parts and is gratefully left alone by grazing cattle. The stalks, flower stems and pinnate leaves are covered in a rough layer of hairs and so are well protected from grazing animals. Before flowering the bud is covered in two boat-shaped sepals. These then fall, the bud opens, the four red petals with black spots at the base open out and the stem straightens. From this species the Reverend Wilks evolved the 'Shirley' poppy series (see below). It is thought that it came from Europe, not the Arctic region, and spread as corn did through the lands.

Climate changes during the early years of the earth's creation accommodated certain flowers, including the poppy. The climate changed from tropical to subtropical to temperate, and hardier plants migrated south. During the Tertiary Period known as the Oligocene (38 million to 26 million years ago), poppies became evident in the far south of England including the Isle of Wight.

Papaver somniferum, the opium poppy, has oblong-lobed leaves producing large single blooms in shades of red, pink, purple and white. Some occur in double form.

Whilst these two well-known varieties remain so popular it is important not to forget other alternative varieties, even if they do not carry the history or symbolism of their eminent forefathers. Perhaps as time goes by they will engender their own folklore:

P. ATLANTICUM	a short-lived perennial with oval, toothed, hairy leaves and single dull orange flowers
P. BURSERI	semi-evergreen with fine cut grey leaves and single white flowers
P. COMMUTATUM 'Lady bird'	A fast-growing deeply lobed plant with single red flowers with a black blotch in the middle
P. NUDICAULE	the Iceland poppy from the northern sub-Arctic regions; the hairy stems carry a single white and yellow flower
P. ORIENTALE	the Oriental poppy from America produces brilliant vermilion flowers with dark blotches at the base of the petals
ESCHSCHOLZIA CALIFORNICA	The Californian poppy, also member of the Papaveraceae family, provides a vivid splash of orange in gardens

Papaver somniferum

ORIGINS

Nature is never brash or loud in its creations, and sometimes a plant exists for a long time before people notice it. The poppy has been on the earth since the beginning of plant life as we recognize it. It was one of about 130 species that thrived in an area covering what we call today Central Europe to Northern Africa, in post-glacial history. Many species found in southeast England spread no further due to climate and soil barriers, but about 20 hardy plants – including the poppy – crossed this barrier, and while the conditions were not ideal, they managed to adapt and survive.

One can presume that poppies have been blooming amidst the corn since the birth of agriculture. In the Middle East some seed evidence has been found in the remains of the Kahun Twelfth Dynasty in Egypt, flourishing before 2500 BC. The Assyrians called them the 'daughters of the field'. (The association between flowers and the feminine principle appears in many civilizations and stories. Traditional Chinese culture viewed all flowers as female and gave them female names, while in Europe roses were associated with queens and goddesses. Many flowers are also associated with the Virgin Mary in Christian cultures.)

It is possible that the poppy reached Britain mixed with the grain crops carried by nomadic Neolithic settlers. The planting of the seed for them symbolized stability and dwelling, the seed in folklore symbolizing life and the fertility of Mother earth.

Papaver somniferum was native to Middle Eastern and Mediterranean countries. When the Romans expanded their Great Empire to other shores they took seeds with them, possibly in fodder or on the hooves and hair of horses, and so the sides of their famous roads became strewn with poppies, along with other plants.

Medieval crops also hosted the blooms, along with cornflowers and marigolds. During this period most people called poppies 'corn roses', and the field or corn poppy came to be confused with the opium poppy and was believed to induce sleep or headaches.

The poppy is often featured in the great flower paintings of the 15th and 16th centuries. These flower pieces were accurate and finely detailed floral or horticultural catalogues as well as being intricate and exquisite designs in their own right. Amongst the roses, peonies, iris, tulip, fritillaria, marigolds, dianthus, larkspur and auricula, a poppy would be found. In Dutch vanitas style, which highlighted the transience of life and the sins of vanity and pleasure, it symbolizes sleep and oblivion.

Varieties of the opium poppy were bred from the 17th century onwards. The horticulturist of that era, John Parkinson, notes double varieties originally from Constantinople. It was grown in the early 19th century in Britain for opiates and poppy seeds. Whether it was to provide the active ingredient for medicinal laudanum is a debatable point, however conditions in Britain were never sufficiently good for the sap to form. *Papaver orientale*, a frequently planted bloom, was native to America and was introduced to Britain by George London a little before 1714.

A popular and well-known cultivar of the Papaver genus is the 'Shirley' poppy, named after the South London village of Shirley. The Reverend William Wilks, a Victorian priest, first found the wild forebears of his produce spreading from surrounding fields into his vicarage garden. One day in August 1880, he found that one flower had petals with a narrow white edge. He saved the seed and from 200 plants that he raised, a few had the same coloured petals. Over the next few years Wilks infused white into the stock so that the seeds of the final strain produced blooms that varied from scarlet to white, with all the tones of pink in between.

The Californian poppy (*Eschscholzia californica*) was named after the Estonian botanist Friedrich Eschscholtz. The plant originated in California and was introduced into Europe in 1790.

In 18th-century Britain the blooms were nick named 'soldiers' and 'redcaps' as they stood proud and erect in the many corn fields. It was the sea of red blooms in the fields, churchyards and cliff heads set against a blue sea that caught Clement Scott's eye in 19th-century Norfolk. He was drama critic for the *Daily Telegraph* newspaper, and nicknamed this area of Norfolk 'poppy land'. His writings in the paper started a craze that resulted in thousands visiting the area using the Great Eastern railway, on a line that was quickly rechristened 'the Poppy Line'.

If one studies the Latin names of many wild flowers and plants, one finds that many have as a second name *arvensis*, the Latin for 'field', thus indicating the habitat they grow in. In the vernacular some plants are prefixed with the word 'corn' to suggest their closeness with the crop.

Ideas change, as do priorities; in early arable farming days the production of a good crop was not an issue and so the appearance of weeds, especially poppies, in the crop were not seen as a threat – the more colourful the field the better. Plants like the thistle were a threat, however, and were pulled out:

> *Each morning know the weeders meet*
> *To cut the thistle from the wheat*
> *And ruin in the sunny hours*
> *Full many wild weeds of their flowers*
> *Corn poppies that in crimson dwell*
> *Call'd 'head achs' from their sickly smell.*
> JOHN CLARE, *THE SHEPHERD'S CALENDAR*

Clare spoke of a time 120 years ago when some areas left poppies in crops, others removed them in an action called 'Poping'.

PLANT LORE AND HISTORY

> *But pleasures are like poppies spread*
> *You seize the flower the bloom is shed.*
> ROBERT BURNS 'THERE WAS A LASS, THEY CA'D
> HER MEG'

What makes the poppy so important in our folklore and history? Why do so many myths exist about this flower growing so unashamedly on the wings of life, as it were? In its natural habitat it never takes pride of place, yet its place is proud and the colour more noticeable than many other wild flowers.

Poppies have long been symbolic of ephemeral pleasures, sleep and oblivion. It was known to exist as long ago as 6000 BC when Swiss lake-dwellers were found to have used morphine. It has been emblematic of new life and bloodshed since far-off ancient Egyptian times. It is a plant that belongs to our lives and culture, that is if a plant can belong to us – we do not own our plants, trees and any other part of nature; we can only ever be guardians to these beautiful creations; their life-force will far outshine ours, unless by our jealous and demanding lifestyle we rob plants of what they need to live – the earth and the air.

In Egypt's New Kingdom of *circa* 1570–1085 BC, the poppy was one of the main constituents of Egyptian gardens; evidence has been found in garden remains from Pompeii. The Egyptians saw an unchanging and unending truth and strength in nature and they used the poppy, along with the cornflower, mandrake, lotus and papyrus, in their formal bouquets. Certainly the most popular three garden flowers for the Egyptians were the poppy, cornflower and mandrake, so it is not surprising that these important flowers for the gardens of the living should be used in funeral tributes for the dead, who were to go on, with the flowers, to the next life. Symbolism was important to the Egyptians; if the poppy meant sleep and oblivion it was most apt for a civilization that looked to resurrection to a new life after rest. Similarly, the early Arabs saw the poppy as the 'Father of sleep'.

Sometimes plant identification is difficult to glean from early civilizations, where languages, scripts and cultures differ widely. The word 'lotus' is an awkward one to deal with, for example. In Greek culture the word 'lotos' was used for a number of varying plants. It is possible that the 'lotus-eaters' or *lotophagoi*, a group Odysseus came upon on the Libyan coast, were actually ingesting the opium poppy – hence the forgetfulness that overcame those who partook of it. Another discrepancy in names is found in Dioscorides, who uses the Egyptian name 'nanti' to refer to two different Poppy species, *rhoeas* and *somniferum*.

But we need not rely on ancient texts alone to discover the poppy's history. Works of art from bygone ages show the goddess Demeter being crowned with a wreath of corn ears and poppies. In ancient days her 'corn' symbolized the universal cereal crop, including wheat and barley, which is evidenced in agricultural areas such as the fertile crescent that stretched from Syria and Turkey to Iran, where the original ancestors of our cereal crops grew in large forest clearings among the oak trees. Cereals are an important pivot for civilization, they give life in the form of food, starches, proteins, oils and salts – a staple human diet, in other words.

In myth Demeter was also named Ceres, the Roman corn goddess. Seeds were used as offerings in a ritual where she would be asked to safeguard the subsequent year's crops. Garlands of poppies, barley and bearded wheat adorned statues of her. It is said that she taught man to till the soil, to sow and reap. Demeter had a beautiful daughter called Persephone who was snatched from the earth while gathering flowers by Hades and taken to his kingdom in the underworld. Demeter was grief-stricken and searched for her daughter in vain. As her grief grew, the crops suffered. It is said the poppies were sent to grow at her feet to ease her pain and lull her to sleep. Maybe it was Hypnos, the god of sleep who is depicted wearing a poppy garland, who caused these blooms to grow. In any case, the opium poppy worked and Demeter slept. It is worth noting that the Greek name for the bloom is *nepenthes*, meaning 'that potent destroyer of grief'. The Greeks drew on the comparison between the heads of dying warriors and the poppies in the fields, heads similarly drooped. Crowns of poppies were put on the heads of those who had recently died, to effect the perfect everlasting sleep.

Whilst Demeter slept, Zeus persuaded Hades to let Persephone return from the underworld at the end of each winter for two-thirds of the year. So Persephone would live with Demeter and the earth goddess would bestow fertility back to the fields and be at peace for two-thirds of the year, then when Persephone returned to the underworld for winter, Demeter would mourn and the earth would grow cold and barren. In this way the poppy came to be associated with renewal of life, with regeneration and activity after sleep. The seed head contains enormous numbers of seeds and this abundance further enhances the association with the gift of life, fertility and Demeter. Because of the association between this story and the poppy, the Greeks also consecrated the bloom to Nyx, the goddess of dreams.

Pliny (born AD 23) wrote prolifically on natural history and refers to the habit of sprinkling egg-brushed bread dough with poppy seeds prior to baking. This practice continues to this day, although its original purpose – to enhance the bread (and whoever ate it) with the restorative power of the poppy seeds, has been all but lost.

The Roman invasion to the shores of Great Britain and the spread of the Great Roman Empire changed the face of British horticulture and gardening. The opium poppy was one of the crops used by the first monks, cultivated in their gardens and infirmaries. In monastic horticultural writings the poppy always appears within the first nine plots of the kitchen garden.

From 17th-century European battlefields to those of the First World War there has been a continuing legend that the poppy springs from the blood of the fallen. There is even a much earlier reference to this, in an account of the 1389 Battle of Blackbird Field in Kosovo. The armies of the Turkish Sultan had defeated the army of the younger Serbian monarchy. It was a battle with much bloodshed; locals to this day report that so much blood was spilled on the ground that the poppies growing close to the convent of Gracanica, where the conflict was heaviest, are a darker red than elsewhere in the area. Time and time again death, blood and the flower appear together in each era and civilization of our history.

In the 19th century red poppies appeared in the ground after the battlefields connected with the Battle of Waterloo had been ploughed. At Ypres and the Somme during the First World War, yet more blood was shed by man and beast on to the earth. Poems by writers such as Gurney recounted the terrible destruction:

> *The songs I had are withered*
> *or vanished clean,*
> *Yet there are bright tracks*
> *where I have been,*
> *And there grows flowers*
> *for others' delight.*
> *Think well, O singer,*
> *Soon comes night.*
> IVOR GURNEY, THE SONGS I HAD

War artist William Orpen visited the battlefields in 1917, a mere six months after the Somme battles:

No words could express the beauty of it. The dreary dismal mud was baked white and pure-dazzling white. White daisies, red poppies and a blue flower, great masses of them stretched for miles and miles – It was like an enchanted land, but in the place of fairies there were thousands of little white crosses, marked 'Unknown British Soldier' for the most part.

Another person among the many to also notice the plethora of poppies was Colonel John McCrae, a Canadian medical officer who was helping the wounded after the second battle of Ypres. The poppies made such an impact on him that he composed a poem about them. It was sent anonymously to *Punch* and printed on 15th December 1915:

In Flanders' fields the poppies grow
Between the crosses, row on row,
That mark our place and in the sky
The larks, still bravely singing, fly
Scarce heard amid the guns below.
We are the Dead. Short days ago
We lived, felt dawn, saw sunset glow,
Loved and were loved, and now we lie
In Flanders' fields.
Take up our quarrel with the foe;
To you from failing hands we throw
The torch; be yours to hold it high.
If ye break faith with us who die
We shall not sleep, though poppies grow
In Flanders' fields.

This poem was adopted worldwide and reprinted everywhere. When the British Legion was formed in 1921, it was approached by someone whose American friend Monica Michael had been wearing a poppy ever since reading the poem. This friend, a member of the YMCA, showed the British Legion artificial poppy samples. In France a Madame Guerin was also caught up with the poppy symbolism and in November 1918 she set up poppy manufacturing, and so the first poppies used by the British Legion were imported from France. By 1922 five disabled ex-servicemen were making lapel poppies, wreaths were brought into use in 1924 and in 1933 a white lapel poppy was promoted by the Co-operative Women's Guild as a pledge to peace. Sadly, Dr McCrae caught pneumonia and died. Each year on the anniversary of his death a bouquet of poppies is lain on his grave – a fitting tribute to the man who penned what many believe to be the greatest poem in English occasioned by the First World War.

If the blooms are evocative of our feelings for the fallen souls who were our salvation, they have also served as reminders of some wonderful folklore that has sprung up around them. Children would be warned about picking the delicate blooms, as it was said that if the petals fell off while the plant was being picked, the picker would evoke storms and be struck by lightening. Early vernacular names for the poppy were Thundercap, Thunderflower or Lightning, echoing this ancient weather lore.

In some areas of the countryside the flower was called Headaches, Touchaches and Earaches – if the blooms were put to the ear a violent earache was said to result. The species *rhoeas* had further body-centred names, including Blind eyes and New eyes. It was said blindness would follow if the blooms were worn, and warts would appear if the blooms were handled. It was also a risk to smell the blooms, as a mere sniff would cause nosebleeds which could only by stopped by putting spiders' cobwebs up the nose! No doubt many of these tales were circulated by adults to stop children gathering the attractive blooms from amongst the crops and treading on precious cereal grains underfoot.

However far-fetched some of these beliefs seem to us now, there is always an element of truth behind them. The blooms can cause headaches and blindness (albeit temporarily). Soldiers from the First World War had to endure long marches through a countryside thick with the red blooms, which did affect their eyes, making them see red for days afterwards. In the 19th century there were more military tailors who went blind than their civilian counterparts – remembering here that the regimental colour was scarlet.

Spare picked flower heads were carried in the pockets of hopeful young ladies as an augur of love. The plant was said to have a 'prophetic leaf', and one's success in love was measured in direct proportion to how fresh the leaves and petals stayed while in one's pocket. Young folk already courting could take a leaf or petal and hold it on top of the hollow of the palm of the left hand and then strike it with the right hand. A good clear resulting sound was said to indicate a good relationship:

By a prophetic leaf I found,
Your changed affection for it gave no sound,
Though in my hand struck hollow as it lay
But quickly withered like your love away.

ANON

HEALTH AND WELL-BEING

The moment man walked the earth he needed sustenance for the body, stimulation for the mind and healing for both. The poppy held relief for his every need. *Papaver somniferum* yields morphine, a naturally obtained painkiller, in fact the greatest painkiller that nature can produce. Apart from morphine, the raw opium, which is the white latex exuded by the green seed head, can also, if necessary, be extracted from the leaves and stems.

As one would expect from such an ancient and world-wise plant, physicians have been administering and experimenting with the poppy for many centuries.

In Sumeria in 4500 BC, small opium balls would be rolled and eaten or taken with wine by those needing morphine. Its analgesic properties relieved intense pain. Nowadays it can be taken in conjunction with other drugs. Several hundred tons of opium alkaloids are used worldwide each year. What is quite sobering to realize is that it cannot be synthesized chemically; nature is the only source of supply. It is also a highly addictive, deadly and destructive drug – the source of heroin.

The property of the plant to stimulate expression was known thousands of years ago by the classical world. Prospero Alpini expounded on the effect of opium in Egypt, its effect in stimulating men in war and love and creating spectacular dreams. Egyptians used opium in large quantities, which created comatose, lethargic and inconsistent behaviour in its users.

The poppy was referred to as *Spn* in medicinal Egyptian texts. *Spn* seeds and fly dung were mixed together, strained and given to crying children to ease their tears. Unguents were made in vast quantities for various health problems. A popular mix was boiled hippopotamus skin, fat, *Spn* seeds and a carob pod. A less repulsive medication came in the form of skin powder made from *Spn*, minerals, myrrh and chalcedon.

In the 11th century, Mesue, an Arabian physician, administered the syrup opium for coughs, and it was still in use in the 17th century as a preparation called 'syrupus de Meconio Mesuae'. The strong syrup contained morphine, codeine, papaverine, narcotine, meconic acid, thebaine and narceine.

The theory behind the Doctrine of Signatures, which originated very early on in history, was expounded by the German Theophrastus Bombastus von Hohenheim, who was born in 1493. The Doctrine was based on the belief that the Creator had provided plants imprinted with signs to help man use them to cure ills, so the plant was either marked like a disease or grew in the shape of part of the body that it would cure. The poppy's red petals were thus believed to be a good remedy for nosebleeds and those spitting blood. A Dutch *Pharmacopoeia* listed *Petala Rhoeadas*, petals of the field poppy, and *Sirupus Rhoeadas*, syrup of the same for healing. A further extract from the syrup was used to dye cheese, so it became a useful by-product of the healing concoctions.

An infusion of powered capsules was often put externally on sprains and bruises, and proved to be a successful reliever of the pain. As has been seen, opium syrup cured coughs; the poppy also had effect on other chest and throat problems. Petals were often used in gargles for sore throats and tonsillitis; the leaves soothed and relaxed chest spasms and stomach pains. The plant will also give pain relief in the case of pain produced from a nervous origin, as in headaches, neuralgia and shingles.

In 1905 morphine was first commercially isolated from raw opium. It was present in medications such as laudanum, and writers such as Coleridge and Elizabeth Browning were among the many who became addicted. Britain also played a rather dark role in the addiction of thousands of Chinese people at this time. The Chinese produced wonderful and much sought after tea and silk. The British East India Company used the opium from poppies grown in Burma and India, and smuggled it into China to exchange for silver bullion with which to buy the tea and silk. In the mid-19th century this trade led to the Opium Wars.

Experimental techniques led to the discovery of heroin in 1898. Effective as a painkiller and a better cough suppressant than codeine, it was readily available in North America until 1917. It took until the Second World War for morphine and heroin addiction to be recognized as serious problems.

In homoeopathic medicine, opium from the poppy is used to relieve 'insensitivity' of the nervous system, sleeplessness and stupor. The essence from the bloom helps redress the balance in life between rest and activity, the physical world and the spiritual. It also provides escapism for all who cannot face life's realities; the field poppy belongs exclusively to those who live in a world where they cannot express fear or emotion.

However hit and miss some of the cures were, there is an element of consistency that runs throughout the ages. The Elizabethan physician Gerard recommends the poppy for 'pleurisie' in a drink from the leaves. Culpeper is keen to endorse the ancient throat and chest cures. He notes the poppy, which he says is influenced by the moon, as keeping catarrhs and defluxions of 'thin rheums' from the head from travelling into the stomach and lungs (a forerunner of consumption). He suggests oil from the seeds for hoarse throats, and the empty seed heads themselves, once boiled in water and used to bathe the temples, to effect rest, sleep and relaxation.

Physicians over the ages used knowledge that had gone before them to endorse their treatments. Later on, however, experimentation with organic chemistry led to new insights. In the 19th century Justus von Liebig (1803–73), referred to as the father of physiological chemistry, introduced the concept of metabolism, a development of organic chemistry. This pioneering science had already produced morphine from opium in 1806.

The early settlers to America and the Native Americans used parts of the Californian poppy to cure toothache, neuralgia sciatica and colic. On the other side of the Atlantic the housewives of the English Fen areas were concocting poppy teas made from white poppy blooms. It was administered for all in the family to relieve problems ranging from rheumatism to teething pains.

OBSERVATIONS

The French writer Gerard de Nerval wrote in the 19th century: 'Each flower is a soul blossoming out to nature.' The poppy is one flower that encapsulates and breathes soul. It epitomizes the struggle we undergo, as mortals, to understand the order of creation, and the importance that each simple unit of life has, seeds waiting for the correct conditions to grow, prosper and give pleasure before returning to oblivion.

The poppy also poses an interesting and deep question on the belief of coincidences. Are there coincidences in life, or are some things and events predestined? Was the poppy seed set in the soil at the time of creation, to find its way to all the points of the world where man could find it and have morphine, and setting into motion the deep symbolism the flower commands.

The poppy, irrespective of its species, hides a force behind its dainty paper-thin petals. If one tries to personify the poppy, it has to be as a woman. A delicate and gentle exterior that hides a depth of wisdom, strength, tenacity and healing power. Poets have long seen this and used the poppy in their work to describe the affinity that the flower has with creation and the heart of the earth.

For those whose lives are spent the flower epitomizes their eternal rest and relief from pain. For those who live and suffer the bloom provides relief from pain, rest and healing. For those who are free from pain and are out in the world, the poppy gives them a chance to wonder at its beauty, love its symbolism and take the opportunity to drink in its beauty and bathe in its fitness to occupy the fields of the summer earth, at peace.

SNOWDROP

Galanthus nivalis

BOTANICAL

The snowdrop is one of the first early spring flowers. As its name tells us, it is often found pushing its head up through settled snow.

The Latin name for snowdrop is *Galanthus*, and the genus belongs to the *Amaryllidaceae* family. The word *Galanthus* comes from the Greek words *gala*, meaning 'milk', and *anthos*, meaning 'flower'.

There are many vernacular names for this fair bloom: 'the Fair maid of February', 'Snow princess', 'White queen', 'Dingle dangle', 'Mary's taper' and 'Candlemas bells'. The French call the bloom *Perce neige*, meaning 'snow-piercer'.

The snowdrop is familiar to thousands of people; with its drooping head and pristine white blooms it is certainly a welcome sight after long winters. It is sometimes difficult to know whether to attribute the bloom to winter or spring, as it sits on the cusp of both. In general terms, the wild plant that is now cultivated as a garden plant is native mainly to central and southern European areas, although it has been introduced successfully elsewhere, where it prefers a soil rich in nutrients and humus so often found in mixed deciduous woodland areas.

Each bloom has three outer and three inner petals, the outer being the longer. It flowers earlier in milder parts of the world, and it is a flower that responds directly to climatic conditions. Whilst immediately recognizable there are in fact several species of the bloom, though their differences are so minute that it often takes an expert botanist to tell them apart.

Galanthus nivalis is the common snowdrop, the term *nivalis* coming from the Latin word for 'snowy'. This bloom, produced from a bulb is native to most of the eastern parts of Europe, spreading from Russia to Sicily and Spain. It is usually found in damp woods, by streams, and in land rich in humus and nutrients. It is certainly found naturalized in England, Scotland, Holland, Belgium and even Scandinavia. In England and Scotland it is quite often called 'flower of hope'. This may be because the way it bursts above the ground, even in frost, is an indication of life returning to the earth after the long winter.

Various horticulturists have produced garden hybrids such as 'Magnet', 'Atkinsii' – named after one James Atkins of Painswick in Gloucestershire in England – and 'Allenii Baker', named and produced by a snowdrop grower called James Allen who lived in Somerset in England during the late 19th century. Other varieties of *nivalis* include 'Lutescens', which originated in the 19th century in Northumberland, England, and 'S. Arnott', a variety named after Samuel Arnott Provost of Dumfries during the 1800s.

The genus carries many more species, some of which grow in British gardens, others scattered throughout Europe (and in America – though not native there, some were brought by early settlers):

GALANTHUS BYZANTINUS	native of northwest Turkey
G. CAUCASICCUS	native of the Caucasus and Caspian coastal area
G. ELWESII	found growing in Yugoslavia, Romania, southern Ukraine, Greece and Turkey. This species is named after Elwes, an English plant collector who was also an eminent sportsman
G. FOSTERI	found in Turkey and the Lebanon

G. IKARIAE	native to the Aegean islands, Tinos and Ikaria
G. PLATYPHYLLUS	native in the alpine meadows of central and western Caucasus
G. PLICATUS	native to western Russia, eastern Romania and the Crimea. Some of these bulbs were no doubt collected during the Crimean war and brought back with the troops

It is quite possible that bulbs from the genus growing in gardens are mixtures from all these various overseas species, however it is *Galanthus nivalis* that is found in British woods, churchyards and near streams today. Over the years some of this species has undoubtedly spread to neighbouring gardens, where it has been moved, or shared with other gardens.

ORIGINS

The snowdrop, along with plants such as box, daphne, woad and a few orchids, poppies and honeysuckle, was one of at least 130 plants that were post-glacial arrivals which settled in an area spreading from Europe to North Africa because of the suitable climate and soil conditions. As with so many plants it is difficult to establish whether snowdrops arrived in an area after surviving the ice age, or were *in situ* before that time. It is probably safe to say that *Galanthus nivalis* is native to Britain and that the other species have become happily established in British soil after being introduced from Continental Europe and Asia Minor.

The alteration of names over the years quite often makes tracing their origins difficult, and the snowdrop is no exception. Whilst there is no record of the plant growing wild in Britain until the beginning of the 1770s, there is evidence that it existed in Britain a long time before that, known under the name bulbous violet (or to give it its full name, 'timely flouring [flowering] bulbous violet'). In the original version of Gerard's *Herbal* of 1597 there is a drawing and description of a plant that can be nothing other than the snowdrop, which he calls the bulbous violet. It is possible also that the plant had been known for a long time within religious circles. The flower has links with the feast of Candlemas, which falls in the Christian calendar on February 2nd. The Catholic church acknowledged the link between the bloom and the Virgin Mary, and Candlemas celebrates the feast of the purification of the Blessed Virgin Mary. Religious shrines and churches were decorated with the bloom.

It is also quite possible that the flower was grown in monastic gardens, or encouraged to spread on religious land, including burial ground.

During the Italian Renaissance, the snowdrop was depicted in religious artwork to symbolize the Virgin Mary, the way it hangs its head in sorrow seen as calling to mind the sorrow of the Virgin at the crucifixion of Christ.

Many churchyards in Britain lay host to this delicate bloom. Maybe this had practical reasons: the bloom encourages insects to pollinate them, including the hibernating bees in monastery hives, who might sense the sweet perfume and be encouraged to start making honey earlier.

Nor are the 'random clumps' seen in the countryside as random as the eye perceives. They may well be all that is left of a garden, or old markers of paths useful on barren winter landscapes, especially for pilgrims en route to shrines and wells dedicated to the Virgin Mary.

The Victorians encouraged mass plantings of the bulbs in areas of their gardens they designed as 'rooteries'. A rootery was created in an area that needed a shady and somewhat damp atmosphere to create a feeling of wildness. Clumps of snowdrops growing at the base of old tree roots created just the wild woodland environment required within the constraints of a Victorian garden.

One myth about the origin of the snowdrop concerns the first biblical pairing, Adam and Eve. When banished from the garden of Eden, Eve mourned when she saw the flowerless landscape they'd been cast into. Because nature mourned, too, at their expulsion from the garden, she sent snow to cover the land as a funeral pall. An angel saw Eve's sorrow and appeared in front of Eve, held out a hand and, catching a falling snowflake, breathed upon it. At that instant the snowflake took on the form of the snowdrop. The angel gave the flower to Eve, telling her, 'this is in earnest, Eve, to thee,/that sun and summer soon shall be'.

This tale about the origin of the snowdrop may explain why the flower is often an emblem of death, a belief that is linked to the physical shape of the bloom – it is said that the shorter three inner petals resemble a folded shroud. On the other hand, the snowdrop is also a powerful emblem of hope:

> I've bought some snowdrops; only just a few
> Not quite enough to prove the world awake,
> Cheerful and hopeful in the frosty dew
> And for the pale sun's sake.
> CHRISTINA ROSSETTI, 'THE MONTHS, A
> PAGEANT'

PLANT LORE AND HISTORY

For the Victorians the snowdrop symbolized hope, as it was one of the first plants to appear each year. But for a flower so linked with hope and new life, a great deal of the plant lore associated with it concerns fear and bad luck.

One fairytale tell us of Oberon's daughter Kenna, who fell in love with the son of King Albion. Unfortunately Oberon objected to the couple's love, and banished Kenna's lover from fairyland. He returned with an army to fight defiantly against his banishment, but was wounded. Kenna rushed to heal his wounds, putting 'herb moly' on them, but where the juice touched his skin it turned to snowdrops, and sadly he died.

The Victorians viewed the bloom as being more to do with death than life, because the blossom grew so close to the bare earth and therefore to those buried and long gone. It was considered bad luck to bring even a single bloom into the house; if this were to happen it was a sure omen that a member of the household would die before 12 months had passed. In some areas of Britain it was felt that, although a single bloom brought into the house was bad luck, a whole handful was not. And some legends have it that happiness will come to a house where the flower blooms in borders just beneath the windows. And a planted bowl of snowdrops (not the cut blooms) in the house was said to harm neither man nor beast.

The flower, being pure and pristine, was also used as an emblem of virginity. Over-zealous young men would be warned off by young ladies carrying in their pocket, or on their person, an envelope of snowdrop blooms.

HEALTH AND WELL-BEING

Despite the snowdrop being mentioned in Gerard's *Herbal*, it is not used greatly in healing. Gerard praises only the 'sweetnesse of their smell'. The plant did have medical uses, however, albeit just a few. Crushed bulbs made into a poultice were often used on cases of frostbite. The bulb contains most of the alkaloids, among them tazettine, galanthamines and lycorine. The bulb can be used as an emetic.

Nivaline, a preparation made from the plant, is thought to help complaints that feature nerve-tissue decay. Research has certainly shown that the plant may contain constituents that help to regenerate nerve tissue.

It is important to remember that the whole plant is poisonous.

OBSERVATIONS

White as a colour symbolizes innocence, hope, truth, purity and simplicity. It was the colour favoured by the first clerics and the Druids. With the snowdrop comes a wealth of plant lore, and superstitions associated with its colour and its name. It is difficult to understand the human psyche, however the unravelling of these plant superstitions at least helps us to understand ourselves and those around us. In its simplest and most obvious sense, the snowdrop carries an incredible strength which can give hope to all. How can one seemingly small delicate bloom push its way through frosted earth which will not allow a spade to penetrate, and appear unblemished? Maybe that is the message of the flower – hope, that despite all the trials and tribulations life brings there is a season of perfection, enjoyment and rest to come.

LILY

Lilium candidum

BOTANICAL

The Lily, or *Lilium*, is a genus of approximately 100 species of bulbous perennials. The word 'lily' is common to most languages in the world, although particular species may have their own common names. In the wild, lilies are found in a wide area round the northern hemisphere, in the temperate zone. Some species, such as *Lilium candidum*, have been in cultivation for over 3,500 years, but it was not until the start of the 20th century that the genus was developed commercially.

In the *De Proprietatibus Rerum* of 1240, the cleric Bartholomaeus Anglicus says, 'The Lely is an herbe wyth a whyte floure. And though the levys [leaves] of the floure be whyte: yet wythin shyneth the lykenesse of golde.'

The lily bulb itself is made up of thick overlapping fleshy scales, which are leaves adapted for food storage. As the bulbs are stem-rooting, they need to be planted deeper than other bulbs. An average lily bloom has two circles of three petals, often with very prominent stamens. In fact the structure is similar to that of the iris.

The colour range of the blooms is vast, and every colour of the rainbow appears, except blue. The size of the blooms varies from 1 to 10 inches across, and on the whole most blooms are found at the top of the stems.

Bulbs are now classified into nine divisions, used by the Royal Horticultural Society and the North American Lily Society:

1   Asiatic hybrids
2   Martagon hybrids
3   Candidum hybrids
4   American hybrids
5   Longiflorum hybrids
6   Trumpet and Aurelian hybrids
7   Oriental hybrids
8   All hybrids not belonging to any other division
9   All true species and their botanical forms and varieties.

The lily has been part of life for so long that it is difficult to know where its true botanical roots lie, but it is a plant that does thrive if undisturbed. No lily root likes to be transplanted and it is also better to replace new bulbs than move existing stock.

Flower scents have been used for many centuries, and in 1893 Count von Marilaum categorized floral scents into six main groups. The flowers in the groups were categorized according to the chemical that predominated in the perfume. These six groups were later increased to ten. The lily perfume comes under group 5, the 'heavy' group, containing flower scents related to any blooms which carry the essential oil that contains indole; the flowers perfumes here are therefore part of the aminoid group. The scent tends to be very sweet, although it does have the disadvantage of becoming unpleasant at close quarters over a long period of time. Most of the scents in this group come from white or cream-coloured blooms.

Many of today's horticulturists produce unusual hybrids of original species, and the list is ever growing. However, all these blooms come from the original ancient plants, and again their names tell us a great deal about their characteristics:

LILIUM AURATUM	golden rayed, a native of Japan; in the wild it often grows in volcanic ash, and is suited to warmer climates
L. BOLANDERI	native to the Siskayou mountains of south Oregon and north California
L. BULBIFERUM	from central Europe, Poland and Yugoslavia
L. CANDIDUM	'the White lily', often called 'the Madonna lily', growing naturally in southern Yugoslavia and Greece towards the Lebanon
L. CARNIOLICUM	native to the southeastern Alps of Italy and Austria, and on south to Greece
L. COLUMBIANUM	native to western North America, spreading from central British Columbia to northern California
L. CROCEUM	'the Orange Lily', a saffron-coloured bloom
L. ELEGANS	'elegant'
L. HANSONII	named after Hanson, an American who introduced seeds of various plants to the Carolinas in the 18th century
L. HENRYI	named after Dr A Henry, who discovered it in western China
L. KELLOGGII	native to northwest California
L. LANCIFOLIUM	originates from a hybrid and is a garden lily grown for a long time in Japan; the name refers to the lance-shaped leaves
L. LONGIFLORUM	'long-flowered'
L. MACKLINIAE	native to Manipur, discovered F Kingdom Ward in 1948 and named after his wife
L. MACROPHYLLUM	native to Nepal, Tibet, Bhutan and Sikkim
L. MARTAGON	native to France and Portugal, east to Turkey, the Caucasus and Siberia, sometimes called 'scarlet Turk's cap', the martagon lily carries an old name with no definite origin
L. MONADELPHUM	found in the Crimea, the northern area of the Caucasus, from the Black Sea to the Caspian Sea
L. MONADEPHOUS	'the stamens are united'
L. PARDALINUM	'panther spotted'; native to northwestern America from northern California to British Columbia

L. PARRYI	from southern California and Arizona
L. PARVUM	native to California and southern Oregon
L. PHILIPPENSE	of the Philippine islands
L. POMPONIUM	meaning 'much splendour'; found in southern France and northwest Italy
L. PYRENAICUM	from the French Pyrenees and Spain; naturalized in Scotland and northern England
L. REGALE	meaning 'royal'; magnificent blooms from China
L. SPECIOSUM	'showy'
L. SUPERBIUM	'superb'
L. TESTACEUM	referring to the colour of the flowers (pale brown), this variety is one of the oldest hybrids still in cultivation, having been catalogued in records before 1841
L. TIGRINUM	the Tiger Lily
L. TSINGTAUENSE	native to northeastern China and Korea
L. WILLMOTTIAE	named after a Miss Willmott

Believe it or not, this list gives but a small indication of the botanical spread of this genus, part of the *Liliaceae* family.

ORIGINS

The elegant lily and its beauty have always been known, and are named in both the Bible and the Talmud. Its beauty and charm have reached many civilizations throughout history. Some of the oldest cultures – the Sumerian, Babylonian, Assyrian, Phoenician, Egyptian, Greek and Roman – all wrote of this ancient flower.

The 18th-century German author and philosopher Johann Gottfried Herder often wrote tales in the style of old legends, plotting the origins of flowers. He wrote this of the lily:

When the earth was still wasteland, a group of charming nymphs came to a bare rock to brighten the barren soil with flowers. The nymphs shared out their jobs; under a blanket of snow on the cool grass the nymph Humility [also known as Thalia] created a modest violet, then Hope [Euphrosyne] created the calyxes of the hyacinth with a beautiful perfume. When Humility and Hope had finished their jobs, a whole variety of new flowers were created, tulips raised their heads and narcissus nodded dreamily. When Venus had seen this she said to the two Graces: 'What are you waiting for, sisters of charm, hurry up and create the flowers of your tenderness.' The Graces went down to earth, and Aglaia, who was Innocence, created the lily. Thalia and Euphrosyne, seeing the lily, created a sister for the lily, the rose, a flower of love. From that time it is said the rose and the lily have flowered together because they were made by the sisters of Grace.

The Greek poet Homer called the lily *Leirion*, from the word *lerios*, meaning 'pale and delicate'. *Lerion* soon changed to *Lirium*, and then to the word *Lilium*, thought to be its Roman name. There are tales that trace the origin of the lily to the Garden of Eden. It was said that it was the only thing there totally pure and innocent, as it sprang from tears shed by Eve as she was expelled from the garden. The lily was certainly plentiful during the biblical times of Palestine. Some feel that it may well be the lily referred to in the Song of Solomon (2:2): 'As the lily among thorns, so is my love among the daughters.'

Certainly there is evidence of the bloom in the Holy Land from 3000 BC. It was a sacred emblem in Crete, and the *Lilium chalcedonecum* was certainly native to the eastern Mediterranean areas, and may well be the lily referred to in another verse of the Song of Solomon (6:2): 'My beloved is gone down into his garden, to the bed of spices, to feed in the gardens, and to gather lilies.'

Interestingly enough Semitic lands did not have flowers predominating; if space were given to flowers it would be the highly aromatic blooms that would be given precedence. *Lilium candidum* would then bloom alongside *Narcissus tazetta* and *Pancratium maratimum*.

Religion has over the centuries used the perfumes of flowers in religious ceremony to please the gods, the word *perfumum* itself meaning 'through smoke' or incense. Certainly the pungent lily aroma was used in this way from about 700 BC.

As history progressed so various civilizations relied upon the lily. Egyptian paintings depict the bloom, with several other tall flowers chosen for their ornamental qualities such as the iris, chrysanthemums and delphiniums.

The exquisitely shaped bloom was a popular image on Cretan pottery; fragments over 3,000 years old attest to this. The Greeks and Romans were more than familiar with the bloom. Homer wrote of it, as we have seen, and in the Roman city of Pompeii the blooms were used on tombs of the dead as a 'momento mori'. Yet there is historical evidence that lilies have been forbidden from certain religious ceremonies because of their links with pre-Christian beliefs. Clement of Alexandra, who lived around 150 AD, forbade the use of lilies and roses in crowns for this very reason. It may well have been that the use of the blooms to adorn the walls of ancient Greek palaces had swayed his decision, or the fact the lily, for the Greeks, was the flower associated with Hera/Artemis, the moon goddess.

In the 10th century the lily was mentioned in *The Benedictional* of Saint Ethelwold of Winchester. It may well be that Roman legionnaires brought some species of lilies to the British Isles. Certainly Crusaders returning from the Mediterranean would have helped spread the bloom. In medieval times the Madonna lily, *Lilium candidum*, was grown in borders in rows, against fences and walls and alongside roses. In 1333 a painting of the Annunciation painted by Simone Martini depicts the Madonna lily, and these blooms were often used to decorate churches on July 2nd, the feast of the Annunciation.

The Tudors were fond of lilies, the 'scarlet Turk's cap' being particularly popular. Gerard in his *Herbal* goes to great lengths to talk about lilies, dividing them into white lilies, red lilies and mountain lilies. He quotes quite precisely that the English white lily grew in most English gardens, while the other white lily found in England grew naturally in Constantinople, 'that being the origin of the plants in our English gardens'. He refers to one white lily as *Rosa Junonis* or 'Juno's rose'. The red lily, he says, is common in English gardens but originated in the ploughed areas of Italy and Languedoc.

In religious iconography, archangels represent the divine energy, the principal Christian archangels being Michael, Rapheal, Uriel and Gabriel, always shown carrying either a sword of divine judgement, a staff for protection, a book for wisdom or a lily for mercy.

Of course the *Fleur de Lys*, the stylized lily flower, was the royal emblem of the kings of France. The *Fleur de Lys* symbolizes a triple ideal, God's majesty in triplicate: his majesty, creation and royalty. The *Fleur de Lys* also symbolizes the trinity of mind, body and soul. The stylized lily bloom appeared in heraldic devices and was used by the first French kings as the *fleron* seen at the end of the sceptre. It was said that the lily motif used for the *Fleur de Lys* arose from a humble hermit's vision, when an angel appeared to him holding an azure shield on which were three golden lilies shining like stars. In this vision the hermit was told to give the shield to Queen Clothilde. The story goes that when the vision ended the Queen herself entered the hermit's small room, received the shield and gave it to King Clovis (whose emblem up to this point had been much less aesthetically pleasing, three black toads). King Clovis carried the shield into battle and was victorious wherever he went.

The red and white lily was also an emblem for the city of Florence in Italy, one of the world's most important trading centres during the Middle Ages and Renaissance, with its own currency on which the lily appeared. Florence is often referred to over the ages as 'the city of lilies'.

The bloom became more strongly associated with riches and royalty during the late 1400s and early 1500s. During the reign of Louis XII the flower became a national bloom and appeared in all French gardens. Earlier rulers had created Orders of the Lily, military awards for bravery. The last Order of the Lily was founded by King Louis XVIII at the end of the 1700s; the symbol of this order was a white silk ribbon from which hung a silver lily.

Oriental lilies were introduced into Europe in the 19th century. The Tiger Lily (*L. tigrinum*) was introduced from Japan via China in 1804 by one William Kerr. In 1910, Ernest Wilson, nicknamed 'Chinese Wilson' because he spent so much time in China, almost lost his life to the lily. On a trip there to collect lilies, having gathered the bulbs he started his homeward journey by mule train when his party were hit by an avalanche. Wilson's leg was shattered in the accident. He recovered but was left with what he referred to as 'a lily limp'.

A feature of many of the lilies that have been naturalized in Europe is the multitude of heads on one stem. This proved to be a very good omen at harvest time. Traditionally, in some areas the lilies were grown near wheat fields, and they acted as a guide for the grain price when sold. The more blooms per stem, the better price the grain would fetch when harvested. In some areas one bloom was equivalent to one shilling per bushel. Women seeing a plentiful crop of lilies would prophesy that bread would be cheap for the next few months.

Lilium tigrinum

PLANT LORE AND HISTORY

Symmetry in creation and life has always been important to man, and the perfect shape of the lily symbolizes for man the spirit or essence of creation. The flower's perfection was noted by Homer who described the skin of Ajax as being as delicate as a lily. In approximately 2130 BC the Sumerian ruler Gudea of Laygash used a perfect lily bloom to decorate a seal cylinder, possibly to indicate that the importance of the seal contained in the cylinder matched the perfection of the illustration on it.

Most of the tales surrounding the lily concern themselves with the symbolism of the white Madonna lily, *Lilium candidum*. The flower could symbolize many attributes: sincerity, common sense and youthful innocence.

It was not until the 2nd century AD that *Lilium candidum* was dedicated or consecrated to the Madonna, and this lily was certainly not referred to as 'the Madonna lily' until at least 100 years ago. The bloom was said to epitomize Mary, its white petals symbolizing her spotless beauty and purity, and the golden anthers her soul within, sparkling in divine light. It is said in folklore that three days after her death, Mary's tomb was visited and found empty, save for an abundance of lilies. *Lilium candidum* held a vitally important position within religious symbolism, symbolizing divine innocence. The plant was encouraged to grow in profusion in monastery gardens and religious grounds to provide blooms for church and cathedral decorations during June and July. And it was not only the Virgin Mary who was associated with the lily; it is said that her husband Joseph's staff produced lilies, and the bloom is also linked with John the Baptist and St Aloysius, as a symbol of their innocence. St Catherine also has the lily as her device, commemorating the conversion of her father Costis to Christianity, when he witnessed the miracle of a scentless lily being given a perfume.

In history the lily is quite often illustrated in a vase; this is a very important symbol because in this the lily takes on the feminine principal. The bloom is also dedicated to St Anthony, the protector of marriages. It appears as a crusading image upon the heraldic arms of the blessed Virgin Mary and as a church decoration to guard against evil. For the bloom to be successfully used in church in ancient times, the stamens and pistils had to be removed, effectively 'gelding' the lily and rendering it asexual.

The Victorian language of flowers includes a yellow lily which could symbolize either falsehood or gaiety. For the Victorians the Tiger Lily (*L. tigrinum*) was associated with the phrase, 'For once may pride befriend me.' The Victorians were great lovers of the lily, and the Tiger Lily often features in Victorian poetry:

> *I like not ladies slippers*
> *nor yet the sweet pea blossoms,*
> *nor yet the flaky roses,*
> *red or white as snow;*

I like the chaliced lilies,
the heavy eastern lilies
the gorgeous tiger lilies, that in garden grow.
THOMAS BAILEY ALDRICH

Because of its ubiquitous associations with the church and religious festivals, the lily also came to be associated with death. Thus superstitions about the lily were perpetuated. In folklore there was the belief that the soul took on the form of a lily and appeared on the chairs of those about to depart this life. A lily bloom brought into the house was said to be followed quickly by the death of one of its inhabitants. White lilies were said to spring up from the graves of those wrongly executed, thus attesting to their innocence and wrongful death. Three lilies were said to spring up from the graves of maidens, which none but their lover should cut. Any lily was said to be tended best by an innocent soul wrongly accused – this belief grew up from the common assumption that the garden of Gethsemane hosted lilies as well as olive trees.

This link between the lily and the afterlife is also seen in the belief that the soul transmutes to become a lily at the time of the funeral, thus symbolizing the purity of the soul after death.

If the soul travels to heaven then it will meet the 'Queen of Heaven', the Virgin Mary, or in pre-Christian symbolism Juno, who was also considered queen of the heavens. In ancient Greek myth, Hercules, Zeus' illegitimate son, suffered at the hands of Hera (Juno as she was known in Roman mythology). This famous hero had been humanly vulnerable at birth and his mother, Queen Alcmene the Tyrrhenian, had hidden him. His hiding place was discovered, so Zeus sent Hermes to save the young child, putting him to sleep on the breast of the sleeping Hera so that her milk would grant him immortality. The infant bit her breast by mistake; the startled goddess awoke and pulled the child away so fast that the milk flowed all over the heavens. The drops that fell to the ground became lilies – 'Juno's roses', as the Romans called them – and one drop fell into the sky and became what we now refer to as 'the Milky Way'.

The lily also appears in Scandinavian legend. Thor carries lightning in one hand and his sceptre, crowned with a lily, in the other.

Oberon, fabled king of the fairies and elves, was also said to carry a lily, as a magic wand. Each lily has its own elf, who is born with it, lives in it and dies with it.

The art world places its part in the plant lore and history of the lily, too. The association between the Virgin Mary and the *Lilium candidum* is evident in a great many paintings. Floral symbolism was popular during the time of the Italian Renaissance, and from the 12th century onwards much money and time were invested in religious art. The lily, along with a few other key symbolic blooms, appears with regularity, and most everyday folk understood the symbolism of the blooms much better than they could read church Latin or even their own tongue. Before the 14th century paintings portraying the Annunciation were rare, but after that time the white lily appears – always depicted between the messenger, the angel Gabriel, and Mary. In some of the earliest of these paintings, the lily was in Gabriel's hand; latterly the lily appears in a vase, the symbolism here supporting the feminine principal.

The orange lily (*L. croceum*) also had a link with Christian art and was often used to symbolize Christ. In the Portinari Altar Piece by Hugo van der Goes (1440–82), several flowers are included to pass on a symbolic message. In a vase sits the orange lily (symbolizing Christ), an iris (for the Queen of Heaven), iris leaves (the spear used at the crucifixion), violets (for humility), three carnations (the Holy Trinity) and a stem of aquilegia (for the seven sorrows of Mary or the seven-fold gifts of the Holy Spirit).

The lily was one of Shakespeare's favourites for representing purity and chastity:

Now by my maiden honour, yet as pure as the unsullied lily ...
LOVE'S LABOURS LOST V.II.352

To gild refined gold, to paint the lily, to throw a perfume on the violet ... is wasteful and ridiculous excess.
KING JOHN IV.II.11

As fascinating as the history of the lily is, its plant lore delights and entertains. It is interesting to see how closely the flower is linked with women. In the garden they will only flourish with success, so it is said, if tended by a good woman or by a mistress who is the master! How delicate is the balance between men and women where the lily is involved – If a man should tread on a lily it will follow that there will be a loss of purity for the women of his household, a sober warning for many a clumsy-footed man.

It may well be that in the past people have been tempted to bring the blooms indoors, however doing so was said to mean permanent spinsterhood for any unmarried girl in the home. A woman who dreamed of the lily would be granted good luck and solitude if she needed it. The purity of the lily meant that it could counter witchcraft; if planted round about the house it would deter ghosts and unwanted evils. One legend held that if powdered yellow lily were secretly administered to a woman she would betray her chastity unless she passed water within several hours of drinking the doctored potion. This devious method was often used by prospective husbands to 'test' the chastity of their brides.

The strangest use of the lily in plant lore was as a means of revenge on people who had done wrong. A lily and the sap of a bay tree could be mixed together and left to rot in a pile of manure. The worms from this heap would later be collected and hidden in the pocket of the guilty person, who would be granted no sleep or rest until the worms quit his or her pocket.

The orange lily (L. *croceum*) is linked with the Irish Ulster Orange Lodges, who march to mark the defeat of King James II by William of Orange at the Battle of the Boyne, 1690. The blooms were found growing on the site of the battle, and so their association with warfare echoes that of the poppy.

HEALTH AND WELL-BEING

Perfume was very important to the ancient Egyptians. The distillation of alcohol was unknown until the 4th century BC; before this time scents were gleaned from plants by steeping them in oil to obtain their essential oil. During the 18th Egyptian dynasty, an ointment infused with essence of lily was much prized, and the more intense the perfume, the better and more highly regarded it was. This ointment had a mollifying and warming effect, and was used for 'female problems'. Yet preparing this lily ointment was an arduous and time-consuming process, requiring 1,000 lilies! A typical 'recipe' of the time went something like this:

9 lb 5 oz oil (1,130 drachme of oil, the drachme being the measurement of weight used by the ancient apothecaries)
5 lb 3 oz (632 drachme) sweetflag
5 oz myrrh (40 drachme) in scented wine
3 lb 6 oz (414 drachme) cardamom in rain water
1,000 lilies
honey
salt
herbs
9 oz (69 drachme) best myrrh
1 1/4 oz (11 drachme) crocus
9 1/2 oz (76 drachme) cinnamon
saffron

Pliny's use of the lily was slightly less extravagant. He mentions using it as a cure for foot and skin problems, and suggests to amateur gardeners that soaking the bulbs in red wine will produce purple rather than white blooms. The Romans endorsed Pliny's use of the lily and often used the juice of the crushed bulbs on corns. The plants were often cultivated near Roman outposts as an important supply of 'materia medica'.

Many centuries later the bloom was encouraged to grow in monasteries and church grounds. Godorus Serjeant, surgeon to Queen Elizabeth I, successfully treated many people with dropsy by combining the juice of 1 lily root and barley flour together, baked into cakes and taken with meat as a replacement for the usual bread.

Gerard's *Herbal* includes a good deal of information on white, red and mountain lilies. He notes that lilies of all descriptions can be 'wild, from the field, tame or from the garden'. Gerard is very conversant with the fact that some lilies originated from Constantinople and other parts of the world. He also reminds us 'that no floure so lively sets forth the frailty of man's life as the lily'.

Gerard used the root of his garden lily to mend severed sinews. For this the lily was first covered with honey and then applied to the wound. He used the roots of the red lily for different medical complaints: a red lily root, roasted and mixed with rose oil, cured burns; a similarly roasted root covered with honey removed wrinkles and facial deformities, whilst the leaves of the red lily were good for serpent bites and, when boiled and mixed with vinegar, healed wounds and ulcers.

Culpeper knew that the lily was governed by the moon and had the ability to expel poison, reduce pestilential fevers and, if the roots were bruised and boiled in wine, then drunk, would be beneficial 'for it expels the venom to the exterior parts of the body'. He advises baking the lily roots with barley meal and eating as bread if dropsy was a problem, and recommends an ointment made from the root mixed with hog's grease for 'scald heads' and ulcers. As would be expected for a flower linked with women, Culpeper advises its use to speed up birth and to reduce swellings in 'delicate areas'.

The Madonna lily (*L. candidum*) has been used from very ancient times for skin problems; however, as it is so scarce in the wild and difficult to cultivate reliably it is seldom used for this purpose today. Its use in the past was sometimes attributed to cures enacted by the Virgin Mary; ointments and salves made from the Madonna lily were said to invoke miracles on boils and burns.

The flower has long been used in folk medicine to treat boils, whitlows on fingers and toes and to heal external wounds. The petals would be crushed and applied to burns, stings and cuts. The bulb could be cooked and then, when soft, mixed with milk and flour to create a

poultice to be applied to abscesses, chilblains and many other skin eruptions. The lily used for this last cure is thought to have been the orange
lily (*L. croceum*).

The Tiger Lily (*L. tigrinum*) was a well-known food plant in China
dating back over 2,000 years. In China and Japan many lilies were
harvested as vegetables. In herbal medicine, the Tiger Lily was used as a
remedy for female reproductive problems – this was in direct response to
its ancient associations with fertility and purity. It was recommended for
nausea during pregnancy. It was also used for heart problems, palpitations and arthritis, while the small bulbs formed at the leaf axils were
used for colic and wind.

In homoeopathic medicine the Tiger Lily was used for female reproductive problems and the heart. The Tiger Lily flower essence is a good
female remedy essence giving inner calm and serenity.

Because the *Lilium candidum* is erratic when grown commercially, its
scarcity means it is not much used in healing now. The Native Americans
had a long history of using it for medicine, however, as an astringent, to
soothe and heal damaged tissues, and for burns, abscesses, chilblains,
ulcers and alopecia.

OBSERVATIONS

The symbolism of the lily is sometimes contradictory: it can be a proud and
regal bloom or it can be humble, especially when it is used to represent the
simplicity and purity of the Virgin Mary. The bloom can represent both
motherhood and virginity because it is the flower of the Virgin Mary. It was
said that most of the flowers growing in the garden of Gethsemane understood Christ's anguish and hung their heads in sympathy – except the lily,
who stood with her head towards the stars. But when the lily saw Christ
kneel down carefully, moving the flowers aside lest he should damage them,
she was humbled and wept. From that day to this, so it was said, each lily
flower carries a small tear at the base of the bloom, symbolizing grief and
penitence.

Many people still associate the lily with death, as illustrated by its prevalence at funerals. Many brides of today shy away from having lilies in their bridal bouquets or church decorations, applying this superstition wholesale to all species of lily.

For those who are familiar with the bloom, who have touched its wax-like petals, stared at its perfect symmetry and breathed deeply its exquisite perfume, the true majesty and magic of this bloom is evident. A rather touching and pertinent tale about the lily concerns the King Solomon. Queen Sybil of Sheba tested the King's wisdom by presenting him with a bunch of lilies, one of which was made of silver, and challenging him to identify the impostor without touching it (the story tells us that it looked identical to the real lilies). The king placed the flowers by an open window, then watched and waited. He found the artificial bloom instantly, as not one bee visited it.

FOXGLOVE

Digitalis purpurea

BOTANICAL

The tall and elegant foxglove is a native biennial or perennial in British woods, hedgerows and open places, although hybrid strains have been produced and appear in gardens. The plant, being so popular, is easily recognized – particularly *Digitalis purpurea*, the common foxglove. The stem of the foxglove is straight and covered in hairs, as are the underside of the ovate-lanceolate leaves. The flowers are spotted internally and form spikes or racemes often 5 foot high. The individual flowers all face the same way. On *purpurea* the drooping flowers are often 2 inches in size, are violet and covered with dark red spots surrounded by a white ring. These rings act as a honey guide for bees, who enter the flowers from below. The downward-pointing flowers are protected from rain and the bees can enter the protected innards. The pollination of the bloom is only carried out by bumble bees, which have to crawl right into the flowers to reach the nectar and thus pollinate the flower.

The seeds of the foxglove require light to germinate and sometimes lie dormant for years until a clearing appears in a woodland, when thousands will spring up. They have adapted to grow happily in shady places.

The genus name, *Digitalis*, is named after the finger-like blooms. The genus belongs to the *Scrophulariaceae* family, a name that refers to the disease scrofula, which plants of this family were said to cure (it could also be cured, so legend had it, by a monarch's touch).

The wild foxglove, *Digitalis purpurea*, is occasionally found in gardens, there are also several cultivated varieties:

D. FERRUGINEA	red/brown flowers; native to southern Europe
D. GRANDIFLORA	cream/yellow flowers; sometimes called ambigua; from Europe and the Caucasus and Siberia (native to mountain chains)
D. LUTEA	yellow flowers; from southwest Europe and northwest Africa; cultivated in the Netherlands as a garden plant
D. LANATA	native to the Balkans

ORIGINS

Today the foxglove is very much a typical part of the country scenery during May and June. In the British Isles it is more commonplace in the West Country, although it can also be found on scrub land, heaths, mountains and wooded areas. It was possibly introduced into central Europe from the thinner wooded areas of southern and western Europe, certainly by people who discovered its medicinal properties.

The common foxglove is not always purple and sometimes can be found in lighter or darker shades, or even with white flowers. Another frequent foxglove is *D. lanata*, which again has become common in a lot of herb gardens. The plant was certainly one of the most important in medieval 'physic gardens'; in Victorian gardening's heyday, designers such as William Robinson used the foxglove to promote the 'natural' garden look. It is a plant that is still today planted in gardens to create a timeless countryside appearance.

The bloom has a very long and deep association with fairy folk, and its name has various origins. The French call the flower *Gantes notre dame*, while in Britain it is often referred to as 'Our Lady's gloves' or 'Our Lady's thimbles' in reference to the notion that the Virgin Mary could have worn the flowers upon her hands for protection. This link with the hands is very important. In 1542 Leonhard Fuchs named the bloom *Digitalis* from the Latin *digitus*, meaning 'finger', a direct indication of the shape of the flower. The flower has also been called 'fairy bells', the Welsh called it 'fairy's glove', and the Irish 'fairy bells'. The name 'fox' is actually a corruption of the word 'folks'; the flower was the 'folk's glove' or 'the glove of the good folk', the good folk being the fairies. In Saxon times the bloom was called 'foxes glofa', the word 'fox' referring to the reddish colour of the bells. In Anglo-Saxon the bloom was called 'foxes gled', referring to the shape of an ancient musical instrument. A slightly less pleasant name was the Gaelic 'Ciochan Nan Cailleachan Marblia', meaning 'dead old woman's paps'.

Foxglove plants were imported from Europe to the Americas in the 18th century, this again after its much sought-after medicinal qualities had been discovered. The plants soon became naturalized in the Americas, but certainly not to the extent they are in the British Isles.

PLANT LORE AND HISTORY

The foxglove in plant lore and history conjures up a magical image, based in part on the fact that it is sometimes found in woodland areas, far from human habitation. As with any of the flowers associated with magic and fairies, it was said to have good and bad portents. It was said that the fairy folk would smile favourably on any gardener growing the foxglove very tall so that it would nod in the garden – the taller and the more nodding the plant, the happier the fairy folk would be. Wherever the foxglove was found growing, weeds and disease would be kept at bay.

The foxglove has a very close relationship with its surroundings; if allowed to flower freely then the surrounding trees and flowers of the fields and woodlands would be happy and would flourish. Plants and flowers of all description are very highly tuned to the atmosphere, to thought waves and to energy levels. It was said that the foxglove possessed the ability to tell when it was in the presence of a supernatural person or being: the foxglove would bend its tall flower spike to pay homage and respect to any such person.

As has been seen, the foxglove carries many vernacular names. Northumberland refers to the bloom as 'witch's thimble'; other names are 'dead man's bellows', 'bloody man's fingers', 'fairy cap' and 'fairy petticoat'. In the Freiburg area of Switzerland the flower is called 'dey'di diablho' which means 'the devil's thimble'; it was said that he used the flower petal upon his fingers.

It is quite interesting to see how the pendulum sways for this flower between associations with good and with evil. For a flower that provided hats for elves and resting places for the fairies, it was also said to protect mortals from fairies. An ancient belief that children could be stolen by fairies engendered the method of 'testing' whether an ill child was real or had been 'replaced' with a fairy child. Three drops of foxglove juice (made by pounding down the bloom) would be placed on the child's tongue, three drops in his ear. The child would then be sat upon a large shovel and swung in the doorway of the family home three times, while being challenged, if it were indeed a fairy, to leave; if human, then the healing process would start. In Welsh homes a large black cross would be etched in juice on the kitchen floor to keep evil spirits away and deny a witch or devil access.

Despite being used to keep evil at bay, the foxglove was also thought to bring bad luck if picked and brought into a home. No true sailor would contemplate having the bloom anywhere near his ship. These superstitions stemmed from the belief that the flower would allow the devil access – perhaps, given its common name 'devil's fingers', it was thought that he clung to the picked blooms. The fear that the bloom was unlucky was also evidenced in the belief that it was a portent of war, and that the tall erect racemes of flowers were in fact soldiers in disguise ready to go off and fight.

In the Victorian language of flowers the foxglove symbolizes insincerity or adulation. Yet to dream of them meant that you would be lucky in love.

Country children, even as recently as just a few decades ago, would use the foxglove as a plaything. The individual bloom could be picked and then inflated, sealed and burst with the finger, rather like a balloon. From that action the plant earned the nickname 'pop dock' or 'claquet'. The belief that fairies lived in the bells of the foxglove flower might have sprung from the fact that bumble bees have to spend a long time in the bloom, crawling deep in for nectar. The buzzing and movement in the bloom may well have fired people's imaginations to believe that an elf or fairy was busying around inside the flower. A noisy child was often likened to an angry bumble bee in a foxglove.

In Northern legends, wicked fairies were said to put the flowers on foxes' paws so they could prowl in chicken runs unheard, and the marks on the inside of the blooms were said to be elves' fingerprints.

HEALTH AND WELL-BEING

There is no description or evidence from Greek and Roman medicinal writings that the foxglove was used, and in fact it has no classical name that has ever been recorded. It was in 1542 that Fuchs named the flower *Digitalis* and warned that it would be a violent medicine. Gerard's *Herbal* describes it as being bitter, hot and dry, and he quotes the ancients that is has no use in medicine at all. In folk cures, however, the plant was well known for medicinal properties, and was believed to cure tuberculosis. In country regions, children suffering from scarlet fever would have the leaves of the foxglove put into their shoes, to be worn for a year as a cure for the disease. The leaves were also used to heal cuts. It is interesting at this point to remember that it is the leaves that contain digitalin. The leaves were also put into bath water to create a 'moody response' from the bather – for example a lethargic person might experience a positive response. A concoction made from the foxglove was said to cure drunken and frenzied behaviour. Foxglove tea is mentioned in George Eliot's *Silas Marner*. And it was foxglove tea that led to the discovery of the true potential and importance of the foxglove. In country circles foxglove tea had long been used to cure dropsy. After several years research in 1785 a Dr William Witherings published *The Foxglove and some of its medicinal uses*. This publication detailed various treatments, and also noted that the dosage was closely related to the amount of toxic side-effects that developed. Thus it was deemed a very powerful and dangerous drug. Further developments discovered that the cardiac glycosides (enzymes acting on the heart) known as digoxin and digitoxin were also contained in the plant.

The drug digitalis is found in the rosette of basal leaves which are created in the first two years of the plant's life. The most prolific producer of glycosides for medicine is *D. lanata*. The amount of chemicals contained in the leaves is in direct proportion to the amount of photosynthesis that the plant has participated in, it therefore follows that the best substances are found in the leaves during the afternoon when the sun is at its hottest. At night, when the activity of the plant changes, the chemicals change and travel to other parts of the plant.

The powdered leaf of *D. purpurea* is used in tablets for various medical problems. There is evidence that the common foxglove was used in Ireland in the 5th century AD, and from the 11th century in Europe. What has to be remembered and is most important is that this plant is poisonous. While using an external poultice of leaves upon a wound for healing is permitted, quantities have to be adhered to without fail. What can improve a failing or inefficient heart can in the wrong hands cause a healthy heart to cease.

OBSERVATIONS

The foxglove is best experienced first-hand, as very few artists succeed in bringing the beauty of the bloom to life on canvas. In some respects the foxglove takes on where the bluebell finishes, as woodland glades move from a sea of blue to a deeper sea of the wild purple foxglove. Despite the fact that some gardeners have produced enormous spikes of pastel shades, the common foxglove can never lose its unique magic.

HONEYSUCKLE

Lonicera periclymenum, the Woodbine

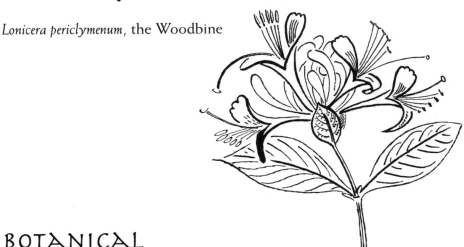

BOTANICAL

The honisuckle that groweth wylde in every hedge, although it be very sweete yet doe I not bring into my garden, but let it rest in his owne place to serve their sens[es] that travell by it, or have nor garden.

JOHN PARKINSON

The Latin name for honeysuckle is *Lonicera*, after one Adam Lonicer a 16th-century German botanist. The *Lonicera* genus belongs to the *Caprifoliaceae* family. The word Caprifoliaceae can be broken down into its several parts: *Capri* (the goat), *foli* (from *folium*, for leaf) and *aceus* (like), so indicates a family of plants that is 'goat-like'. In the case of the honey-suckle this refers primarily to the fact that it is the favoured food of goats!

The common name 'honeysuckle' has not always been used for this plant, which has in its time been referred to as 'suckling', 'caprifoly' and 'woodbind' or 'woodbine', referring to its habit of growing very tightly around host trees or bushes. 'Honeysuckle' refers to the honey dew often found on the leaves of the plant. With any of the honeysuckle family the exquisite perfume is stronger at night, leaving the plant to be pollinated by the nocturnal limehawk moth. Only insects with long tongues can pollinate the plant in any case; bees have to crawl a long way into the nectar tube even when it is filled to its highest level in the afternoons, and as evening falls so the level of nectar drops, leaving successful gathering only to nocturnal moths with incredibly long tongues. The plant guards against self-pollination by making sure that the male and female parts mature entirely in turn. After ripening each berry houses many seeds.

The *Lonicera* genus contains about 200 species of deciduous and evergreen shrubs and climbers. The blooms are tubular with lips that diverge. The following species are some of the many from this genus: Many of the Latin names help us learn a little bit more about the habitat, growth patterns and description of individual blooms:

L. ALPIGENA	the alpine honeysuckle, native to the European Alps
L. AMERICANA	a semi-evergreen hybrid from north America
L. CAPRIFOLIUM	the 'goat leaf' honeysuckle, from Europe and naturalized in Great Britain
L. COERULEA	the blue honeysuckle, native to the European Alps
L. ETRUSCA	from the Mediterranean
L. FRAGRANTISSIMA	from China, a 'most fragrant' winter-blooming plant
L. INVOLUCRATA	from Canada and the western United States, with yellow flowers and strong green bracts
L. JAPONICA	from Japan, China and Korea; very fragrant white to pale yellow blooms
L. NIGRA	the black honeysuckle, native to the European Alps
L. NITIDA	shining, glossy leaves
L. PERICLYMENUM	the 'woodbine' from Great Britain, Asia Minor, the Caucasus and Western Asia; the most familiar and well-loved honeysuckle in the UK, it will sometimes live for 50 years; its vernacular name is 'woodbine'
L. PILEATA	from China, having a cap (the berry is topped with a strange calyx)

L. STENDISHII	from China
L. SYRANGANTHA	from China
L. TATARICA	from southern Russia and Turkestan
L. TRAGOPHYLLA	the Chinese 'woodbine'
L. XYLOSTEUM	the fly honeysuckle, native to the European Alps; the name comes from the Green *xylmon*, meaning 'wood', a reference to its woody stems

ORIGINS

Possibly the earliest reference to the honeysuckle was in AD 659, when the plant is listed in the Chinese book *Tang Ben Cao*. At times it was a plant of great predictability, as its growing pattern was always the same: it would wind itself sun-wise (that is, east to west) around other plants. One common name, 'woodbine' or 'woodbind', denotes this character, although this is a name given in folklore to several other climbing plants. There is evidence of *Lonicera periclymenum* as far back as the 8th century, named after the ancient Greek hero Periclymenus, one of the Argonauts who could change his shape at will, very similar to the honeysuckle flowers themselves, which frequently change form and colour to attract butterflies by day and moths by night. The origin of the name 'suckling' or 'caprifoly' lies in the fact that the leaves of the honeysuckle are the favourite food of goats.

All cultivated varieties come from the original wild *L. periclymenum*, which has been growing in Britain for many centuries. Gerard in his *Herbal* says that he has it in his garden but has not had it for long because some varieties are rare, difficult to find and only stocked by keen horticulturists. He actually likens the flowers to the noses of elephants.

Several other varieties exist which have their origins in other countries, such as *L. belgica*, an early Dutch honeysuckle. One of the oldest is *L. serotina*, the late red honeysuckle. *L. japonica*, which originated in the 19th century, is a shrubby plant native to Asia. *L. nitida* was introduced to the West in 1908 by the horticulturist Wilson. In 1862 Dr

87

George Hall, an American physician who established a hospital for seamen in Shanghai, introduced a *Lonicera* to America which went on to be something of a garden pest. The beginning of the 20th century saw the introduction of *Lonicera x heckrottii*.

Gardens have long been graced by the presence of pergolas, which have existed since Roman times. A pergola is an extended arbour, some of them wide and long enough to allow horses to canter their length. The honeysuckle is a popular plant to grow up pergolas, providing shade and a beautiful perfume.

While the honeysuckle has been used for many centuries, it was overlooked as an important garden plant until the Elizabethan period; before this time it was familiar in woods and hedges. The Elizabethans used the plant to create shade and cover in a bower or arbour:

And bid her steal into the pleached bower, where honeysuckles ripened by the sun, forbid the sun to enter ...
WILLIAM SHAKESPEARE, *MUCH ADO ABOUT NOTHING* III.1.7

PLANT LORE AND HISTORY

The honeysuckle is associated with love because of its growth pattern (it has sometimes been called 'love bind'). It symbolizes, in the way it clings to plants in the wild, the tight embrace of lovers. The plant also has various other meanings in symbolism, such as 'the bounds of love', 'generous and devoted affection' and 'sweet disposition' – no doubt linked to its wonderful heady fragrance. Fidelity and affection in the language of flowers are often symbolized by the honeysuckle, and in some areas it has been referred to as 'hold me tight'.

Its fragrance is very heady, and there was once prevalent the belief that smelling it filled the mind instantly with images and dreams of love. For that reason in folklore it was banned from being put indoors in the presence of young girls. It was said that the fragrance would make their dreams less than innocent. However, if the person who picked it was considered sufficiently mature, the fragrance would promise them dreams of love and passion. Some folk believed that if the bloom was picked and brought into the house a wedding would follow within the next 12 months – on the downside, however, farmers believed picking the honeysuckle would lead to an unsuccessful second crop of hay. It was also said that bringing it indoors would herald a severe attack of sore throats for the family of the house.

Honeysuckle nectar was popular with animals, insects and humans alike. There was a belief that if the juice from a honeysuckle leaf were spread around a bee hive, the bees would be kept happy and stay for a long time. It was also said that a walking stick made from a hazel stick which had been encircled and marked with honeysuckle would enable its owner to court the lady of his dreams. Much time was spent by young men searching hazel woods for a perfect specimen from which to fashion just such a magic walking stick.

HEALTH AND WELL-BEING

The honeysuckle genus has contributed widely for many centuries to medicine. It has been used to cure a varied selection of problems. The Chinese believed that the plant actually granted an increased life span and linked it very much with immortality. Evidence of the honeysuckle exists in religious places from the 3rd century BC, and has been found decorating the outside of Buddhist temples. It was viewed as a herb of immortality not only to people but also the vegetable world (a reference to its ability to shoot and flourish even when cut right back). Gerard's *Herbal* recommends that the flowers be steeped in oil, left in the sun and rubbed upon the body to cure coldness and numbness. Culpeper recommends the honeysuckle as a cure for asthmatic problems. It can also be used to cure sore throats either as a gargle on its own or mixed with sage, rosemary and plantain. Irish folk often used it to cure jaundice, while in China in the 1950s it was being used as a contraceptive.

L. caprifolium (the Dutch honeysuckle) and *L. periclymenum* (the wild woodbine) have often been mentioned in historical texts as being medicinal plants. *Caprifolium* was said to have laxative and expectorant properties, while *periclymenum* was an expectorant, antiseptic and was used in cough mixtures. Pliny suggested that *periclymenum* could be used to cure spleen disorders if taken with wine; it was also used for urinary and childbirth problems.

Today honeysuckle continues to be used in homoeopathic medicine and herbal medicine, though usually the *L. japonica* and *L. periclymenum* species are used. All parts of these honeysuckles were used in healing: the flower buds of *japonica*, referred to as 'jin yin hua', are used to cure fevers as they can clear toxins from the body. In some Traditional Chinese Medicine the buds are stir-fried to cure diarrhoea. The stems of the plants are used during acupuncture, to dispel colds and dysen-

Lonicera caprifolium

tery, and to take the pain out of rheumatoid arthritis. The wild honeysuckle flowers (*L. periclymenum*) were usually made into syrups to treat coughs and asthma. They appear in some cough preparations today.

What again is important to remember is that the berries of any honeysuckle are poisonous and great care should be taken when using the plant. Of all the species of honeysuckle, only about 12 are used medicinally nowadays. Both the leaves and the blooms contain salicylic acid, a component of aspirin which can be used for colds, aches, pains and fevers. Honeysuckle as a syrup or a tea has long been known as a useful antidote for respiratory problems, and in general the plant calms nerves, eases tension and promotes well-being.

OBSERVATIONS

Anybody who has experienced the exquisite fragrance of the honey-suckle on a warm evening will be able to appreciate how easy it is to become totally intoxicated with the plant. The heady perfume encourages daydreams and relaxation. Fragrant bowers filled with honeysuckles were the meeting places of lovers long past. If a flower can bring to mind a personality, then the honeysuckle flower belongs to those who gain pleasure from thinking about the past, and are happy as they look to the future.

AQUILEGIA

Aquilegia vulgaris, the Columbine

BOTANICAL

The *Aquilegia* genus consists of nearly 100 species, which are hardy, herbaceous perennials. The word *Aquilegia* is thought to come from the Latin *aquila*, meaning 'eagle' – part of the bloom (the flower spear) is somewhat similar in shape to an eagle's claw. The English name 'Columbine' (from the Latin word *columba*, meaning 'dove') refers to the fact that if the bloom is held upside down it looks like a ring of doves dipping into water for a drink. Apart from Columbine, the bloom is also called 'Granny's Bonnet', 'Granny's Night-cap', 'European Crowfoot' or 'Herba Leonis'. In his *Herbal*, Gerard refers to this last vernacular name, explaining that it is a herb that 'the lion doth delight' (though *why* it might have delighted lions is unclear, except that in folklore it was said that young lions ate the plant to give them strength).

The *Aquilegia* belongs to the *Ranunculaceae* family. This name is based on the Latin diminutive *rana*, meaning 'frog'. Frogs prefer to live in damp areas, and as the aquilegia prefers damp wooded areas and fens in its native habitat it is similar to the frog.

The leaves grow on long stalks and the drooping bloom, often coloured purple or blue in the wild, stands at the top of a similarly long stem. The flower is made up of five corolla- or petal-like sepals; inside there are a further five petals and a hooked spur. Any nectar formed in the bloom lies at the end of this spur; insects with long proboscis such as the bumble bee reach the nectar, while some insects with short proboscis try to reach the nectar by making holes in the spur of the bloom. After pollination, Gerard says, 'the floures grow up cods, in which is contained little black and glittering seed'. On the whole the blooms, and indeed the plants, live for a short period of time; however this plethora of seeds ensures that the genus continues.

The *Aquilegia* today consists of many hybrids, alpine species and varieties that are better suited to borders.

A. ALPINA	from Switzerland; prefers light woods
A. BERTOLONII	from Italy, a dwarf species
A. CAERULEA	from the United States, originally dark blue
A. CANADENSIS	from Canada and the US; includes lemon flowers
A. CHRYSANTHA	golden-flowered
A. DISCOLOR	from Spain
A. ECALCARATA	from western China
A. EINSELEANA	from the southern Alps of Italy and Switzerland; sometimes called 'Einsel's Aquilegia'
A. FLABELLATA	meaning fan-shaped; from Japan
A. GLANDULOSA	meaning glandular and 'glauca' (blue-grey)
A. JUCUNDA	bright
A. KITAIBELII	named after the botanist P. Kitaibel
A. LONGISSIMA	from Mexico and southern USA
A. NEVADENSIS	from Nevada
A. REUTERI	sometimes called 'Reuter's Aquilegia', from the southeastern French Alps
A. SKINNERI	named after the botanist Skinner
A. THALICTRIFOLIA	with leaves similar to Thalictrum
A. VIRIDIFLORA	having green blooms

sometimes called the Columbine, native to Europe and England in particular, found in woods, bushy places and limestone areas

ORIGINS

This plant, now sadly uncommon is, in the wild, a perennial. It is more prevalent in ash woods, as the growing habit of the ash allows light to filter to the woodland floor, encouraging a varied selection of seasonal blooms, the aquilegia being one of many. In these woods it is often found growing amongst ramsons (wild garlic,) its blue/purple blooms a vivid contrast with the white of the wild garlic. Old vernacular names include 'aquilinae' and 'ackeley'. The short spurred hybrids (the spur is the pointed back of the bloom) have been created from the native *Aquilegia vulgaris*, whereas the long-spurred hybrids originate from the Canadian rocky blooms discovered in 1864 and those from New Mexico discovered in 1873.

This bloom, so native to Europe, became native also in northeastern America and later came to be the state flower of Colorado, being called 'the rocky mountain columbine'.

There is much evidence that the columbine has been part of our lives for many centuries. Artwork over the ages, and paintings in particular, give us much visual evidence. In 1437 Hans Multscher used it in his painting *Death of the Virgin*; another religious painting, *Adoration of the Shepherds* by Hugo van de Goes (1475), also features the flower. In a less religious setting it is used in a painting entitled *Emilia in Her Garden*, created in 1465 by 'The Master of the Hours of the Duke of Burgundy'. This painting illustrates a medieval French garden, which has in the foreground a border that includes aquilegia. In 1526 Dürer used it in the painting *Albertina*. Further evidence of the bloom is found in 15th- and 16th-century church carvings in several British cathedrals.

Obviously each columbine used in the past has been the *vulgaris* species. It was a popular plant in Elizabethan gardens, where groups of it were used to great effect. The word 'columbine' has its own historical reference and meaning. It is said to came from the Italian word 'columbina' meaning 'a lady love' or 'a coquette of tender years'.

PLANT LORE AND HISTORY

The symbolism of the columbine is not terribly positive. It was once the emblem of 'cuckoldom', the spurs at the end of its nectaria being said to resemble a cuckold's horn. Sometimes it was said to symbolize foolishness, as the bloom resembles a jester's hat. In Shakespeare's day it symbolized worthlessness and ingratitude. Shakespeare uses this symbolism when he links the columbine with rue, another sad plant. Sir Thomas Browne (1605–1682) wrote: 'The columbine by lonely wanderer taken/is there ascribed to such who are forsaken.'

In folklore it was said that any person dreaming of the flower would have a happy adventure, though whether this meant in reality or dreams was never quite made plain. It was a plant that was used to protect young couples from witches, though with its cuckoldry associations one would think that witches were the least of people's problems! Sometimes in folklore it was called the lion's herb because it was said that in springtime young lions ate the plant to give them strength.

In the Victorian language of flowers the aquilegia meant 'folly', the purple bloom meant 'resolved to win', and the red bloom 'anxious and trembling', none very positive attributes. The most positive aspect of the columbine lies in religious symbolism, where the bloom symbolizes the seven-fold gifts of the Holy Spirit: wisdom, understanding, counsel, strength, knowledge, true godliness and holy fear. This symbolism is of course linked to the association of the bloom with doves. While the flower has only five petals, this link with the seven gifts was reinforced by religious painters, who made sure that any bloom depicted in this symbolic way had a stem carrying seven flowers. Van Eyck went one stage further when he painted the Virgin Mary wearing a crown of seven columbines.

HEALTH AND WELL-BEING

The Aquilegia, as a member of the Ranunculaceae family, is poisonous, the seeds fatally so – especially to small children. However, used in proper quantities the plant over the centuries has been used for healing. In folklore various parts of the plant including the seeds were used for spleen and liver complaints, jaundice and dropsy. The juice of the leaf was often used on wounds and skin eruptions, and was also useful for swellings (the leaf could be applied directly onto swellings in the form of a poultice). The plant proved to a be a urine stimulant, and infusions of parts of the plant were used to treat sores in the mouth, sore throats and rheumatic pains. The seeds administered on a biscuit with butter were used to keep boils at bay; this remedy was current in the Netherlands until not so long ago.

Culpeper informs readers that the columbine is a plant of Venus and that taking the seeds with wine would speed up the delivery of a child. He says that the Spanish used to eat part of the root before fasting to cure kidney stones. In 1741 it was recorded in the Wurttemberg *Pharmacopoeia* that *Aquilegia vulgaris* was an anti-scorbutic herb (used to treat scurvy); however, by the 19th century the plant was no longer officially used.

As well as being an antiseptic and astringent, Aquilegia also has sedative qualities and was used for nervous complaints. Aquilegia contains cyanogenic glycosides and vitamin C, but is no longer used internally.

OBSERVATIONS

The Aquilegia is one of the many flowers linked with Christian symbolism, and it is fascinating to see that despite the strength of Christian teaching and example the Aquilegia has not lost its many vernacular names in preference to columbine.

The Church found the association between certain flowers and pre-Christian ceremony and beliefs difficult to accept and accommodate, and so tried to assimilate these flowers into Christian belief by founding stories or symbolism of its own. Lack of knowledge or ignorant fear led to the destruction or suppression of much folk and plant lore. Yet the majority of plant beliefs were not a threat to any particular denomination, and worked within a belief in a creator of the universe with all living things sacred, a belief that the future of creation and nature in particular was the keystone to man's survival and prosperity in terms of food, clothing and shelter. It is these steadfast beliefs which we might do well to return to in today's rather muddled and misbalanced world.

HELLEBORE

Hellebore niger, the Christmas rose

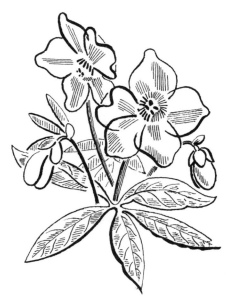

BOTANICAL

Helleborus is the name given in classical form for the hellebore family, a genus of over 20 species, all very closely related. The Greeks used the word *belleborus* for any form of the genus. The genus consists of perennials, some evergreen, some deciduous. In gardens today they are chosen for their winter and spring blooms. In the wild (where they are rare, at least in the UK) they are found in woodlands, where they are a perennial preferring calcareous soil.

The name *Helleborus* comes from two origins: the Greek *elein* meaning 'to take away', and *bora*, meaning 'food'. The root induces vomiting, thus the origin of the botanical name. The *belleborus* belongs to the *Ranunculaceae* family, to which many poisonous plants belong.

The seeds of the plant are spread in several manners. The more unusual method is by snails, who eat the oil covering around the seed and then carry the discarded seeds along in their slime.

As well as the native plants there are several garden varieties of this genus:

H. ABCHASICUS	from the Caucasus
H. ARGUTIFOLIUS	this plant's name is a synonym for the Corsicus Hellebore; from Caucasus and Sardinia
H. ATRORUBENS	from southeast Europe
H. FOETIDUS	sometimes called 'stinking hellebore' due to its fetid aroma, native in Europe, rare in Great Britain, but when found prefers the south of the country; the green blooms are often rimmed with a maroon colour; the plant is poisonous
H. NIGER	in the vernacular often called the 'Christmas rose', which flowers from December to March; from Central and southern Europe
H. ORIENTALIS	the 'Lenten rose', from Greece and Asia Minor, this produces blooms of white, pink and purple
H. PURPURASCENS	from Hungary, this variety is deciduous
H. VIRIDIS	'the green hellebore', from Europe, rare in England and Wales, preferring calcareous woods

ORIGINS

The Hellebore is certainly one of the group of oldest cultivated plants. Seeds to substantiate this have been found in prehistoric tombs. What the plant was used for is difficult to ascertain, it may well have been for medicinal, sacred or even magical uses. The hellebore that appears in history, folklore and superstition is the *Helleborus niger*, a plant that goes by many names: the Christmas rose, the Black hellebore, Black nisewort or Neesewort and the Neesing root among them. It is difficult to explain

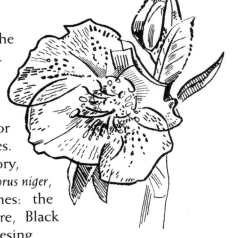

Hellebore orientalis, the Lenten rose

99

all these names, though the plant has indeed a black root, and the white blooms, which can sometimes flower in December, give credence to the name Christmas rose.

The origin of the flower in one tale is that it first grew by the gates of heaven, tended by the angels who called it 'the rose of love'. When Adam and Eve were expelled from the Garden, it became covered in snow (as is found in many floral tales). Sadly all the flowers that had been looked after by Adam and Eve remained in Eden, however the angels asked God if Adam and Eve could take the rose of love to earth as a symbol of God's mercy.

Another association with Christmas comes to us in a tale told of the birth of Christ, although botanists will be quick to point out the bloom is not native to the Holy Land. A small girl wishing to see the Christ child and finding the stable was overjoyed, but had no gift to give the baby. In one version of this tale she cries and her tears puncture the snow; when she stops an angel shows her little roses that have sprung up from her tears. The child picks these 'Christmas roses' and gives then to the Christ child. The other version says that the small girl finds the flowers blossoming from impressions made in the snow by the Virgin Mary as she walked to and fro from the stable.

The Christmas rose has a far more ancient name, that of *Melanpode*, which originates from a physician called Melanpus who lived in approximately 1400 BC. This medical man was said to have cured the daughters of Proteus, King of Argus. The daughters had been cursed with madness by the goddess Hera, whom they had insulted. The ancient physician, aware of the healing power of the Christmas rose (he had observed its calming effect on the goats who ate it), fed it to the girls to effect their cure. The Greek historian Herodotus (approximately 484–425 BC) was instrumental in informing us of this tale and the origin of the ancient name of the bloom.

It is said the plant was given the name helleborus by the Romans after a river of that name; the Romans also used the word 'helleborus' to describe someone who was insane. In those days the plant was considered the best medicine for curing insanity, and the best Christmas roses were recorded as growing in many Aegean coastal villages.

An Arthurian legend tells us of King Arthur's half-sister Morgan-le-Fay, who in folklore possesses the dual role of healer and wicked sorceress. It was said that she concocted a potion that prevented Queen Guinevere from conceiving, and that this potion contained hellebore roots among other plants such as lovage, vervain, penny royal, rue and wood sorrel.

The Elizabethans used the hellebore as a border plant. Gerard chronicles the Bishop of Norwich as having a white hellebore growing in a wood near his house, and also notes that it grew in the Welsh mountains. He speaks, too, of a white hellebore growing in his own London garden, referring to it by the name 'Lingwort'. He says that the black hellebore was far more prolific in London gardens, flowering about Christmas time if the winter was mild. And he informs us that in 'high Dutch' it is called 'Christ's herb'. Culpeper does not have much good to say about the black hellebore, referring to it as 'fetter wort', 'fetter grass' or 'bear's foot'. A similar sounding name, Setterwort, was used for *H. foetidus*, 'the stinking hellebore'.

PLANT LORE AND HISTORY

Roman scholar Pliny the Elder writes that the Gauls used the juice of *H. niger* on the tips of their hunting spears. Once these had wounded their prey the poison killed the animal, however the poison could also taint the flesh and so the carcass had to be handled carefully afterwards.

H. niger, like the mandrake root, had to be dug from the earth with due care and, in the case of the niger, secrecy. On the morning of digging it up, the perpetrator of the deed must drink a glass of wine with garlic in it; this was said to keep any headache created by the deed at bay. The digger must then make a circle around the chosen plant with consecrated chalk, must face the sun and say a prayer, and then sink the spade into the earth at the circumference of the circle. It was vital that even the birds of the air should be unaware and unable to see the digging in progress; if perchance any eagle should circle overhead, disaster would befall the perpetrator, who would die before a year had elapsed. Writing in the 1st century AD, the Greek physician Dioscorides makes reference to this:

> Those who dig it up pray to Apollo and Asclepius by observing the eagle's flight. They say that the bird's flight is dangerous, for it would bring death if it saw hellebore being dug.

In medieval times the hellebore was viewed as a plant of magical properties, and many superstitions grew up around it. The black hellebore was said to bring bad luck to any person picking it, yet as a plant growing in the ground its presence near houses was encouraged as it was believed to purify homes and drive evil away. A hellebore was used by some to measure the success of a forthcoming harvest: a root producing four tufts meant the harvest would be good, but only two tufts meant that the harvest would fail.

While the Hellebore became for some an emblem of purity, in the Victorian language of flowers the Christmas rose signified 'relieve my anxiety', whereas in general a Hellebore meant scandal and calumny.

HEALTH AND WELL-BEING

From the time of the ancient Greeks the Hellebore has been used to cure mental problems and to sharpen the mind. Hippocrates prescribed milk from goats who had been grazing on the Hellebore to cure madness and insanity, with the most severe cases being treated with a brew or concoction made straight from the plant. The Greeks also used it to treat those believed to be possessed by demons.

All species of the genus are toxic and yet over the centuries have been used to expel illness. From the Middle Ages onwards a powdered concoction was used to cure worms in children, though quite often the treatment killed not only the worms but the patient. This practice continued up until the 1800s. The Victorian artist Gilbert White refers to this violent remedy, yet children continued to be given a concoction of the plant before breakfast, as it was said to boost intelligence. The plant was also used to prevent leprosy, rabies, epilepsy and miscarriages, though there is no evidence extant to prove that it worked.

Black nisewort, one of the nicknames for the *H. niger*, points to its use in dried and powdered leaf form to induce sneezing. The black root cured cramps and difficult breathing; a strong dose was said to dispel obstinacy and melancholy. Some people believed that if a home suffered under a heavy, foreboding atmosphere, then a vase of Hellebore flowers would dispel the unpleasantness and bring calm. Christmas roses brought into a house at Christmas would bestow blessings and protection, but only if the blooms were brought indoors still on their roots and not cut.

> *Borage and hellebore fill two scenes,*
> *Sobereign plants to purge the veins*
> *Of melancholy, and cheer the heart*
> *Of those black fumes which make it smart;*
> *To clear the brain of misty fogs,*
> *Which dull our senses and Soul clogs;*
> *The best medicine that e'er God made*
> *For this malady, if well assay'd.*
> ROBERT BURTON, *ANATOMIE OF MELANCHOLY*

In Elizabethan homes, herbs, aromatic plants and flowers would be strewn on the floor to minimize bad odours. However the perfume of the crushed hellebore was considered injurious and was avoided to safeguard health.

Culpeper says that if applied to infected skin, *H. niger* will eat up dead flesh and hasten cure; mixed with cinnamon and taken as an internal potion, it will cure gangrene. Country folk, he says, have long used Black Hellebores for animals that have coughs or who have eaten poison. The cure for these animals was effected by making a hole through their ear and putting a piece of the root of the Hellebore into it. He quotes farriers as using the plant for many animal ailments. Gerard also praises the Black Hellebore for animals, saying it was often called 'consiligo' because husbandmen of his era used it on cattle. He quotes that the root of the white hellebore is also good against poison, sickness and 'cold diseases that be of hard curation'. He says that any medicine made from the white hellebore should not be given to those of a delicate constitution without being diluted first, but that it is quite safe in strong doses for country folk, who are tougher and stronger! A root weighing the same as a two-pence piece of the time, when mixed with honey and wheat flour, was said to cure ague *and* kill rats and mice.

While *H. viridis* and *H. foetidus*, the green and stinking hellebores respectively, were used by herbalists in the Middle Ages, now they are more at home as show plants rather than healing plants. Once used as purgatives, tonics and anaesthetics amongst other uses, the Hellebore is almost obsolete medicinally, apart from a small area of homeopathy where it is used in a tincture against mental illnesses.

OBSERVATIONS

At the core of each tale, folk belief and name for the Hellebore lies the same truth: the plant is ancient, a powerful healer and also a dangerous destroyer. Today the delicate blooms of the Christmas rose (*H. niger*) withstand seemingly impossible conditions, encased in ice yet miraculously standing firm and strong to adorn gardens in the early months of the year. Yet cutting them and bringing them indoors ensure their swift death. They are best left where they can achieve perfection in their natural state. Perfection is only achieved and beauty allowed to shine when one's reason for being is not compromised or self-centred.

PEONY

Paeonia officinalis

BOTANICAL

The peony, sometimes spelt paeony, is named after Paeon, who was a physician in ancient Greece. The genus, which is made up of herbaceous and shrubby perennials, belongs to the *Paeoniaceae* family. The plants fall naturally into two groups, the first group having developed from the large, full-bloomed Chinese variety, and the second with twisted exaggerated petals in the Japanese-based group. Today the flower shapes fall into four distinct groups:

1   single – cup-shaped flowers with one or two layers of incurving petals
2   semi-double – flowers as single groups but with twice as many rows of petals
3   double – rounded blooms with two outer rows of incurving petals, the rest smaller and densely packed
4   anemone form – sometimes called Imperial or Japanese, with one or two rows of incurving petals, the centre a mass of densely packed narrow petaloids developed from stamens.

Many species exist:

P. ARIETINA	from southeast Europe
P. EMODI	from northwest India
P. LACTIFLORA	from Siberia and Mongolia, sometimes called 'albiflora', meaning 'white-flowered', a true species
P. LOBATA	from Portugal and Spain, sometimes called peregrina
P. LUTEA	from China and Tibet, meaning 'yellow'
P. MASCULA	a single variety sometimes called 'corallina', meaning 'coral coloured'
P. MLOKOSEWITSCHII	from the Caucasus
P. OBOVATA	from Siberia and China
P. OFFICINALIS	from France to Albania, a true species often called 'the red apothecaries' peony'
P. SUFFRUTICOSA	from China, sometimes called 'Moutan', the Japanese name referring to the tree peony Meutang, the King of Flowers

The majority of peony plants in gardens today are hybrids of original true varieties.

ORIGINS

The peony is one plant that possesses many names from very many countries – in Latin *peony*, in the vernacular *pinny*, in Chinese *chishaoyao* for the red peony or *sho yu*, meaning most beautiful. This is a flower that is beautiful both in sight and perfume.

The Latin word *peony* comes from two origins. The first is that it was discovered by a chieftain called Paeon. The second origin of the name is more complicated and is retold by Pliny the Elder, who says that Apollo's mother Leto gave Paeon a peony flower on Mount Olympus, which is where he based his healing powers when he cured Pluto, god of the underworld and Ares, god of war. These stories are recorded in Homer's

Iliad. Some tales add that in fact Paeon was changed into a plant to save being mortally wounded himself.

The peony has long been popular in the gardens of China, Japan, Asia, Europe and America. *P. lactiflora* has been grown and tended since 900 BC in China. In the 3rd century BC the Modan, as the peony was called, appeared in jade carvings in temples. The tree peony *Paeonia suffruticosa* attracted a craze and a large following, becoming a symbol of wealth. Other peonies attracting a large following were the herbaceous peonies such as *P. officinalis*; gardens in Yangchow hosted thousands of plants which people travelled far and wide to see. For the Chinese the peony was an important flower in art; during the 'Five Dynasties' (907–60 BC), flower painting became a recognized branch of art. The peony in these pictures symbolized prosperity; it also appeared in poems that accompanied these paintings. Some of these paintings and poems took on an erotic nature because the peony was linked with the female and her form. In the 17th century a tree peony painting by Yun Shouping was accompanied by a poem describing the cut bloom in the painter's hand as a woman dancing – thought to be a reference to his favourite concubine.

It is possible that some of the first plants came from China to Britain via Europe with the Romans; this could have been *P. mascula*, sometimes called the male peony. Certainly *P. mascula* was in evidence in the monastic healing gardens of medieval England. *P. officinalis*, the medicinal peony (considered the female peony) was introduced to Britain from Crete. It is thought that an Augustinian historian and medically trained monk called Gildas lived on the small island of Steepholm in the English Channel in the 6th century, and that plants from his medicinal beds, including the peony, spread into the surrounding grassland there, where the ocean climate encouraged its growth. In his *Herbal*, Gerard mentions the existence of the plant growing wild in Britain – this has not been substantiated but Gerard was clearly knowledgeable about the plant's healing properties. He gave it two other names: *Cynospastus* and *Aglaophotis*, or Bright Shine, in reference to the seeds, which glow slightly in the dark. In the Tudor and Stuart ages, *P. officinalis* was a common plant in borders.

P. lactiflora, from eastern Asia, was thought to have been introduced to the west in the 18th century. British shipmasters are thought to have brought peonies from the equivalent of Chinese garden centres back to England – Robert Fortune, superintendent of the Royal Horticultural Society's Chiswick Hothouse, spent 20 years visiting China and Japan bringing back peonies (it was also he who encouraged and developed the tea industry in India).

In 1870 William Robinson published *The Wild Garden*, a book which encouraged the planting of various non-native plants in English gardens to grow in the wild without any care or supervision. He quotes the success of peony species growing amongst the long grass. During this time, French hybridizers took the beautifully perfumed Chinese peonies and created new varieties. So it was not really until the beginning of the 19th century that the peony was used as an ornamental garden plant, although Joseph Banks, then based at Kew, had already received *P. lactiflora* from Pallas, a German who had noted the importance of this plant for healing in China.

As people began to settle in America they took plants over the seas with them, including the peony – for its decorative rather than medicinal value. Followers of the bloom set up the American Peony Society, creating collections of many different varieties.

PLANT LORE AND HISTORY

The beauty of the peony bloom is symbolized in the roots of its name, Paean, meaning 'hymn of praise to Apollo'. Some plants are said to live up to 100 years at a time and are often found growing amid the rubble of houses and homes long gone, soul survivors of things past. They prefer to grow undisturbed; it was considered great bad luck to uproot a plant. It was said that they lost their dignity as a result of such a move and would refuse to flower until they had regained this lost dignity. Such was the fear of uprooting a peony at the wrong time that great myths grew up round this practice. A complicated manoeuvre was developed so that no human hand need uproot the plant: a hungry dog would be tied to the base of the stem at the point it entered the ground. The hungry dog would then be coaxed with meat, would strain at the rope and thus uproot the plant, without human intervention. If the seed pods of the plant had to be collected then it was most important that this was done well away from birds such as woodpeckers – any picker spied by a woodpecker would shortly lose his eyes, or so folklore warns us. And of course any picker was aware that because the plant had such beauty it was chosen by the nymphs, who would hide in its leaves – so picking the plant, and thus ousting the nymphs, would be courting disaster.

The seeds in the peony were very useful – if the picker had managed to avoid the woodpecker, that is! They were used in cooking as a spice to flavour meats, as is quoted in *Piers Plowman* by Langland. Seeds were also used for protection. They would be gathered at dark by shepherds, who found the seeds easily because they were said to shine like candles in the night. The seeds were strung upon white thread and worn around the neck to ward off evil spirits, and when soaked in wine and worn as a necklace, or even just kept by the bed, were said to dispel nightmares.

The roots were also important. They would be dried, carved and then fashioned into protective amulets to be worn around the neck. The onset of Christianity saw the amulets becoming beads worn in a rosary. Sailors would always make sure that peony in some form was on board; when a storm was at its height sailors would burn peony as an incense, to ensure better weather to come.

This plant, with its perceived ability to ward off the forces of darkness, was strongly linked with the moon. In some folklore tales it was believed that the peony was created by a moon goddess so that the plant would reflect the moon's beams throughout the night. As protective as it might be, it was also considered a harbinger of death. It was once a well-known 'fact' that if the blooms on a peony plant amassed to an odd number in the garden of a home where a death had occurred, there would be further deaths before the next 12 months had elapsed.

In the Victorian language of flowers the peony symbolized shame and bashfulness, and yet in Chinese folklore it was symbolic of love and the blooms were given as love tokens, as noted in the *Book of Odes* by Shaoyao. The tree peony (*P. suffruticosa*) was above being a mere token of love, however, because it was considered the King of Flowers and held an exalted position, symbolizing honour and prosperity. Its image was often used on art objects such as vases, paintings and screens. Branches of the blooms were arranged in large vases in reception halls, and the plant was grown in gardens in grand raised marble beds. During the 18th century, the popular Chinese blue porcelain was traditionally decorated with bamboo, chrysanthemums and peonies. These illustrations were changed for the European market, the branching twigs were simplified, as were the peony blooms, which became first buds and then onion shapes – hence the famous 'onion decorated' porcelain evolved, which remained a very popular and collectible commodity.

HEALTH AND WELL-BEING

About an infants neck hang peonie,
It cures Alcydes cruell madadie.
This plant also prevents the mocking delusions the fauns bring on us in our sleep.

PLINY

Pliny used the peony in many medical recipes for varied problems. Named after the Greek god of healing, it was used to stop bleeding. It has been used in folk medicine for many centuries. The root of *P. mascula* worn as a necklace was thought to prevent convulsions and improve dental health in children. It was used in attempts to prevent 'the falling sickness', spasms, epilepsy, lunacy, cramp and many other nervous afflictions. The seeds were said to dull the pain of childbirth. In medieval literature it was quoted as curing jaundice as well as stomach upsets, and much is written about it in the *Materia Medica*.

P. mascula, with its long roots and pinnate leaves, was considered the male plant. It was this species that was grown in medieval monastic healing gardens. *P. officinalis*, introduced to Britain in 1548 from Crete, was considered the female plant and thus used to cure female complaints.

Over the centuries the medicinal use of the peony declined in the west, but remained important in traditional Chinese medicine. In Chinese medicine a cultivated root is called *Bai-shao*, while the wild root is *Chi-shao*. Today the peony is still valued as an important healer in Chinese medicine. The root of *P. lactiflora* cools the blood down, moves clots and relieves pain and has been used (taken internally) to cure eczema in children. A distinction is made between the red flowering *lactiflora*, used for the problems mentioned above, and the white flowering species, often used as a women's tonic. In Chinese medicine the white flowering species is called *Bai-Shao Cyao*. *P. officinalis*, the common peony, is used as a

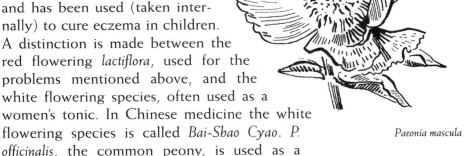

Paeonia mascula

diuretic and a sedative. *P. suffruticosa*, the tree peony, is an antibacterial; the bark of the root is used for sores. It can also be used for cleansing poor circulation, but it is, as with all the peonies, only used with great care and knowledgeable advice.

OBSERVATIONS

The peony is a plant of contradictions. It is immensely important in healing and yet, as with many other plants, too much brings disastrous results. It is a plant ruled by the sun and yet, as folklore would have it, created by the moon. It can bring relief from nightmares and yet in the language of flowers symbolizes nothing more strong than bashfulness. It is a plant that is sometimes linked with the whole body and its healing, and at other times associated specifically with the female form. Maybe this is where the magic and the strength of the plant lies, in its ancient history and its adaptability. Because it is associated with both the sun and the moon, perhaps this gives it the power to dispel negative thoughts and to heal both mind and body. In the Middle Ages lunacy was dealt with by covering the 'lunatic' with peony leaves and petals. It was believed that if the patient were left for a time to breathe in the flower's aroma, he would come to his senses. Whether this 'healing' worked because it was believed to work (the placebo effect has always been with us) or by the material components of the plant itself, any contact with nature could only have been beneficial. Perhaps we need not go so far as to lie covered in peony petals, but we do need to spend time in contact with the natural world. Just lying on the grass on a summer's day listening, breathing and feeling works wonders for our health and well-being.

CHRYSANTHEMUM

Chrysanthemum indicum

BOTANICAL

The chrysanthemum belongs to the *Compositae* family, the largest family of plants. *Compositae* comes from the description 'put together', the over-all characteristic of all blooms in this family being that they carry a dense head of florets very close together. The word *Chrysanthemum* comes from the Greek *chrys*, meaning 'golden', and *anthus*, a flower. So it would seem that these blooms were originally golden.

The genus is made up of annuals and perennials, some evergreen, some deciduous semi-shrubs used for their blooms. Each bloom is called a flower, although in fact each is made up of a large number of individual flowers or florets. The genus also includes *C. pyrethrum* and *C. tanacetum*, plants such as the tansy, feverfew and pyrethrum daisy, but for this chapter we are concentrating on the decorative Chrysanthemum blooms that originated in China.

These chrysanthemums fall into several categories:

- the florists' chrysanthemum, common as a commercially viable crop available all year round in single heads and spray-headed varieties
- disbudded – these can be single anemone-centred, incurved or reflexed. They are single blooms, where all other blooms have been removed to concentrate on one single large head.
- Non-disbudded; these are multi-headed spray varieties which include the single daisy type, pom-pom and double heads.

Species include:

C. ALPINUM	from the European Alps; bears daisy-like blooms
C. BOSMARIENSE	from Asia Minor; like C. *alpinum* but with a further daisy-like head
C. CORONARIUM	from the Mediterranean, meaning 'crown' or 'wreath like'
C. CORYMBOSUM	from Europe, Caucasus and Asia Minor
C. FRUTESCENS	from the Canary Islands, meaning 'shrubby'; sometimes called 'the Paris daisy' or 'Marguerite'
C. INDICUM	from India, often called 'a greenhouse chrysanthemum'
C. MAXIMUM	from the Pyrenees, often called 'the Shasta daisy'
C. MULTICAULE	from Algeria
C. PARTHENIUM	from Great Britain, often called 'feverfew'
C. RUBELLUM	from Japan
C. SEGETUM	from Great Britain, meaning 'of cornfields', often called 'the corn marigold'
C. SINENSE	from China; the border and greenhouse variety
C. ULIGINOSUM	from Hungary and Eastern Europe, meaning 'moisture lover'

ORIGINS

For the Egyptians of the 18th Dynasty (1567–1320 BC), the chrysanthemum was one of a few blooms used to adorn Egyptian gardens. In the Ptolemaic period the *Chrysanthemum coronarium* was used to make bouquets and crowns to decorate religious altars. In 500 BC Confucius mentions small yellow chrysanthemums.

The chrysanthemum originated in China and, though popular, always took second place to the peony. As China opened its doors to visitors and to export, the plant spread to Japan, possibly between the 8th and 12th centuries. In the period of Chinese history called the Six Dynasties (220–581), the chrysanthemum existed as a monograph of the day. By the 12th century there were 25 cultivars known, and by 1708 at least 300. Most hybrids that came in the 18th century to European borders and greenhouses were colourful hybrids created by Chinese and Japanese gardeners from native species. The Japanese at one point proved to be better cultivators of the plant. The 4th-century Chinese poet Tao Yuan-Ming is reputed to have had a magnificent chrysanthemum garden to retire to, and often the chrysanthemum symbolized a scholar in retirement.

In about 400 AD it was said that Zen Buddhists introduced the chrysanthemum from China to Japan, where it became a symbol of the Mikado. Its representational form (actually a 16-petalled chrysanthemum) looked a little like the rising sun. This image was used as a decorative motif in 1186 on the Japanese Emperor's sword. An Order of the Chrysanthemum was created, and it was an award of the highest merit. The bloom became a flower of inspiration in Eastern art, poetry and music.

In Chinese lore it was considered to be the 'Fourth Gentlemen of Flowers' and appeared in various colours and shapes. It was the flower for autumn, joviality and an easy life. It could appear to be defiant and frail or triumphant, and it was said that anyone painting it would have a proud disposition. Chrysanthemum festivals were popular, and as the chrysanthemum's lucky number was nine, the festival would be held on the ninth day of the ninth month. This flower festival was called *Kiku-no-seku*, the festival of 'the Queen of Japanese flowers'.

In 1789 Monsieur Blanchard brought chrysanthemums from China to Europe, and in 1795 one of the first garden chrysanthemums was shown in England. In 1860 the plant-hunter Robert Fortune brought chrysanthemums to England from Japan; these were in the form of the large-flowering species. And so the chrysanthemum craze began.

There is evidence of a chrysanthemum originating in Persia, where an insect powder existed that was made from chrysanthemums (the dust was lethal to insects but not to humans). In France, Italy and southern Germany the chrysanthemum became linked with the dead and was a prime flower to be offered to the dead especially at the beginning of November for the feast of All Saints. The chrysanthemum then became known as *Fiori dei Morte*.

Throughout the late 19th century the chrysanthemum was a popular cottage garden flower, providing colour in autumnal border plantings. On the other side of the world, in New England, the chrysanthemum became a popular flower in church arrangements – put there, it was said, as an aid to meditation which would help to keep the congregation awake during the long services!

PLANT LORE AND HISTORY

The chrysanthemum is very popular in the Far East, being the national flower of Japan, symbolizing the sun and life. It is called *Ki Ku*, meaning 'sun'. In ancient Japan it was only the Emperor and extremely high-ranking nobles who could grow or wear the bloom; any person overstating their position by growing or wearing the chrysanthemum would suffer a fate worse than death. This plant, which symbolized for the Chinese human perfection, was worn by Japanese warriors as a 'golden pledge of courage' during the War of the Dynasty in 1357.

In the Victorian language of flowers the bloom symbolizes cheerfulness and optimism. The red chrysanthemum symbolizes love, the yellow slighted love and the white truth. The chrysanthemum was occasionally referred to in the West as *Diosophrya*, meaning 'God's eyebrow'. In the East the chrysanthemum meant contemplation and autumn. In Europe it was considered unlucky to bring chrysanthemums indoors – it was said that you were then being wished dead because of the flowers' close association with funerals.

C. *coronarium* was made into garlands and worn as a protection from evil. According to Japanese legend, the Emperor had a favourite servant, Keu Tze Tung, who one day through no fault of his own accidentally offended the Emperor, who banished the poor youth from court. Tung travelled along until he found the valley of the chrysanthemum through which flowed a stream, which on either side was carpeted in flowers, the dew from which dripped into the stream. It was said that anybody who drank from the stream would become immortal (other cultures also believe that all who drink from water that flows between chrysanthemums will live to be 100).

By 1840 in Victorian Britain, many horticultural societies had set themselves up to support the growth and production of fine buds, blooms and fruits; from the late 1860s onwards the chrysanthemum was included as a prime show bloom.

HEALTH AND WELL-BEING

Chrysanthemum morifolium, often called the florists' chrysanthemum or mulberry-leafed chrysanthemum, came into the west in about the 18th century and was accepted as a popular decorative flower. However in the East it had been used in medicinal circles from at least the 1st century AD. Because the Chinese believed that if you drank from a stream that flowed between the blooms you would live for 100 years, the bloom had a link with longevity. Chrysanthemum tea was a very popular beverage, as was chrysanthemum wine, and the petals and leaves, infused, produced both wine and medicine. The tea was said to produce a cooling effect, while even the dew from the leaves would help promote good health and long life. Quite often chrysanthemum tea was drunk before periods of meditation and deep thought, as it was said to clear the head as well as remove headaches and depression.

China's Chong Yang festival (sometimes called Chong Jiu Double Ninth), held on the ninth day of September, was a time for the ceremonial drinking of chrysanthemum wine. This coincided with vast displays of chrysanthemum blooms, all to celebrate the flower and induce longevity. The Chinese used petals in salads, whilst in Italy it was viewed as a herb. The Koreans used the roots rather than the leaves as a cure for depression and vertigo; a tea made from the roots also cured vertigo as an emotional problem, and helped steady the paths of those whose lifestyle was too fast and too 'heady'. The flower essence was often prescribed to dissolve spiritual blockages.

Today the chrysanthemum leaves are often called 'chop suey greens' – these come from *C. coronarium*, or in Chinese *Shungiku*. The flowers of *C. morifolium* are called *ju hua*; they are quite bitter, and used as an antibacterial, anti-inflammatory and to increase blood flow. It can also be used for colds, eye and liver problems and hypertension.

OBSERVATIONS

The concentration in this chapter has been on the more obvious chrysanthemum – that is, the florists' chrysanthemums that are found in gardens and borders and were used by the Chinese many centuries ago. What is fascinating is that the bloom could not be introduced to the western world until China became more accessible to the rest of the world. Many other treasures lie hidden on this planet, there for the finding.

In Great Britain, two chrysanthemum species grow wild: *C. leucanthemum*, the ox-eye or dog daisy, a native found in grassland and at roadsides once used to cure chest complaints; and *C. segetum*, often called 'gold' or 'the corn marigold', an annual seen (and sometimes most unwelcome) on arable land. *C. segetum* is thought to have been introduced to Britain in the Neolithic era. Henry II decreed an ordinance against this 'guilde weed', calling for its destruction. It was an invasive weed and unwelcomed.

Many more of the chrysanthemum genus have long and varied histories, such as *C. vulgare* – tansy, *C. parthenium* – feverfew, *C. cinerariifolium* – pyrethrum and *C. balsamita* – alecost (sometimes called costmary). However, as they are classed as herbs they have been omitted from this book.

As with all ancient blooms there are tales that do not necessarily have any basis in fact but nevertheless are delightful. One comes from Germany, where a peasant travelling home on Christmas Eve found a child lying in the snow. The man, cradling the child, took him home and shared his Christmas with him. On Christmas morning the boy revealed himself to be the Christ child before promptly vanishing. The man despaired at the child's departure, but when next he passed the place he had found the child he saw wonderful flowers growing from the snow. He gathered them up and took them home, naming them 'the gold flowers' which is what the name 'chrysanthemum' means.

By far the most delightful tale is one of a girl in love. It was decreed by the gods that her husband would only live to match, in years, the number of petals on a flower. The girl spent long hours trying to find the bloom with the most petals. She eventually found a carnation which had many petals, more than she'd found on other flowers – but for her still not enough. So she took a sharp instrument and after much toil managed to slice each petal into its smallest possible sections, thus creating the chrysanthemum.

In the western world the bloom greets the autumn, a time that is certainly active, not passive. Trees that are deciduous make an effort to shut down and physically throw off their leaves, but not before providing nature with a mantle of reds, rusts and golds. The earthy-smelling chrysanthemum fits well into this world of damp leaves, ripening fruits and shortening days; autumn brings a certain scent into the air which anyone being in tune with the earth can sense. The autumn becomes a time of preparation, of stocking up, of inward thought and contemplation. This and more are held within the many-petalled chrysanthemum.

BUTTERCUP

Ranunculus acris

BOTANICAL

The vernacular name 'Buttercup' crops up time and time again in the countryside. Buttercups are actually botanically referred to as *Ranunculus*, a genus belonging to the *Ranunculeceae* family. The genus includes annuals, perennials, evergreens, semi-evergreens and aquatics. Over the years very many species have been hybridized and made more 'suitable' and showy for garden borders. Very few native buttercups are greeted kindly in gardens. We are probably more familiar with two of the more popular species from the countryside: *Ranunculus acris*, the common buttercup, and *R. ficaria*, the lesser celandine.

The word *Ranunculus* comes from the Latin *Rana*, for 'frog', as many of these plants prefer damp ground. The word 'buttercup' describes admirably the shape and the colour of the bloom, whilst the word 'celandine' has come from the Greek *chelidon* meaning 'a swallow' – this name is said to have been granted to the bloom because it starts to bloom at the same time that the swallows arrive from their migratory journey. It is important at this point to remember that the lesser celandine belongs to the *Ranunculeceae* group, while the greater celandine belongs to the poppy (*Papaver*) group.

R. ACRIS	the meadow buttercup or meadow crow-foot, from *acris* meaning 'sharp' or 'bitter'; from Europe including the British Isles, where it is a perennial throughout the countryside
R. ALPESTRIS	from the Jura, the white alpine buttercup
R. ARVENSIS	corn crow-foot or corn buttercup; a native annual in the British Isles, especially in southeast England
R. BULBOSUS	from England, Ireland and Scotland, the bulbous buttercup; found in meadows and grassland
R. GLACIALIS	from the Alps and damp rocky areas; 'the glacial buttercup'
R. PARNASSIFOLIUS	from Switzerland and the western Alps; 'the grass of Parnassus'
R. PLATANIFOLIUS	'the plane-leafed buttercup' from the Alps
R. PYRENAEUS	'the Pyrenean buttercup' from the central and southern alpine region
R. REPENS	'the creeping buttercup', native to Britain, a weed in gardens
R. SEGUIERI	from Switzerland, the eastern Alps, Jura and the Dolomites; 'the seguieri buttercup'
R. THORA	a limestone-loving plant, the poisonous buttercup

R. ficaria is the lesser celandine. It is the first flower of spring. The celandine, a member of the *Ranunculus* family, is on equal merit in the countryside with the buttercup. The flowers have 8 to 12 petals and plenty of nectar for the bees. The blooms open and close with the sun. The word *ficaria* means 'fig shaped', a reference to the root tubers which the plant uses to spread vegetatively. Small bulbils often get washed away in flood water from the damp areas the plant prefers, and thus the plant spreads without producing many seeds.

ORIGINS

R. acris, the common buttercup, is thought to have been flowering on this planet since the Oligocene period before the Ice Age, approximately 18 to 26 million years ago. Fossilized remains tell us this quite accurately. It certainly is a common sight in the British Isles and is the plant used in the game *'Do you like butter?'*, in which a bloom is held under the chin – if a golden glow is reflected on the person's chin, this reveals that he or she indeed likes butter.

R. arvensis, the cornfield buttercup, is not now such a familiar sight in cornfields due to careful weed irradiation. *R. repens* (the creeping buttercup), however, is still an invasive visitor. Gerard in his *Herbal* was quite familiar with the buttercup, calling it 'Crow foot', 'Lobel', 'King knob', 'Gold cups', 'Gold knobs' and 'Butter floures'.

R. ficaria, the lesser celandine, has origins dating back at least 10,000 years. Named for the Greek *chelidon*, there is a tale from the time of Aristotle that says that female swallows used celandines to restore sight to their young fledglings who had after some mysterious occurrence had their eyes 'put out'. The 17th-century mystic William Coles writes:

> It is known to such as have skill of nature, what wonderful cure she hath of the smallest creatures, giving them knowledge of medicine to help themselves, if haply diseases annoy them. The swallow cureth her dim eyes with celandine.

The celandine originated in Europe up to the Arctic areas, north Africa and western Asia. It, like the common buttercup (*R. acris*), has many vernacular names, including 'Golden stars', 'Spring messenger' and 'Pile wort' – this last name is from the Latin *pila*, 'the ball', a reference to the ball-like tubers upon its roots. In America the celandine is called 'Swallow worts'.

PLANT LORE AND HISTORY

And cuckoo buds of yellow hue, do paint the meadows with delight.

Ranunculus ficaria, the celandine

So wrote Shakespeare in *Love's Labour's Lost* (V.ii.904), 'cuckoo buds' being a nickname for buttercups. Shakespeare was right in his description of the blooms carpeting meadows. In the countryside, vast areas of yellow, then and now, greet the viewer with delight. Buttercups have too acid and unpleasant a flavour for cattle to eat. Country folk used to believe that the amount of buttercups in a field would indicate the quality of the butter (the more there were, the better the butter). While of course the buttercup has no bearing on butter yield in a direct way, indirectly it helps because cows choose to eat more suitable grass rather than the acrid leaves.

The species name *acris* indicates that it is toxic; the plant contains protoanemonin, which can make pasture land acrid and limits other plants' growth. In folklore it was said that any cow lying down among the buttercups would receive a bewitched udder, and buttercups were often thought to invite a form of negative magic. A very ancient nickname for the bloom is 'crazy', due to the fact that folk believed insanity would follow if you smelled the bloom too deeply and too long.

In plant lore many golden blooms are associated with the sun and positive thought. There is one such myth regarding the buttercup, in that it was thought useful for divining the truth. Instead of holding it under the chin to find out whether one liked butter or not, it was held under the chin to distinguish the truth. With the bloom in place, questions would be posed about anger, love and friendship. If the answers given were the truth, the bloom would reflect its yellow colour on the respondent's chin.

123

In the Victorian language of flowers, the buttercup symbolizes ingratitude and chilliness. May Day has always had important links with plant lore, and in Ireland the buttercup was part of May Day traditions. Farmers were said to rub the buttercup over the udders of their cows to increase milk yield. While the plant could not possibly yield better milk production directly, it did so indirectly, as the bitter taste left on the udders would encourage calves to wean earlier, and thus leave more milk for butter making.

As with all tales of flowers, one can take and use what one needs from them. In this vein a rather interesting little tale exists about the 'birth' of the *Ranunculus*. *Ranunculus* was a young boy dressed from head to foot in gold and green silk, who spent his days in the forests running around among the trees singing in a beautiful, clear, high-pitched voice. This was lovely for a short while, however he never ever stopped running or singing, and after a while the wood nymphs realized that this was disturbing the peace of the forests and so they turned him into a buttercup to bring peace and balance back to their woods. Thus *Ranunculus* was sent out to the open meadows to live.

In the Middle Ages, *R. ficaria*, the lesser celandine, was called 'Chelidonium the Minus' to differentiate it from 'Chelidonium the Majus', the greater celandine, to which it is not related botanically. The lesser celandine was said to be a barometer for plant sowing – folk would start sowing their seeds when the first celandines appeared in about April. In the 13th century celandines were evident in church architecture; there exist friezes in Notre Dame cathedral depicting celandine leaves amongst other blooms. The celandine was certainly a plant that would have appeared in medieval flowery meads. In ancient alpine and Pyrenean areas there is evidence that celandine juice was used on arrows to ensure that any prey shot would be poisoned; several other plants of the *Ranunculaceae* family also possess this ability.

People in the past have used the tender young leaves in salads, and the closed buds have been used as a spice, in the absence of capers. In the Victorian language of flowers, the celandine symbolizes joys to come, perhaps because the plant helps to greet the spring. In 1613 Browne in his *Britannia's Pastorals* talks of Celandine, a shepherdess of 'matchless beauty' – perhaps his inspiration came from the delightful blooms of pure golden beauty decorating the meadows and grasslands.

HEALTH AND WELL-BEING

Like many members of the *Ranunculaceae* family, buttercups and celandines did not play a big part in folk medicine or healing due to their poisonous nature. An ancient name for the buttercup was 'accursed crow foot'; the French called it *Mort aux Vaches* ('cows' death') or *Herbes Sardonique* ('bitter plant'). All these names referred to the burning and blistering nature of the sap. This characteristic was well known by beggars of old, who would rub the plant upon their body to open up sores, enabling them to gain more sympathy from passers-by and hopefully collect more alms. The distastefulness of the sore had to be engineered carefully – too many sores or too large might resemble leprosy, a feared illness in Britain, and then no one would come near.

In ancient healing rheumatism was thought to be improved by rubbing buttercups on the skin over the affected area, so that blisters would be induced. The blisters were said to ease the rheumatic pain. An easier cure was used for madness. Bags of buttercup blooms were made and hung round the neck of anyone showing signs of insanity, to relieve symptoms.

The lesser celandine once went by the names 'Fyg wort' or 'Pile wort' – according to the Doctrine of Signatures, the root system or tubers were thought to look like haemorrhoids, and so were meant to cure the problem. Even today this plant, in tablet form, plays a part in the treatment of piles.

In the Netherlands, the root tubers were worn as an amulet around the neck to keep piles at bay. The leaves were said to be a common cure for scurvy, jaundice, ringworm and warts. The plant was also used by falconers, who maintained that the eyesight of both the handler and the hawk would be improved if treated with celandine. Many is the time that a pot of celandine flowers has graced a sick room, as it was a common belief that if the celandine died the patient would recover. If however the celandine lasted, then there would be no recovery.

OBSERVATIONS

For a plant that is so widespread it is perhaps surprising that no great use for it has been found. Perhaps its use in healing is yet to come; maybe its chemical composition has healing properties yet to be accessed.

The link with butter is fascinating because it is almost without rhyme or reason – the cows don't eat the buttercup and so the butter is made no richer or yellower by the flower in the long run. Surely here its colour is the key. Yellow flowers have always been considered to denote wealth, and butter remained the prerogative of the rich for many centuries. The lesser celandine is also worth thinking about. Sometimes, but very rarely, you find flowers having similar vernacular names. Thus there exists the lesser celandine (*Ranunculus ficaria*) and the greater celandine (*Chelidonium majus*), which are similar only in the colour of blooms. The juice of the greater celandine is, however, important historically, having been used by alchemists in their attempts to make 'the philosopher's stone', which would grant immortality. The name *chelidonium* does, after all, come from the Latin *donum caeli*: a gift from heaven.

MARIGOLD

Calendula officinalis

BOTANICAL

The marigold is known in Latin as *Calendula officinalis*, and belongs to the *Compositae* family. The *Calendula* genus consists of approximately 20 or more shrubs and annual herbaceous varieties. *C. officinalis*, sometimes called 'the pot marigold' or 'common marigold', is the most common. It is not found in the wild in Britain and on the whole its occurrence is the result of self-sowing. It has a long flowering period – this fact is reflected in the meaning of the word *calendula*, which comes from the word *calends* meaning 'throughout the months'. *C. officinalis* is found in southern Europe, it has light green obovate leaves and bright orange to yellow freely occurring blooms. The common name 'marigold' is not to be confused with French and African marigolds, which belong to the *Tagetes* family, are native to Mexico and appear in gardens during summer months as bedding plants.

ORIGINS

Calendula officinalis and its few cultivars have been cultivated for several centuries. The plant, a native of the Mediterranean, has been used since the time of the ancient Greeks, and even before that by distant Arabic and Indian cultures. As a garden plant it has been evident in Europe since the 16th century. In 1584 it is mentioned in a writing entitled *A Handeful of Pleasant Delites*. In this piece of writing, the marigold is mentioned as being 'for marriage'. It has, over the years, been cultivated to act as an ornamental bloom in the garden, used in cookery and medicine.

The name *Calendula* has already been discussed, however there is another theory as to its origin – that it comes from the Latin *calendae*, meaning 'first of the month', as it was said that the bloom was always in flower on the first of each month in ecclesiastical gardens (in its native Mediterranean climate). The plant follows the sun, opening early in the morning and closing as the sun begins to fall from the sky.

The bloom has been popular with many eras in history. In the 5th century it was popular in the garden of Gallic nobles, with the Romans and used at Indian weddings and Muslim ceremonies including Dassera, where it was used in festival garlands. In the Middle Ages it was used in church festivals – one of the vernacular names for the bloom was 'Mary's gold', dedicated to the Virgin Mary – and many ancient churches had 'marigold windows' in their Lady Chapels, dedicated to the Blessed Virgin Mary. The plant was also used in May Day celebrations, strewn at cottage doorways and made into garlands.

In his *Herbal*, Gerard describes the marigold at length, making reference to the large double blooms being 'vulgar sort of women' and naming the plant 'Jacke-an-Apes on horseback'! One quite old cultivated variety was nicknamed 'hen and chickens'.

The marigold was once miscalled 'the sunflower' – quite often a flower's origin is not appreciated because of this kind of misnomer. Other ancient names for the flower include 'gold' and 'rudde'.

The flower can be traced back to the time of a venerable legend. In the wild, the Greek marigold was either *Calendula arvensis* or *Calendula officinalis*, and both are thought to be the 'sunflower' referred to in the legend of Clytie and Apollo. The god Apollo was deeply loved by a water nymph called Clytie, however he spurned her attention and love. The sad nymph pined day and night, refusing food. She sat for nine days staring at Apollo, the sun god, as he rose each day. Her face would follow his movement until at last the sun chariot set at night. The gods pitied Clytie and turned her into a sunflower, her face becoming the bloom and her neck the stem, constantly following the sun.

PLANT LORE AND HISTORY

In general the marigold symbolizes pain and grief in plant lore, while under the dominion of the sun. In South American and Mexican lore the flower was linked with the killing of the Aztecs by the Conquistadors in their search for gold; it was said that the red flecks that occasionally appear on the blooms are the blood shed by the Aztecs. The pain and the grief that the bloom seems to symbolize can be dispelled, so it is said, by mixing marigolds in a vase with roses, this then symbolizes the sweet sorrows of love.

The ancient tale of Apollo and the love-forsaken nymph resurfaces in another form in the tale of a maiden called Caltha, who spent all her days watching Apollo. His rays melted her so that all that remained was a marigold upon the grass, symbolizing the sweet sorrows of love.

The marigold also symbolizes constancy in love, and it was a popular bloom long ago in bridal bouquets. On St Luke's Day maids would take marigold blooms, mix them with marjoram and wormwood, simmer the concoction over a low fire and then before going to bed bathe in the brew. It was said that doing this would ensure they would dream of their true love. A marigold bloom picked and worn between the breasts was said never to fade and would ensure one's sweetheart's love.

Another story tells of a young slave girl who collected the earth that had been below the feet of her true love, put it in a pot and sowed marigolds on top, so that as the flower bloomed so their love would grow and strengthen.

The origin of the nickname 'pot marigold' came from the practice of using the plant in cooking as a substitute for the rather exclusive saffron. The marigold was also used to replace saffron for colouring butter, puddings and cakes. In folklore it was said that the pot marigold would help you see fairies dancing in front of your very feet. The marigold could also (like the buttercup) be used as a divination flower, and its colour was said to ward off witchcraft. The bright yellow colouring denoted riches and the marigold was considered a true flower or herb of the sun.

For the Hindus the marigold was a holy flower, and in the east when combined with poppies it denoted 'I will soothe your grief.' It was grown quite a lot in monasteries and on church land; being a flower of the Virgin Mary it was often used to adorn altars and statues to her.

Picking the bloom had to be done carefully. In folklore it was said that picking the bloom or even looking at it courted disaster in that one might succumb to the weakness of liking strong drink – the very old vernacular name 'drunkards' echoes this myth. Quite often the bloom was also called 'husbandman's dial' and was considered a powerful aphrodisiac, although in German plant lore it was considered unfavourable as a love flower, denoting pain, anger and grief, and in the language of flowers when mixed with other blooms it denoted 'the changing tides of life from good to ill'. Being a flower of endurance meant that it tried its best, and in gardening was known as a 'companion plant', one that was planted to help other garden plants. The marigold was said to keep white fly at bay and kill nematodes in the soil, thus encouraging potatoes and tomatoes to be plentiful and bountiful.

In the 16th century the plant was used as a successful hair dye. A rather more useful purpose for the marigold was as a means of telling the time – an origin of the name 'husbandman's dial'. The marigold could be used as a (very primitive) clock. The Victorians were said to set their clocks by the marigold, believing that it opened at 9 a.m. and shut at 3 p.m. Weather lore held that if the bloom had not opened by 7 a.m. the day would see rain and thunder before sunset.

HEALTH AND WELL-BEING

The marigold is a fairly diverse bloom as far as health and well-being is concerned. It is usually the flower head or individual florets that are used, never the whole plant. It is used in cosmetics and perfumery as well as healing. The Romans used marigold tea to relieve fevers, and used the juice to cure warts and other skin irritations. In the Middle Ages, Albert the Great and St Hildegard were using the marigold to cure snake and insect bites, liver problems and intestinal upsets. In the 12th century, Macer's *Herbal* mentions the marigold as being the plant to use to clear the head and to induce cheerfulness. A century later the physicians of Myddfai offered this advice:

> Take marigold, pound well with good wine, vinegar, strong mead, or strong ale. Strain carefully, and drink a good draught in the morning fasting, whilst the pestilence lasts. If you are taken ill, you will need no other than this as your only drink. It is a good preservative against the foreign pestilence called the plague.

During the 16th and 17th centuries, marigold infusions were used in the form of a tea to heal toothache and eye problems. Bee and wasp stings were treated with the juice, applied directly to the wound. Marigold water soothed eye problems, and powdered marigolds gave ease from agues. Gerard and Culpeper both describe the marigold as a 'comforter of the heart and spirits'. Gerard recommended a conserve made from marigold, flour and sugar, to be taken in the morning for heart tremors. He prescribed the dried flower preparation for 'broths, physical potions and for divers other purposes'. In fact such was the demand for marigold flowers that they were sold for a penny a pound ready dried from shops.

The marigold also lent itself well as a combination healer: mixed with witch hazel (*Hamamelis*) it was used to treat varicose veins; mixed with Saint John's Wort (*Hypericum*) it healed bruises.

During the American Civil War, field doctors used marigold juice to cure and give ease from wounds.

131

The marigold has recuperative properties and will heal sunburn; the juice, combined with a cream base, will keep skin soft and supple. The flowers have an astringent quality and will stimulate and help the body fight infection. Its antibacterial properties will treat fungal infections. A hot infusion helps the body release toxins – in this role marigold has been known to 'bring out' measles and chickenpox from the body (in some parts of southern Britain the flower was nicknamed 'measle flower', though this led to some people believing you could catch the infection by handling the blooms). Inhaling the scent or partaking of distilled water from the flower was said to relieve depression and headaches.

This flower, associated with the dominion of the sun, was also believed to have magical properties. It was said that those who had been robbed would see the thief before them if they wore the flower, and many wore it as protection from the plague.

Bowls of the bloom kept in the kitchen are said to absorb and negate any unpleasant or strong cooking smells, while the spicy taste of the flowers makes it a useful addition to soups and stews. The younger leaves make an interesting addition to a summer salad.

The constituents of the marigold as a volatile oil – calendulin, saponins and yellow resin – promote healing, relieve stomach problems, stimulate the liver and ease gynaecological problems. Marigold can relieve arthritis and rheumatism and heal wounds.

OBSERVATIONS

One of the beliefs associated with the marigold was that even to smell it or gaze upon it would aid and lift depression and ease a sorrowful and heavy burden. Perhaps this belief arose because the bloom is linked to the sun: it looks like the sun, and tracks the sun's movements, opening and shutting in time with the sun's journey across the heavens. The plant also plays an important part in gynaecological healing in herbal and homoeopathic medicine. The marigold is also associated with femininity, being the flower of the Virgin Mary and the subject of many works of art and literature, where it serves to represent the female imperative:

THE MARIGOLD
When with a serious musing I behold
the grateful and obsequious marigold,
how duly every morning she displays
her open breast, when Titan spreads his rays;
how she observes him in his daily walk,
still bending towards him her small tender stalk;
how, when he down declines, she droops and
    mourns,
bedewed, as 'twere with tears, till he returns;
and how she veils her flowers when he is gone,
as if she scorned to be looked on
by an inferior eye; or did contemn
to wait upon a meaner light than him.
When this I meditate, me thinks the flowers
have spirits far more generous than ours,
and give fair examples to despise
the servile fawnings and idolatries,
where with we court these earthly things below,
which merit not the service we bestow.

GEORGE WITHER

DAFFODIL

Narcissus pseudonarcissus

BOTANICAL

The daffodil comes from the *Narcissus* genus, all of which are bulbs, the majority of which are ornamental and hybrids of a few native basic species. The word 'daffodil' comes from the Greek *asphodel*, a name for some form of lily. The word 'daffodil' is synonymous with the majority of flowers in the *Narcissus* genus. The word *narcissus* is said to come from the Greek word *narkao*, meaning 'to deaden'. This may well be an allusion to the plant's narcotic properties.

The genus belongs to the *Amaryllidaceae* family. This name comes from the classical name for the shepherdess Amaryllis, mentioned in works by Virgil and Theocritus.

The genus is a popular group of spring flowers, each individual species tending to be given the title 'daffodil'. All species are botanically narcissi, however those with a long trumpet are called daffodils. Two species are natural: the wild daffodil (*N. pseudonarcissus*), and *N. obvallaris*. These two species are native to England and Wales but not so much Scotland or Northern Ireland. Other parts of the world host other species native to their shores. These native species were the progenitors used to create the diversity of daffodils that exists today.

Hybridization, which changed the form of the bloom, started in 1820 when a Reverend Herbert started cross-pollinating different species. *Narcissus hispanicus*, which came into England before 1600 from France and Spain, was one of the species most used to create today's characteristic blooms.

Today the *Narcissus* genus is divided into 12 sections or divisions, according to cup or trumpet size:

Division 1 – trumpet	One flower, one stem, the trumpet/corona as long as the petals
Division 2 – large cups	One flower, one stem, the cup/corona shorter than the petals but more than 1/3 their length
Division 3 – small cups	One flower, one stem, the cup/corona less that 1/3 the petal length
Division 4 – double	Several rings of petals, cup unnoticeable
Division 5 – triandrus-style	Multi-headed
Division 6 – cyclamineus style	One flower, one stem, long-trumpeted drooping heads, reflexed petals (that is, petals that are bent or curved back onto themselves)
Division 7 – jonquil	Multi-headed, short cup with a sweet perfume
Division 8 – tazetta style	Multi-headed, short cup, fragrant
Division 9 – poeticus style	One flower, one stem, small cup
Division 10 – wild species	
Division 11 – split-cupped	
Division 12 – miscellaneous	

Some of the most noted varieties are:

N. ASTURIENSIS	from Spain and northern Portugal
N. BULBOCODIUM	from Algeria, Morocco, Spain, Portugal and southern France, 'the hoop petticoat', from *bolbos* meaning 'bulb' and *kodion* meaning a 'little fleece'
N. JONQUILLA	from Europe and northeast Africa, the wild jonquil
N. MINOR	from the Pyrenees and northern Spain
N. OBVALLARIS	a very old native of European origin
N. POETICUS	from the mountains of central and southern Europe, preferring mountains or damp meadows, 'the poet's narcissus'
N. PSEUDONARCISSUS	from Europe, including Great Britain, the wild daffodil or lent lily, 'the false narcissus'
N. TAZETTA	from the Canary islands, southern Europe, north Africa, Persia, China and Japan; multi-headed bunched blooms, sometimes called polyanthus narcissus

ORIGINS

The daffodil has been cultivated for many centuries, and the genus is found throughout Europe, especially in Spain, Portugal, France, Switzerland, the former Yugoslavia and North Africa. There are about 60 true species, half of which are naturalized hybrids, and approximately 100 wild varieties. Thousands of cultivars exist as do several old varieties, such as the Victorian 'Weardale Perfection', 'Empress', 'Pheasantseye', 'W. P. Milner' and the 'King Alfred' daffodil (this last originated in 1899).

The origin of the name daffodil is difficult to pin down. Some say it is named after Saint David, the patron saint of Wales because it is always in bloom by March 1st, St David's Day. The daffodil has been called 'affodil', 'lent lily', 'jonquil' and 'daffodilly'. The genus name *Narcissus* comes from the myth of the Greek youth of that name, who rejected the love of a nymph called Echo. She died of a broken heart, leaving nothing but her beautiful voice. Narcissus fell in love with his own reflection in a pool; in his attempts to get to the beautiful youth reflected there, he drowned, to return as a flower growing by the water. It is from his name we also get the words 'narcissism' and 'narcissistic', to denote someone vain and self-absorbed.

The UK hosts two native wild daffodils: *N. pseudonarcissus* and *N. obvallaris* (the latter sometimes called the Tenby daffodil). The 'Queen Anne' daffodil is named after Anne of Austria; another favourite, *N. tazetta*, originated in Asia.

The native daffodils prefer woodlands rather than open spaces. In Great Britain they are found in prolific numbers in the Lake District (where they gave Wordsworth the inspiration for his ode to the flowers), in the North Ridings of Yorkshire and the Royal Forest of Dean on the Gloucestershire/Herefordshire border.

There was once a belief that the daffodil, sometimes called lent lily, was not yellow but white. Greek myth tells us of Persephone, who would pick daffodils in spring. One day whilst picking she became tired and lay down and slept. Pluto, god of the underworld, saw her and, smitten with her, carried her away to the underworld to be his bride. It was said that his sulphurous touch caused every white flower to turn yellow. Some of the blooms accidentally tumbled into the underworld river of Sorrows, called Acheron, where they seemed to prosper. This association with the underworld may explain why daffodils are often used at grave sites. Pliny and Theophilus documented that ghosts love daffodils. In some sources daffodils are said to carpet the fields of the dead, known in myth as the Elysian fields.

The first Sunday in April is known in some quarters as Daffodil Sunday, a day that originated in the Victorian era when most well-off Victorians went visiting the sick, bringing flowers to cheer them.

The blooms, growing in the wild, often pinpoint the location of long-gone Christian sites. The blooms were often grown in ecclesiastical environments, one such community belonging to St Gregory, which coined the name 'Gregories' for the bloom. Quite a lot of wild daffodils today grow in woods called 'Abbey woods', a reminder of habits and times long passed. The thought of the blooms growing wild spurred the Victorians to run 'daffodil specials' with the help of the Great Western Railway. These trips fed the mania for collecting blooms from the wild.

In the 1930s a 'daffodil special' line ran between Gloucester and London's Paddington Station, so that folk could come and pick to their hearts' content at Dymmock and the Royal Forest of Dean.

In 1910 the English Daffodil Society was formed, recording over 2,000 cultivated species. The flower has always been popular, in fact the Spanish traded anthracite for daffodils. Many legends abound about the flower during the Greek and Roman periods. For the Greeks it was a funeral flower; for the Chinese it symbolized purity and a good and prosperous new year. The Romans discovered the plant's mucilaginous properties and used the sap as a wound healer. During times of famine the Greeks ate the bulbs. Calcium oxalate, an irritant, exists in the sap – great care has to be taken when daffodils and other flowers are placed in the same vase, as this irritant can harm other plants.

The collectors' craze for daffodils existed even in the mid-16th century. At this time the plant was common in all European gardens, where both the white and yellow types were produced. In 1614 the pharmacist K Porret was producing interesting varieties from his garden in Laden, the Netherlands. One C Clusius was growing *N. tazetta* and other jonquil varieties from Gibraltar. The blooms prospered in the Netherlands where the Dutch used *N. tazetta* as a valuable trading commodity.

Gerard in his *Herbal* refers to several daffodil species. One he called 'Primrose Peerelesse' seems to have been common in British gardens. He also cites 'purpled corrinetted' blooms growing in Swiss meadows, and 'British Junquillias' with several heads per stem.

PLANT LORE AND HISTORY

In plant lore the word 'daffodil' stands for the native *N. pseudonarcissus*. There are very many different meanings to the words 'jonquil', 'narcissus' and 'daffodil'. All daffodils belong to the narcissus family, and are therefore narcissi, however not all narcissi are daffodils. The distinction depends on which division (see page 135) they belong to. The word 'jonquil' originates from the Spanish word *jonquillo*, meaning 'rush', a reference to the rush-like appearance of the leaves.

In the Victorian language of flowers the daffodil symbolizes regard, and is associated with the afterlife, death and burial.

The Egyptians believed that the strong perfume of the narcissus was redolent of the underworld; the flowers were often found in Egyptian funereal wreaths. The Egyptians associated the word 'narcissus' with *narkao*, meaning 'to numb', an indication of the narcotic properties of the perfume. The daffodil soon became a very strong symbol of death – in very early ritualistic societies the corpses of human sacrifices were bedecked with daffodils as a further sacrificial symbol. In Greek myth, as mentioned earlier, the asphodel/daffodil symbolized the death of Persephone; at this time the bloom also became known as 'affodil', and was for many decades thereafter spelled without the initial letter 'd'.

In 1648 in his poem *Hesperides*, Herrick writes:

> *When a daffodil I see*
> *Hanging down her head t'wards me,*
> *Guess I may what I must see:*
> *First, I shall decline my head;*
> *Secondly, I shall be dead;*
> *Lastly, safely burried.*

It was considered extremely bad luck if the first daffodil of the season that you saw had its head drooping downward towards the ground instead of upright. In medieval times a drooped daffodil was considered an omen of death.

The Arabs considered the bloom or its perfume to be an aphrodisiac. The Indians used the oil produced by the flower as a sacred ointment which they used to rub upon their bodies in preparation for prayer.

The belief that the flower was a powerful portender of grief also had a positive effect. Seeing the first daffodil of the season was a positive sign, and folk were recommended to start new projects in direct response to how well the bloom thrived. To see the first daffodil of the year also meant that you would be granted more gold than silver in the coming 12 months – if, that is, the bloom was facing you. Bringing one bloom into the house reinforced this luck, however bringing a bunch of flowers into the house meant that no chicks would be produced by any hens sitting on eggs at that moment. However, the luck was good as far as goslings were concerned, because the number of flowers in the bunch would match the number of goslings hatched, providing the blooms were brought in well before the eggs actually hatched.

Daffodils were used in dream divination; it was said that love and happiness would soon come to anyone who dreamed of the flower.

Despite the fears of having the blooms in the house, many people did so, and children were often seen selling the blooms – though not for money. It was considered bad luck to exchange daffodils for cash, and so pins would be exchanged on the market – this then became an origin of the term 'pin money'.

HEALTH AND WELL-BEING

Daffodils are very rarely eaten by animals, as the sap prevents the flower from becoming a favourite treat. The sap cantains calcium oxalate, a skin irritant. However, man has overcome this and has in history used the bloom for healing. Galen in his *Herbal* says that the roots dried and ground down were used to 'consound and glew wounds'; the concoction could also be used on cuts, veins, sinews and tendons that were damaged. The potion had a cleansing effect and, when mixed with honey, could be put upon burns, cuts and sprains. If then to the dried roots and honey nettle seed was added, it became a perfect cure for sunburn. If the ground roots and honey had darnel (*Lolium temulentum*) added, then it could be used to draw out splinters, thorns and other foreign bodies under the skin. The oil was used to cure epilepsy and hysteria, and the fragrance helps focus the mind and ease an agitated spirit, having a calming effect.

Latterly in Britain the bloom has been used as a symbol for cancer care in fund-raising and advertising activities.

OBSERVATIONS

When spring comes to the earth after a long and often hard winter, it is seen as a rebirth. Many of the blooms of the spring herald new hope, new life and new beginnings, and the daffodil is at the forefront of this symbolism. Its appearance, radiant colour and beauty have been welcomed and used as an inspiration for art and literature from ancient times to the present day. It is a bloom that makes an impression on people, and sometimes its profusion is such that the onlooker can only stand in awe. Yet they are ephemeral, short-lived beauties, as Herrick says in his poem *To Daffodils*:

> *Fair daffodils, we weep to see*
> *you haste away so soon:*
> *as yet the early-rising sun*
> *has not attain'd his noon.*
> *Stay, stay,*
> *until the hasting day*
> *has run*
> *but to the even-song;*
> *and, having pray'd together, we*
> *will go with you along.*
> *We have short time to stay, as you,*
> *we have as short a spring;*
> *as quick a growth to meet decay,*
> *as you or anything.*

IRIS

Iris florentina

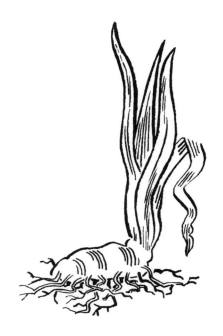

BOTANICAL

The iris belongs to the *Iridaceae* family, the genus *Iris* consisting of 300 species growing mainly in the northern hemisphere. Irises prefer temperate areas and none are found growing wild in the southern hemisphere. Most species are now grown in cultivated circumstances. The spread of the iris is from the Mediterranean, northern Iraq, Turkey, Israel, the Caucasus, Afghanistan and Asia.

The flower's botanical construction is based on the number three: there are three falls (the outer petals) and three standards (the inner petals). In some species the falls have a number of hairs; these irises are then referred to as 'bearded'.

Because the genus is made up of a variety of different blooms, they have been classified into sections. There are four main sections, all of which have subgroups:

Bearded/*Pogon* Iris	Blooms with hairs on the falls, rhizomatous roots and flat leaves. Also includes the *Arillate* group and *Eupogon* sub-section
Beardless/*Apogon*	Blooms with no hairs, smooth falls, rhizomatous roots and thin flat leaves. Also includes *Californicae*, *Hexagona* and *Laevigate* sub-sections
Crested Iris	Blooms have flesh-like crests instead of hairs. Thin rhizomes at surface level with flat shiny leaves.
Bulbous Iris	A bulbous root with foliage that dies quickly. Includes *Juno*, *Reticulata* and *Xiphium* sub-sections

There are two irises found as native perennials in Britain. *I. foetidissima* is prevalent in the south of England; it was later introduced into Ireland and Scotland and is sometimes called the Stinking Iris or Gladdon, a vernacular name for an Iris. *I. pseudacorus*, another native British perennial, prefers damp and wet country and is common throughout the British Isles. Its species name means 'False Acorus', to distinguish it from *Acorus calamus*, the original Acorus. *Iris germanica* is sometimes called the Flag Iris. *I. versicolor* is found in northeastern North America and is sometimes called the Wild Iris or Blue Flag.

As with many flowers, the species name sometimes gives us an indication of the physical or growing characteristics of the plant:

I. CHAMAEIRIS	ground or dwarf-growing
I. CHRYSOGRAPHES	gold-veined
I. FILIFOLIA	narrow-leaved
I. FOETIDISSIMA	having a fetid odour
I. FOLIOSA	well-leaved
I. GRACILIPES	thin-stalked
I. HISTRIO	from the Latin for 'actor' – the bloom is highly decorative
I. LAEVIGATA	smooth
I. PALLIDA	pale-coloured
I. PUMILA	small
I. TENAX	tough, referring to the physical attributes of the leaves
I. VERSICOLOR	many-coloured

I. XIPHIUM   this refers to the Greek name for the *Gladiolus segetum;* the name's origins are unknown. This variety is the English iris.

ORIGINS

It was Linnaeus who first named the iris. The legend of Iris was first written by the Greek poet Homer in about 700 BC. Iris was goddess of the rainbow and a messenger, and is often depicted carrying a Caduceus, something similar to a sceptre, in her left hand. Whenever the gods intended acting, the rainbow was sent as a bridge between the heavens and earth. It was Iris who would bring messages from the gods. Iris is also said in mythology to accompany the souls of women to the place of 'Eternal Sleep'. Quite often in art she is depicted as being very beautiful. As she travels on her journey on the rainbow she is sometimes depicted as holding a container of water to give to the clouds. Linnaeus used the name to emphasize the brevity of the bloom's life.

The iris also symbolizes life and the resurrection, again a link with the belief of the accompanying of souls. It is a flower connected with Osiris, who was the first Egyptian Pharaoh to be immortal. Most of the grand border irises today have actually been created by German, American, French and British horticulturists and are in no way natural or native. Certain species names give us some idea of the origins, or in some cases of the plant-hunters who found them:

I. BULLEYANA	after A K Bulley
I. DELAWAYI	after Delaway
I. DOUGLASIANA	after the explorer and botanist Douglas
I. FLORENTINA	from Florence
I. FORRESTII	after Forrest
I. GERMANICA	the Flag Iris, from Germany
I. HOOGIANA	after Hoog, a nurseryman from Holland
I. JAPONICA	from Japan

I. KAEMPFERI	after a 15th-century physician called Kaempfer
I. LACUSTRIS	of the Great Lakes
I. MISSOURIENSIS	of the river Missouri in the Rocky Mountains
I. MONNIERI	after the French botanist Monnier
I. SIBIRICA	from Siberia
I. TECTORUM	meaning rooftops – this variety appeared growing on thatched roofs in Japan
I. TINGITAMA	from Tangiers

The iris certainly has a very ancient history. *I. florentina*, which originated in southern Europe, was a heraldic emblem and was often confused with the lily as being the inspiration for the Fleur de Lys. In history the Fleur de Lys is very important, but the true origin of the flower is disputed because many centuries ago the word 'Lily' could have applied to the Iris. Artistic freedom abounded and the Iris appeared in very many different styles. It has appeared in heraldry and architecture, and in Britain was in the Royal Arms until the 19th century.

I. florentina has often been called the Florentine Lily and is one of the oldest plants in the history of cultivation, having been used in Egypt in 1500 BC where it appears in tomb paintings in the Valley of the Kings, and also as a decoration piece upon the brow of the Sphinx. Its shape was synonymous with the Royal Sceptre, symbolizing power and majesty.

I. florentina was also a very important flower in that the roots, once dried and powdered, smelled like violets. This powerful and important commodity was 'Orris root', and with alcoholic extraction produced 'Frangipani', a very important perfume. The dried roots contain Irone, also found in violets, thus the perfumes are similar. The ancient Greeks often called the Iris 'xiphium' from their word *xiphos*, meaning sword – this was in reference to the shape of the iris leaves.

The Yellow Flag, *I. pseudacorus*, was very important in medieval times, where it was christened with the unusual vernacular names 'Duck's Bill' and 'Sheep Shears'. It was found growing by ponds, streams and rivers.

Today's tall bearded flowers have come to us from horticultural breeding of different species including *I. pallida*, a highly perfumed variety introduced into England during the Elizabethan era. *I. germanica* was very popular in Elizabethan gardens, while I. *sibirica* was another favourite Elizabethan bloom.

Some sources maintain that the iris was introduced to Europe by Charlemagne from various original territories. *Iris versicolor* is native to North America, where it was used as a medicine. It is the state flower of Tennessee. There some iris species native to American soil; the rest came to America from Europe. The famous American poet Henry Wadsworth Longfellow used the iris to illustrate the earthly passage of life:

> *Thou art the Iris, fair among the fairest,*
> *Who armed with golden rod*
> *And winged with the celestial azure, bearest*
> *The message of some God.*
> *Thou art the Muse, who far from crowded cities*
> *Hauntest the sylvan streams,*
> *Playing on pipes of reed the artless ditties*
> *That come to us as dreams.*
> *Oh flower-de-luce, bloom on, and let the river*
> *Linger to kiss thy feet!*
> *Oh flower of song, bloom on, and make forever*
> *The world more fair and sweet.*

PLANT LORE AND HISTORY

In folklore the word 'iris' appears often, but it is sometimes difficult to ascertain which species is referred to. It was I. *pseudacorus* that gave pleasure to children who used its thick wide leaves to make small boats to sail on streams. Many bygone communities used this species to produce a dark green dye. It was also strewn before the bride and groom at wedding ceremonies, to be crushed underfoot and release its lovely aroma.

Over the centuries children have been warned not to bite the iris root. It was said that doing so would produce a lifelong stammer.

The iris is one of the Virgin Mary's blooms. It denoted purity and majesty to the early Christians. In some works of art Mary is shown wearing a crown of iris heads supported by cherubim. It appears, too, in representations of the Christ child.

The white iris has long been planted on Muslim graves, as white is the colour of mourning.

In the Victorian language of flowers the iris symbolized a message – this hearkens back to the myth of Iris, who travelled the rainbow taking messages between the gods and the mortals below.

I. pseudacorus is a very important flower in the Iris family, and seems to have had many uses ever since it was introduced into medieval Britain in the 9th century. As well as producing a black ink, its seeds could be roasted and used as a substitute for coffee. It produces an oil with a perfume that can act as substitute for *Acorus calamus*, the sweet rush-like strewing herb, an important part of any medieval or Elizabethan home, used to keep the air fresh and free from fetid odours.

HEALTH AND WELL-BEING

In his *Herbal* Gerard calls the iris Floure-de-Luce. He used the ground root mixed with rose water to relieve bruises, making sure that any delicate skin was first covered with a fine silk to avoid a rash. *I. foetidissima* was used successfully as a herbal purgative, mixed with ale. Sometimes this species was known as 'Stinking Gladdon', the 'Stinking' part referring to the smell of the crushed leaves (resembling the odour of beef), and 'gladdon' from *gladius*, the Latin word for 'sword'. Some iris roots were said to cure sunburn – the resulting potion was called *Calamis*, a forerunner of today's modern Calamine lotion.

I. germanica was found to contain, amongst other things, starch, resins and tannins. Dried, cleaned roots were peeled and given to children to chew on to help them cut their teeth. The same root, powdered, was a constituent in soap, toothpaste, skin powder and snuff. Today *I. germanica* rhizomes are used for coughs, deep wounds and diarrhoea, as well as breath fresheners.

I. versicolor, the wild iris or Blue Flag, has been one of the most well used of all the irises, and was listed between 1820 and 1895 in the *American Pharmacopoeia* as an excellent purgative and emetic. It is a herb that can act upon the gall bladder and liver, and as a diuretic and laxative. It is used today for psoriasis and acne, arthritis, fibroids, gland problems and septicaemia. The fresh root, however, as opposed to the dried, often causes sickness and diarrhoea.

The iris as a species can be harmful if eaten, especially the rootstock – how right early peoples were to warn children from eating this in its raw state!

Iris germanica

OBSERVATIONS

The moon is up, and yet it is not night;
Sunset divides the sky with her; a sea
Of glory streams along the Alpine height
Of blue Friuli's mountains; Heaven is free
From clouds, but of all colours seems to be, –
Melted to one vast Iris of the West, –
Where the Day joins the past Eternity.

BYRON, *CHILDE HAROLD'S PILGRIMAGE* CANTO IV, 27

The iris symbolizes a message, the rainbow linking heaven and earth, sun and rain, one world with the other. It is also a flower that links the living

148

and the dead, as the goddess Iris would escort the dead to the afterlife awaiting them.

Of course we all have an iris within us, in our eye. It is believed by some that the eye sees both ways: it looks out at what is going on, the image reflected on the retina, taken in and stored for deep contemplation – and it takes our thoughts within and uses these to inform what we see.

We have a 'mind's eye' that can sometimes be perceived by the onlooker. How often have our eyes given forth what we are truly thinking when our face does not reflect our true thoughts? In mythology, Iris the messenger sometimes brought news that people did not want to see. In the Bible there is a passage that tells us that it is easier for a camel to pass through the eye of a needle than for a rich man to enter the kingdom of heaven. When the true meaning of 'the eye of a needle' is understood, this passage makes sense. The 'eye of the needle' in countries such as Egypt was a low arched doorway set into a larger door. So it was possible for a camel – but only one unburdened of its riches and burdens – to pass through this eye. If we rid ourselves of the burdens and trappings of modern life, we can enjoy the richness offered by nature, as exemplified in the short-lived but vivid iris.

GERANIUM

Geranium robertianum, the Herb Robert

BOTANICAL

The word 'geranium' is used for two entirely different flowers from two very different genera. While both are part of the *Geraniaceae* family, the garden geranium, sometimes called Crane's Bill, belongs to the *Geranium* genus, and the other belongs to the *Pelargonium* genus. The name 'geranium' used for the brightly coloured summer plant is technically incorrect, but has over the years become the more usual name for flowers in the *Pelargonium* genus.

The name 'geranium' was first used by Dioscorides and comes from the Greek *geranion*, or *geranos*, which means 'crane'. The fruit of this flower was thought to resemble the bill of a crane.

The name 'pelargonium' comes from the Greek word *pelargos*, 'stork-like'.

Both genera produce seeds that have bird-like attributes. So it is small wonder that confusion arises between the Crane's Bill and Stork's Bill.

For the purposes of this chapter, plants belonging to the *Geranium* genus will be referred to as Crane's Bill, those of the *Pelargonium* genus Stork's Bill.

CRANE'S BILL

The Crane's Bill genus consists of approximately 350 species. Some are annuals, some perennials and others sub-shrubs. Some are suitable for garden borders. They tend to prefer temperate regions of the world.

G. CINEREUM	from the Balkans, a small Alpine plant.
G. COLUMBINUM	a native annual found in southern England; has a characteristic long stalk
G. DISSECTUM	a native annual of southern Britain; has deeply cut leaves
G. ENDRESSI	a French variety introduced as a perennial into gardens, named after the botanist Endress
G. LUCIDUM	a native annual in the British Isles, excluding the Orkneys, Shetland, Hebridean and Guernsey islands. Its name means 'shiny'.
G. MACULATUM	native to northeastern America
G. MOLLE	a UK native annual; the name means 'dove's foot'
G. NODOSUM	a perennial introduced into UK gardens; the name means 'knotted'
G. PHAEUM	a perennial introduced into gardens and now native in the British Isles; the name means 'dusky'
G. PRATENSE	a UK native perennial preferring limestone, found in the south of Britain, rare in Ireland and northern Scotland, also found in the Pyrenees, the Ardennes, Denmark, Finland, Sweden and Russia. Meaning 'meadow', the fruit of the Meadow Crane's Bill most resembles its namesake
G. PYRENAICUM	not a mountain plant, but a hedgerow one; native to southern England
G. ROBERTIANUM	a native annual in the British Isles, also found in Europe, eastern America, northwest Africa and western Asia. Known as 'Herb Robert'.
G. SANGUINEUM	found in Europe, a native perennial of the north English coast. The name comes from *sanguis*, meaning 'bloody', from the red stalk that appears in the autumn. Also known as the Bloody Crane's Bill

G. SYLVATICUM   a native perennial in Scotland, rare elsewhere; the Wood Crane's Bill.

STORK'S BILL

These Pelargoniums are sub-divided into four groups:

1   Zonal: These are plants with rounded leaves with a darker zone in the centre. They have single blooms in five-petalled arrangements.
2   Regal: These are shrubby, round-leaved plants. The leaves are serrated and the plant bears trumpet-shaped blooms.
3   Ivy-leaved: This is a group of trailing plants.
4   Scented. These plants are grown for their foliage. The flowers are small and star-shaped, the leaves are scented, often variegated and textured.

The scented plants cover a wide range of perfumes:

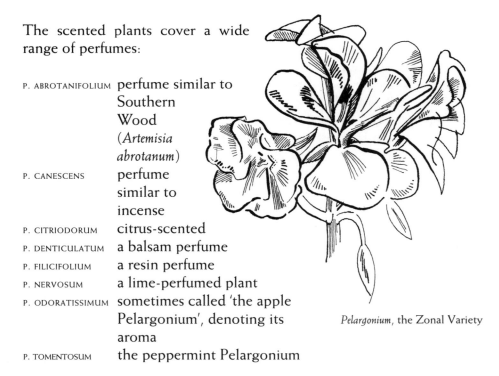

P. ABROTANIFOLIUM	perfume similar to Southern Wood (*Artemisia abrotanum*)
P. CANESCENS	perfume similar to incense
P. CITRIODORUM	citrus-scented
P. DENTICULATUM	a balsam perfume
P. FILICIFOLIUM	a resin perfume
P. NERVOSUM	a lime-perfumed plant
P. ODORATISSIMUM	sometimes called 'the apple Pelargonium', denoting its aroma
P. TOMENTOSUM	the peppermint Pelargonium

Pelargonium, the Zonal Variety

There are many more Stork's Bill plants. Even the so-called 'unscented' ones have a faint perfume, some stronger than others:

P. CAPITATUM	the Wild Rose Pelargonium
P. GRAVEOLENS	the rose Pelargonium
P. PELTATUM	the ivy-leaved Pelargonium
P. QUERCIFOLIUM	the oak-leaved Pelargonium
P. RADENS	the raspberry-leaved Pelargonium

ORIGINS

CRANE'S BILL
Archaeologists have found evidence that the Dusty Crane's Bill, G. phaeum, was in evidence after the Ice Age in various parts of what we now call Europe. The most popular or best known Crane's Bill is 'Herb Robert' (G. robertianum). It is sometimes called Stinking Crane's Bill from the rather strange scent its crushed leaves release; it is also known as Red Robin. In medieval days it was called *Herba Sancti Ruperti*, and was variously ascribed to Saint Robert, Pope Robert or the French Abbé Robert, who founded a Cistercian Order of Brothers in France in the 11th century.

In his *Herbal*, Gerard calls the Crane's Bill 'Pigeons' Foot', 'Dove's Foot', 'Pescolumbinus', 'Pied De Pigeon' or finally 'Geranium Columbinum'.

The American Crane's Bill (G. maculatum) was used a great deal in Native American folk healing. Its spotted leaves gave it the name *maculata*, from *macula*, meaning 'spotted'; it was sometimes called Alum root or the Wild Geranium. Whichever its name it has been in evidence in North America for many centuries.

During the 19th century several species were used at the front of Victorian borders – G. pratense, G. sanguineum and G. sylvaticum being particularly popular.

STORK'S BILL

This plant originated in South Africa, although it is found throughout the southern hemisphere – in the African tropics and Australia, for example – and in the Middle East. The perfumed variety has been cultivated in Europe since the 17th century and has produced thousands of cultivars and hybrids. Francis Masson, a Scot working for Kew Gardens in the late 18th century, brought back hundreds from the wild. The blooms have been coming over from the Cape Province since the early 1600s but remained 'undis-

Geranium pratense

covered' by many until 1847, when the perfume industry in France detected the plants' aromatic properties and sometimes used it as a replacement for Attar of Roses. This perfume was usually made from the plant *P. capitatum*.

As well as France, Italy, Algeria and Russia have all produced an oil from this plant, which is sometimes called Bourbon. The plant was mentioned in the book *Hotus Botanicus*, written by the Dutch botanist Jan Commelin in the late 1600s. Various species are listed in this book.

By 1787 there were so many 'Geraniums' in existence that Charles Louis L'Heritier de Brutelle regrouped the genus in his *Geraniologia*, ascribing the *Pelargonium* genus to the bright showy blooms from Africa, the *Geranium* genus to the Crane's Bill, and the *Erodium* genus to the rock-plant varieties. This last name comes from the Greek *erodus*, meaning 'heron', and so another bird joined the flock!

P. capitatum was used to perfume snuff and was an important commodity, being a popular scent. The Victorians were lavish users of this showy plant, which fitted in well with their summer bedding plans. In the late

19th century the hybrids 'Jewel', 'A M Mayne' and 'King of Denmark' were widely used in large Victorian gardens on a grand scale. Gertrude Jekyll, the eminent Victorian garden designer, favoured *P. tomentosum*, using it to flavour jellies and describing its leaves as 'thick as a fairy's blanket'.

From the end of the 18th century and into the early 20th, several hybrids were produced: 'Clorinda' in the early 20th century, 'Lady Plymouth' (first recorded in 1860), 'Prince of Orange' (well before 1880) and 'Radens' (from at least 1774).

The most unusual tale of the origin of this bright bloom comes to us from an Arabic legend. Mohammed was washing his shirt and then put it to dry on a Mallow Plant bush – such was the bush's shame and embarrassment that it blushed a deep pink, and so the *Pelargonium* was born.

PLANT LORE AND HISTORY

CRANE'S BILL

'Herb Robert' is the Crane's Bill that has attracted the most folk lore and superstition. Associated very much with fairies, the name 'Herb Robert' is in some quarters thought to be a reference to the folklore character Robin Goodfellow, better known as Puck. Robin Goodfellow appears in the folklore of many countries. He is a brownie, a sprite of the house in Scotland, in Germany *Knecht Ruprecht* and for the Scandinavian countries *Nisse god-dreng*.

> *Either I mistake your shape and making quite*
> *Or else you are that shrewd and knavish sprite*
> *Called Robin Goodfellow ...*
> *Those that hob-goblin call you, and sweet Puck*
> *You do their work and they shall have good luck.*
> WILLIAM SHAKESPEARE, *A MIDSUMMER NIGHT'S DREAM* II.I.32

Robin Goodfellow was in some stories a very jolly household sprite or fairy, carrying out mischievous but harmless tricks and practical jokes. In some tales, however, he is positively fiendish. Quite often if the family were good and deserving, Robin Goodfellow would do good deeds for them and would care for the family.

There is also a link with the Robin Redbreast, and the Herb Robert became as revered and sacred as this bird. If a robin was killed then it was said that any cow milked for the murderer would produce milk that would turn to blood. This belief was transferred to the plant, so that to uproot the Herb Robert meant that there would be a death in the family. This sort of belief led to very cautious behaviour as far as the bird and the plant were concerned; due reverence had to be observed.

In the Victorian language of flowers Herb Robert symbolizes steadfast piety; this may well hearken back to the Abbé Robert, whom some people believe it was named after.

STORK'S BILL

The Victorians loved the showy blooms of this genus, and made great use of its fragrant leaves for cakes and puddings. They would also float the leaves in finger bowls on dining tables. Young ladies spent their leisure hours making bookmarks from the scented leaves. They also used the decorative leaves as foliage to back single blooms worn in button holes. Many of the showy blooms held interesting meanings in the language of flowers. In general terms the plant meant constancy and availability, however to dream of it meant that you were due for a very great change of heart – whether this meant in your love life, social life or elsewhere is unclear, but most likely it had to do with love.

The Victorian language of flowers ascribed different meanings to the various blooms:

ivy-leafed (*P. peltatum*)	a bridal favour, often used in bouquets
lemon-scented (*P. citriodorum*)	an unexpected meeting
nutmeg pelargonium (*P. 'Fragrans'*)	an unexpected meeting
oak-leafed (*P. quercifolium*)	true friendship

rose-scented (*P. graveolens*)   preference
'The Flower of Spring', the silver-leafed geranium   recall
'The pencil-leafed geranium',
used to describe any pelargonium with markings on it   ingenuity
any red/scarlet pelargonium bloom   comfort

HEALTH AND WELL-BEING

In general terms this family of plants (*Geraniaceae*) were believed to ward off evil influences and therefore ill health, so it was classed as a protective herb.

CRANE'S BILL
These *Geranium* genus plants contain a lot of tannins, which makes them useful as astringents. Culpeper listed the Crane's Bill as being under the dominion of Venus, and therefore associated with love. Elizabethan love potions consisted of a high quantity of Crane's Bill, and cordials made from the plants were said to lift the spirits. Gerard also used the herb, and said a concoction of the roots (dried and powdered) mixed with red wine or claret could be given to a fasting patient; if carried out over 21 days this treatment would cure any ruptures and internal burstings. He goes on to add that elderly patients should be given the concoction mixed with powdered red snails! He favours the Dove's Foot Crane's Bill, *G. molle*, for this treatment.

In early healing, Herb Robert was used to cure skin eruptions and as an astringent and sedative. It was used in a gargle for sores in the mouth. The American Crane's Bill, *G. maculatum* (sometimes called Alum Root, Spotted Crane's Bill or Wild Geranium), was listed in the official list *American Pharmacopoeia* and was widely used by Native Americans for healing; early settlers in the same areas as these Native Americans also used it. The Blackfoot Indians used the powdered root as a poultice to stop bleeding. The Meskwakis used the root for mouth sores and piles. Cherokees and Iroquis also used it as a mouth wash, and the latter group

157

used it on the navels of newborn babies to promote healing where the umbilical cord had been cut. Early American settlers, thought to have brought over native British varieties, used them to treat children's stomach problems. The root would be boiled in milk to make it more palatable, and it had no negative side-effects.

Homoeopathic treatments of today use *G. maculatum* for stomach upsets, sore throats and some gynaecological problems. A lot of the cures ascribed to *G. maculatum* are for 'female problems' – an interesting fact given that the plant is dedicated to Venus.

Herb Robert is used today to promote healing, internally for stomach infections and ulcers, externally on wounds and skin eruptions.

STORK'S BILL

The pelargoniums have not been used much for healing, at least in Europe. Given that its origins lie in Africa, this comes as no surprise. African tribes, however, did use the roots of some species in the *Pelargonium* genus to cure diarrhoea.

The perfumed pelargoniums are used quite often today, having been found to contain over 20,000 components in their oils.

P. BETULINUM	camphor or birch leaf pelargonium, a digestive and decongestant healer
P. CAPITATUM	the wild rose pelargonium, an internal healer traditionally used in the South African Cape region for digestive problems. The oil is used in aromatherapy treatment.
P. 'FRAGRANS'	the hybrid nutmeg pelargonium, used as a foot or leg rub
P. GRAVEOLENS	the rose pelargonium, an anti depressant and antiseptic which also reduces inflammation. Used for nausea, acne, tonsillitis, bruises and ring worm.
P. ODORATISSIMUM	the apple pelargonium, used internally for gastroenteritis, externally for throat problems, neuralgia and skin problems
P. QUERCIFOLIUM	the oak-leaved pelargonium, used as a cure for rheumatism
P. TOMENTOSUM	the peppermint pelargonium, used in a poultice on sprains

The pelargoniums are also used a lot in the culinary world:

P. ACETOSUM	the Sorrel leaf pelargonium, used in salads and stews
P. CITRONELLUM	used in tea and desserts
P. CRISPUM	used in tea and desserts
P. 'FRAGRANS'	the nutmeg pelargonium, the leaves of which are used to flavour patés and coffee
P. RAPACEUM	a pelargonium with roots that can be cooked like potatoes
P. TOMENTOSUM	the peppermint pelargonium, used as an infusion for tea, added to fruit punches and other desserts

OBSERVATIONS

Crane's Bills and Stork's Bills are worlds apart. Visually you have the splendour, vibrancy and the almost intrusive brightness of the pelargoniums, compared with the unassuming and delicately coloured and leaved Crane's Bills. This diversity is enhanced further because the geraniums originated in cooler, mainly European areas, while the pelargoniums are of South African origin. Between them, however these two genera are capable of curing problems in almost every part of the body.

The beauty of the pelargoniums is short lived, and certainly in Britain instant gardens and window boxes are transient efforts to add gaiety to a drab exterior. The smaller and more unassuming Crane's Bills remind us that despite blazes of glory the less glamorous matters of life have to be addressed in order for life to continue its journey.

VIOLET

Viola tricolor, the Wild Pansy
or Heart's Ease

BOTANICAL

The violet, or viola, belongs the *Violaceae* family and is a genus of a mixture of perennial and annual plants that number about 500 species. The majority live in the temperate regions of the world, many in the European alpine region.

All the flowers have five petals. The violet-type plants have strap-shaped tops, while the pansy-type tops are rounded. Violas have some flowers which do not open and are self-pollinating – this makes them *cleistogamic*.

Over the years many cultivars and hybrids have been produced. The *Viola odorata alba* is the one most widely produced.

Several other sweetly perfumed flowers have, over the centuries, also been called viola, which can make tracing the plant's history and origins difficult.

V. ARVENSIS	a native annual, this plant is common throughout the British Isles but not so much on the west coast. It is sometimes referred to in the vernacular as pansy.
V. BIFLORA	The two-flowered pansy, found in the northern hemisphere
V. CANINA	The Heath Dog Violet, a perennial. It has no perfume.
V. CUCULLATA	from northeastern America
V. GRACILIS	a true species from Asia Minor, very rarely seen in cultivated conditions. The species name means 'slender'.
V. LUTEA	The Mountain Yellow Violet, a native perennial of mountain grasslands. Modern gardens host Pansies that are hybrids produced from *V. lutea* and the wild pansy, *V. tricolor*
V. ODORATA	a native perennial common in southern Britain, rarer in northern Britain and Ireland. Known as the Sweet Violet, often white, it is also found in Asia and North Africa
V. PALUSTRIS	The Marsh Violet, a native perennial of the British Isles, but rarely found in central southern England or central Ireland, where the ground is not boggy enough.
V. REICHENBAICHIANA	the pale Wood Violet, a native perennial in England, less common in Wales and Ireland, not native to Scotland
V. RIVINIANA	The Common Dog Violet, a native perennial throughout the British Isles
V. TRICOLOR	The Wild Pansy, sometimes called Heart's Ease, a native annual and perennial common throughout Europe including Great Britain, slightly rarer in Ireland
PANSY	This is a hybrid plant with larger flowers than the native violet

ORIGINS

One can get incredibly muddled with all the names that are applied to this genus. Are they violets, pansies or violas? The problem is not eased by the fact that some violets are called violas, and some violas are called pansies. The genus name is *Viola*, but there is also a commercially produced plant that we now call the Viola. The commercially created Viola was established by one James Grieve in 1867, when he crossed *Viola tricolor* with *Viola lutea*.

Viola tricolor is known by the common name Wild Pansy, or Heart's Ease, however the common name 'pansy' applies to a modern group of hybrids.

It may be simplest first of all to look at the origins of the name *Viola*. It comes from the Greek word *ion*, said to originate in the story of a young woman called Io who was loved by Zeus. Sadly, Zeus's wife Hera was jealous of this love, and to protect Io, Zeus turned her into a cow, amid a field of violets to eat. Hera became suspicious of this beautiful cow and asked her husband for it; he was forced to agree. Hera is then said to have sent flies to attack the creature, who, unable to rid herself of them, jumped into the Ionian Sea (this sea is also named for her). Zeus promised never to look at Io again in return for her being changed back into a woman.

There are now many, many vernacular names for this simple flower, such as Corn Violet or Corn Pansy for *V. arvensis* (*arvensis* being Latin for 'field'), and Heart's Ease/Wild Pansy for *V. tricolor* – some of the other vernacular names for this species are somewhat bizarre, even farcical:

Kiss me at the gate
Tittle my fancy
Johnny jump-ups
Three faces under a hood
Love in idleness
Cuddle me to you
Jump up and kiss me

All these names arose from the belief that the Heart's Ease could be used to create a potent love potion.

The name 'Pansy' comes from the French *penser*, 'to think'. People once believed that the pansy, with its head hanging down, resembled a visage deep in thought. Another vernacular name for this plant is 'paunce' – probably a mispronunciation or misspelling of the French *menues pensées*, which, roughly translated, means 'idle thoughts'. Another name was *pensée sauvage*, the Wild Pansy.

There are also explanations for the name *tricolor*. In the Middle Ages it was called *Herba trinitatis*, or Herb Trinity. The origin of the name comes from an ancient tale. The *tricolor*, so the story goes, once had a far, far sweeter perfume than the sweet viola, *Viola odorata*. Growing among the crops, the tricolor would be picked in bunches – and as a result when harvest time came many of the crops had been trampled and there wasn't enough food to go around. The plant, so it was said, was very worried and distressed about this, and so prayed to the Holy Trinity to lose its perfume. The Trinity granted the flower's wish, and named it Herb Trinity in recognition of its piety. This same flower also had another vernacular name, 'Flamey', because it was said that colours of it were the same as the colours of wood when first burning.

There are also interesting tales of how the violet came upon this earth. It was said that Cupid loved white violets; envious Venus changed them into purple to lessen his love for them. Orpheus would often lie his lyre on the grass when he was not playing it, and it was said that violets grew beneath it as it rested. A less lyrical tale can be found in Greek mythology. Hector is said to have given Ajax a sword in return for a purple baldric (sword sheath and belt). After Hector had died, Ajax fought with Odysseus and was defeated. In a fit of insanity Ajax killed himself with the sword that Hector had given him. It was said that where his blood fell, violets grew in remembrance of the friendship between Hector and Ajax.

The names for the bloom were still being debated during the time of Gerard in the Elizabethan era. In his *Herbal* he lists the bloom as *Nigra viola*, the Black Violet, and as *Herba violaria* and *Mater violarum*. It may well have been a mispronunciation that led to the name viola, as Gerard says the letter 't' was often missed out of the name *Vitula*, thus creating Viola.

The violet is indeed a truly ancient plant. *Viola rupestris*, sometimes called the Rare Teesdale Violet, is a survivor of pre-glacial history. The plant has over 2,000 years of cultivated history. Muslims maintained that 'the excellence of the Violet is as of the excellence of Islam above all other religions'. In gardening history the bloom has plunged from obscurity to popularity and back again. At the height of its popularity as a garden plant there were over 278 scented cultivars; at the lowest point of its obscurity there were only 13. Many of the highly perfumed cultivars were lost during the First and Second World Wars.

Viola odorata has been produced in Greece commercially since 400 BC. The blooms were sold in Athenian street markets. The Romans were great lovers of the violet, the colour itself being very fashionable in Roman Society. To the Romans the violet species was one of the main chaplet flowers used to adorn the heads of poets, civic leaders and other high-ranking Romans. It was also, with the lily and the rose, traditionally used as a tomb memorial flower. The Romans would drink wines flavoured with violets, and such was their love of the bloom that Horace (65–8 BC) complained that the Romans spent 'more time growing violets than olives'. There is evidence from writings in Pompeii that it was one of the main flowers in gardens there.

In one tale tracing the origins of the colour of *Viola tricolor*, Cupid is said to have shot an arrow right into the Wild Pansy, previously white, changing its colour for ever:

> *Yet mark'd I where the bolt of Cupid fell*
> *It fell upon a little Western flower*
> *Before milk white, now purple with love's wound,*
> *And maidens call it love in idleness,*
> *Fetch me that flower; the flower I shew'd thee once;*
> *The juice of it on sleeping eyelids laid*
> *Will make or man or woman wildly dote*
> *Upon the next live creature that it sees.*
> WILLIAM SHAKESPEARE, *A MIDSUMMER NIGHT'S*
> *DREAM* II.1.165

This tale of Cupid's arrow is also the key to the name 'Heart's Ease', as the flower has long been associated with love.

During medieval times, violets were used to perfume linen. Dried perfumed blooms were added to pot pourri. It became a very important flower in medieval flowery meads and mixed floral lawns. Monks grew the flower in profusion in their herb gardens, to make a fragrant retreat in which to sit and contemplate. They were grown in such profusion that they became as tightly compact as grass, the violet beds coming to be referred to as Violaria.

A flower's perfume sometimes seems to be the overriding factor where naming is concerned, and throughout the ages the names Gillofloures, Wallfloures, Damesfloures and the Marian violet have all been given to the perfumed violet and to other similarly perfumed blooms.

In the early 1830s the cultivated pansy – created from *V. tricolor, V. lutea* and *V. altaica* (this last from Russia) – became one of the celebrated eight florists' flowers.

The Heart's Ease that appeared in art in the medieval era as symbolic of humility was the same that could be found at the beginning of the 19th century, but then the species underwent a change. One T Thomson, a gardener to Admiral Gambier, bred a pansy with a larger, more circular face, and the characteristic lines on the flower's face (bees' honey lines) became 'dark blotches'. With this new strain of plants, clubs sprang up to exchange ideas and raise new cultivars. These 'Heart's Ease Societies' had annual shows, and many new strains were developed.

During the Victorian era the violet enjoyed a similar cult to that in Athens. It was one of Queen Victoria's favourite flowers, and the cut flower was commercially produced to be sold in baskets on the London streets and to be used for the extensive perfume industry. The plant became the basis for a lot of the compact Victorian bedding schemes in gardens, and cultivars such as 'Bullion', 'Blue Stone' and 'Irish Mollie' were very, very popular. The Parma Violet (*V. palmata*) was also extremely popular. It is thought that this perfumed variety originated in the Orient. Such cultivars as 'Marie Louise', 'Duchess de Parme' and 'Swanley White' were popularly grown for their perfume. In 1867 the firm Dicksons of Edinburgh spent a great deal of time and resources improving pansy breeding, and created a variety of violas and pansies. By 1893 a commercial perfume that matched the fragrance of *V. odorata* had been invented, and so mass production of the violet went into decline.

During the Edwardian era Queen Alexandra slightly revived the flower's popularity, having a favourite violet-scented perfume made for her. It became fashionable for ladies to wear a bunch of the flowers tucked either into their sashes or their belts. In the United States, the *V. riviniana* is the state flower of Wisconsin, and violet species flowers are also the state flowers of Illinois, New Jersey and Rhode Island.

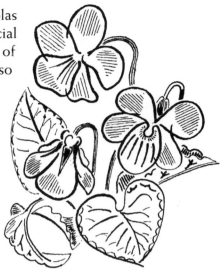

Viola riviniana, the dog violet

PLANT LORE AND HISTORY

Violets belong to the countryside, in fact as a bloom they are very rarely found growing near industry or factories, preferring clear, pure air. Thus many country stories grew up around the bloom.

Quite often the bloom was used to entertain children – in some parts of Britain it earned the nickname Stepmother. While telling the tale of a stepmother and her children, the petals of the flower would be plucked as the story unfolded, with parts of the plant (such as the anthers and stigma) used to portray different characters.

It was considered perfectly safe to bring large bunches of violets into the home, but never just a single bloom. The plant was considered an antidote to evil and witches. Wearing a violet while out hunting ensured that the wearer would not fall from his horse.

Despite the fact that the flower was considered in some quarters as a protection against evil, there was bad luck attached to it as well. It was considered bad to pick any violet that had dew upon the petals – to do so meant the death of a loved one would soon follow, as would the death of any landowner should any blooms flower out of season. In some areas folk believed that fleas lived within the stems of the violet and so they were never ever brought indoors, and it was always considered unwise to pick violets when the weather was fine, because sure as sure bad weather and intense rain would follow.

Necklaces of violets were worn around the neck to protect from deception and, strangely, inebriation. The Greeks and Romans strongly believed that the perfume of the flower would dispel the odours and power of alcoholic drinks, and so the flowers would be crushed into wine. When a child had reached its third birthday safely, celebrations would be held and the child adorned with a chain of violets around its neck, to mark the child's survival through the first, most difficult years of its life.

During the Middle Ages the violet was used in the kitchen to sweeten and fragrance desserts and savoury dishes alike. In fact a lot of the folklore involving violets has to do with the hazards of eating the seeds – however this only holds true when they are white, before they have ripened.

The pansy is strongly associated with love. Anyone wanting to ensure the ongoing love of their sweetheart would carry a pansy about their person. For the Elizabethans the violet symbolized innocence and pure love. This belief was perhaps based on the botanical fact that some violets are self-pollinating, and thus 'pure' or 'virginal'. For the French the violet was a symbol of virginity and innocence; it was traditional to strew violets on the bed of newlyweds. On St Valentine's Day the Wild Pansy/Hearts' Ease (*V. tricolor*) was used to symbolize the cure for broken hearts. In the Victorian language of flowers the wild pansy symbolized thoughts, faithfulness and modesty, while the yellow pansy symbolized rural happiness.

In Christian symbolism the violet meant humility and constancy, particularly (in medieval art) Christ's humility. It was grown in medieval monastery gardens as a protection from evil. The tale is told that all violets were white until Mary turned from watching Christ on the Cross,

167

at which all the violets became purple to echo her mourning – one reason that purple remains the ecclesiastical colour of mourning. In pre-Christian times, the violet was the flower of Sachiel, one of the seven angels of Jupiter.

As with many flowers the violet has a link with political power and influence. It was Napoleon Bonaparte's favourite flower, used as a sign to distinguish his enemies from his supporters. Such was the association between the man and the violet that they were banned in France after Napoleon's defeat at Waterloo.

Time and time again flowers are used for protection and to ensure longevity and happiness. Because flowers in the viola family look so much like faces, it was believed they could be 'read' to foretell the future. In 1847 Thomas Miller published *Language of Flowers or the Pilgrimage of Love*. In it he included a divination code based upon the lines on viola faces – by this time the viola used was probably a pansy, a cultivar of the wild species:

If the petal plucked was pencilled with four lines,
it signified hope; if the centre line started a branch, when
The streaks numbered five, it was still hope, springing
Out of fear; and when the lines were thickly branched,
And leaned towards the left, they foretold a life of trouble;
But if they bent towards the right, they were then
supposed to denote prosperity unto the end; seven
streaks they interpreted into constancy in love, and if the
centre one was longest, they prophesied that Sunday
would be their wedding day; eight denoted fickleness;
nine, a changing heart; and eleven – the most ominous
number of all – disappointment in love and an early grave.

Country folk have always held the violet in great esteem as a sweet-smelling, humble yet important bloom, as William Bullein wrote in 1562:

God send thee Heart's Ease, for it is much better with poverty to have the same, than to be a Kynge with a miserable mind. Pray

God give thee but one handful of Heavenly Heart's Ease which passeth all the pleasant flowers that grow in this worlde.

HEALTH AND WELL-BEING

for they that may not sleep, steep this herb in water and at eventide let him soak well his feet in the water to his aches ... and he shall sleep well by the grace of God.

ROGER ASCHAM

As with such an old and revered flower, the violet is high up on the list of healing plants. In folk medicine it was used to cure pleurisy, jaundice, fevers and rheumatism. The flowers, when boiled, produced a juice that cured headaches and relieved sleeplessness. The roots, tied around the legs, were said to give a person extra strength so that they would never be outrun, and juice put on the eyes meant that your eyes would never ache for a complete year.

The bloom would also be used to predict the course of an illness – bruised petals would be tied to the forefinger of the patient; if the patient slept while the petals were being tied on it meant he or she would recover, but if no sleep came to the patient then the outlook was grim.

The viola has had a very important place in ancient healing as well as folklore. Priscian, a Byzantine physician of the 4th century AD, advised that any person picking the first three violets of the season would suffer no illness for the next year. Since 500 BC it has been claimed that the genus cures cancer; research into this continues today. During the 1930s lung and heart cancer were treated with *V. odorata*.

The Persians and Greeks believed that Heart's Ease (*V. tricolor*) would cure a broken heart, and that a tea made from the flower would dispel dizziness. Hippocrates used the flowers to cure headaches, chest infections, melancholia and hangovers, to name but a few. Pliny used the genus to strength the heart and to calm anger, whilst in the Arabic world the plant was used to cure constipation, tonsillitis and liver problems. In about 1250 the monk and herbalist Bartholomaeus Anglicus said 'The lytylnes ... in substaunce is nobly rewarded in gretnesse of sauour [savour] and of vertue.'

Later on in the history of healing, Culpeper recommended this 'cool plant' to cure heat-related problems such as fevers. He recommended that the violet syrup was the best form of treatment, that the green leaves made excellent poultices, and that piles could be treated with an ointment made of violas and egg yolk mixed together and spread on the affected area. Gerard also recommended the genus for inflammatory problems of the sides and lung, and for 'ruggednesse of the windpipe and jaws'. He said that a syrup made with the plant had been used to relieve thirst.

Today, both *V. odorata* and *V. tricolor* are still used in healing. *V. tricolor* is used to cure skin problems ranging from eczema and nappy rash to ulcers. It can produce an excellent cough expectorant, is a diuretic tonic and an anti-inflammatory. It can also speed up the healing of wounds. *V. odorata* is a purgative and also produces excellent cough mixtures and gargles. The flowers are also used to colour medicines.

The plant also contributes to the pleasures of life: it is used to perfume lotions, soaps and toilet water and is also used to produce a liquor called Parfait D'Amour. Violets have been used in salads, syrups, tissanes and violet vinegar. Jams, jellies and pickles have been flavoured with the blooms, and the icing on the cake, so to speak, is that the blooms can be candied or crystallized and used as a decoration.

OBSERVATIONS

I think the King is but a man, as I am: the violet smells to him as it doth to me.

WILLIAM SHAKESPEARE, *HENRY V* IV.i.106

The violet has universal appeal, and its beauty is there for all of us.

The name 'pansy' has been used in a derogatory way, as a slur for a man who is not considered as robust or 'masculine' as he might. The derivation of this slur is obscure; there are various possibilities. The best and strongest origin of the saying 'pansy' actually comes from the Victorian gardening world. In large gardens many young lads were employed as apprentice gardeners, working their way up through lesser positions with an eye towards, hopefully, being head gardener one day. Along the way they had to tackle many tedious back-breaking jobs. The job of dead-heading the pansies – a task which must be done to remove the seeds and ensure a bumper crop and better flowering time – was tiring, dull and back-breaking, yet required no strength. And so the task was given to the weakest garden lad. Thus, perhaps, the term pansy came to be equated with someone who was not necessarily over-endowed with strength. Over the years and from at least 1929 the word pansy has been used as a derogatory term for gay men. There is however nothing historically to substantiate this. In the 1500s the violet was often worn by many who had no intention of marrying, however this did not imply that they refused to marry because their love was for their own sex; it could well have meant that their true love had died, gone away or was unobtainable, and so they wore the 'Heart's Ease' to help mend their broken heart.

The colour of violets has come to be associated with mourning. Violet is a mixture of red and blue, and so has adopted the strength and power of red and the wisdom and tranquility of blue. It is a truly mystical colour, and is used in meditation. It was a very popular colour with the Romans.

CARNATION

Dianthus barbatus,
the sweet william

BOTANICAL

The carnation genus consists of very decorative and highly perfumed garden flowers. On the whole they are annuals and evergreen perennials, although there are some exceptions that are biennial and semi-evergreen. The genus holds approximately 300 species and includes the very popular carnation, pink, and sweet william. The majority of border-grown plants are hybrids; some – such as the perpetual flowering large carnation, the florists' form – require greenhouse growth.

In their natural habitat they are found in the northern temperate zone spreading from Eurasia to South Africa. The Latin for the genus is *Dianthus*, from the Greek *dios*, meaning Jupiter, and *anthos*, 'flower'. There is one thought that *dios* refers to god or divine rather than Jupiter, therefore the flower is a divine flower. Others refer to it as the flower of Jupiter or Jove.

The *Dianthus* genus belongs to the *Caryophyllaceae* family. The origin of this is again Greek, from *karuon* meaning 'nut' and *phullon* meaning 'leaf', therefore the word means the nut-leaved plant, sometimes known as 'clove tree' in reference to the family's clove-like perfume.

The derivation of the word 'carnation' has long been the subject of debate. Some say it comes from *carnis*, meaning 'flesh', because of the blooms' colours. Others say the name is a corruption of the word 'coronation', in reference to the flowers' popularity as part of chaplets and garlands.

For ease of botanical clarification the genus is divided into five groups, two for the carnations and three for the pinks:

1 Border Carnations: Annuals and evergreen perennials with prolific flower production. The stems carry five or more blooms. Picotee varieties (that is, those with the petals lined in a darker colour) do occur.
2 Perpetual Flowering Carnations: Evergreen perennials with all-year-round flowering, grown in the greenhouse and for cut flowers. Spray varieties available.
3 Pinks: Evergreen perennials growing in clumps, producing many single or double blooms.
4 Old-fashioned Pinks: Mass-blooming summer plants, a 'mule' type is available that is a cross between a border carnation and sweet william.
5 Modern Pinks: A cross between the old-fashioned pinks and the perpetual flowering carnations

The *Dianthus* is very popular, providing cultivars that encompass ingenious colours and patterns, all originating from native species around the world:

D. ALLWOODII	the original hybrid pink named after plant-breeder Montague Allwood
D. ALPINUS	the Alpine dianthus, a small short-lived variety
D. ARENARUS	from Northern Europe, a mass-flowering species
D. BARBATUS	the sweet william from Eastern Europe; *barbatus* means 'bearded'
D. CARYOPHYLLUS	the carnation, from southern Europe and North Africa, sometimes called 'gilly flower' or 'clove pink'. The species name comes from the shrub carnation, the buds of which were sold to produce a clove-like perfume.

D. CHINENSIS   the Indian pink from eastern Asia

D. DELTOIDES   from Europe, the maiden pink;
deltoides means triangular, after the
Greek letter *delta* which is said to
appear on the petals

D. PLUMARIUS   from southwest Europe, the
pink; *plumarius* refers to the
frilled petal edges

D. SUPERBUS   from Europe and northern Asia
spreading to Japan, the fringed
pink

Dianthus allwoodii

ORIGINS

The carnation has epitomized beauty and perfume
since classical times. The first seeds of the flower were said to have originated in China, coming into Europe via Paris in 1705. *Dianthus chinensis* is
mentioned in medical books of the Han Dynasty (AD 23–206).

D. *caryophyllus*, the clove carnation or gilly flower, was said to have
come to England from France as a border plant; once arrived the group
was divided into three sections for ease of clarification: Flakes, Bizarres
and Picotees. Each group was identified by the pattern upon its petals.

Some of the pinks are cultivars from the English alpine (D. *alpinus*) and
European rock dianthus (D. *plumarius*); some of the larger, fuller-petalled
carnations originate from species created from half-French and half-
Japanese stock.

The carnation has gone in and out of fashion throughout the
centuries, as new varieties appeared and old ones died out. Yet again,
with so many ancient blooms this flower has been known by many, many
names, all of which have diverse origins and very few of which can be
confirmed conclusively.

The sweet william (D. *barbatus*) was said to have grown wild in
Normandy and was possibly named after William the Conqueror or

William of Aquitaine by Carthusian monks. It is also said to have been named after Saint William, whose feast day falls on June 25th, at about the time the flower blossoms.

The name 'gilly flower' (for *D. caryophyllus*) has equally obscure roots. In Old English the word 'gilly' meant July, and of course this is one of the months when the bloom is at its most prominent. There is also the link with cloves, as the Old English word *giroflier* means 'clove' or 'clove-like'. In Europe any flower with a clove-like perfume was called a gilly flower.

Then there is the name 'pink', used to describe *D. chinensis* and *D. plumarius*. One theory is that the word 'pink' comes from the Celtic *pic*, meaning 'to peak' or 'come to the height of beauty' – a suitable name for a flower that has such perfection and beauty. We now use the word 'pink' to describe a particular colour; this has only been current since a few centuries ago – previously any colour of this hue was called 'blush' or 'flesh'. A further theory about the name 'pink' comes from the Middle English word *poinken*, which describes the action of making holes in either thick cloth or leather; later on the term was used to describe the decorative edging on leather or cloth slightly pinked and serrated. This edging matched the serrated petal edges of some of the *Dianthus* species.

Gerard's *Herbal* mentions even more names for this genus, such as 'pagients', 'pagion-color' and 'horse flesh blunket'.

During the Greek era the carnation had been a principal flower used in garlands and coronets. Theophrastus (372–287 BC) and Nicander (2nd century BC) were familiar with the flowers, referring to the sweet william as the 'eye-centred flower'. Gerard called it Sweet Job, Job being another name for God, as found in the genus name *Dianthus*.

While one theory holds that the sweet william came originally from

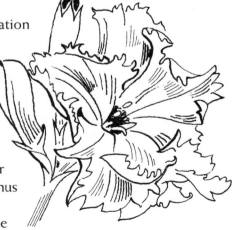

Dianthus caryophyllus

France into Britain, Pliny says that the *Dianthus* was brought to Rome from Spain by Augustus Caesar. In the 14th century there was a very popular drink called 'sops in wine'; this was a deep red, rather strong-perfumed drink made from wine with clove-scented dianthus in it. This drink was thought to have originated in Spain.

During the Middle Ages, garlands were constructed from various *Dianthus* species, the most popular being red and white. By the time of the Tudors, *D. caryophyllus* (the gilly flower) was very, very popular. 'Fenbow's Nutmeg Clove' was the oldest cultivated *Dianthus* species and was planted en masse in Tudor knot gardens. The Tudors chronicled two distinct *Dianthus* – the single (which included the pinks), and semi-doubles (which they called coronations). These two were very important to the 'still-room art', the still-room being the nerve centre of houses of this period. Here the mistress of the household would spend many hours concocting perfumes and sweet-smelling ointments to keep the house smelling pleasant and safeguard her family's health. Homemakers of this period made mouth washes, moth repellents, cosmetics, powders, perfumes and medicines. Some Elizabethans referred to the dianthus as 'Tuggies', after one Mistress Tuggy of Westminster, who possessed one of the largest collections of the genus of that day.

By the Elizabethan era the carnation had reached the height of its popularity. In 1618, William Lawson's *The Country Housewives' Garden* mentions the gilly flower as 'the king of flowers except the rose'. By the 18th century carnations were grown in the gardens of the rich and influential, produced by florists (horticulturists) of the day, and exhibited in large public houses. This symbol of power and royalty also had its place in religious iconography. In France the bloom was referred to as *Oeillet de Dieu*, meaning the flower of God, and in Christian symbolism was used to depict divine love. In the hands of the Virgin Mary it depicted her redemption and her blessed perfume. It was sometimes synonymous with the pain of the Crucifixion, as cloves were often used as symbols of the nails used at the Crucifixion. A painting of the Christ Child holding a carnation had a twofold meaning, symbolizing both his Kingship and his Crucifixion.

As well as a flower of divine love in art it also symbolized earthly or 'profane' love. It was known as a betrothal flower.

The French were very fond of the carnation and it became a symbol of the Bourbons and the French Revolution. By the second half of the 17th century the carnation had reached the peak of popularity in France: red carnations synonymous with the working class and white carnations used on Mother's Day. In the US the carnation is still worn traditionally to commemorate Mother's Day.

The Victorians used the carnation widely, and old cultivars such as 'Mrs Sinkins, 'Inchmery' and 'Paisley Gem' were particularly popular. During the time of the Industrial Revolution, 192 varieties of pinks were grown just by the florists Barlow, Keen and Hugg. The privilege of growing the *Dianthus* was granted not only to horticulturists but to ordinary working men. Many working-class Dianthus Societies sprang up. The Paisley weavers near Glasgow produced a highly decorative edged pink that was referred to as the lace pink.

The Victorians' love of this genus also encompassed the sweet william, so popular in Victorian times that it was made a show plant in many borders.

PLANT LORE AND HISTORY

The carnation is a bloom associated with betrothal, fecundity, marital happiness and, in the case of a white carnation, a woman's love. Giving someone a bunch of carnations would indicate that he or she was truly fascinating. In Italy the carnation symbolized ardent love, while in the Victorian language of flowers the associations covered a vast range of sentiments:

yellow/yellow and pink	disdain
striped red	extremes of emotion
deepest red	alas my poor heart
pink	boldness
red and pink	lively and pure love
striped pink	refusal
white and pink	refusal and departure

177

For many centuries the carnation was believed to be an aphrodisiac; to this end it was traditionally used as a flavouring in the wine served to brides at the wedding reception!

In folklore the carnation's association with love made it prevalent at gravesides and in funeral wreaths. It was also the flower for smart day wear, especially in Britain – think of Oscar Wilde's celebrated green carnation – when businessmen and 'gentlemen' alike would wear the carnation as a button hole.

The sweet william (*D. barbatus*) had its own symbolism, that of gallantry, and was the subject of a story written by Ovid in his *Metamorphoses*. A herdsman who spent much time playing his pipes unfortunately frightened the deer, so that Diana, Goddess of the Hunt, took out both his eyes. Instantly regretting her action, as an apology and in memory to the man she made flowers grow with small dark centres like the iris of an eye.

Traditionally the Greeks and the Romans used the blooms of the *Dianthus* genus at all celebratory festivals, including religious ones. Some say the carnation appeared at the birth of Christ. In Brazil the bloom is referred to as *Cravos de Defunto* – roughly translated meaning 'nails [or cloves] of the dead'. One folk tale provides another link between the *Dianthus* genus and the Crucifixion. When Mary went with her son to Calvary, she wept tears which changed to small flowers as they met the earth. Thus the blooms of the maiden pink (*D. deltoides*), which have a few small white dots on the corolla, are sometimes called 'the tears of the Virgin Mary', and are known as flowers of pain and love.

In France it was considered bad luck to give someone carnations. In Italy a white carnation was associated with death and funerals, and was said to be under the spell of the evil eye.

The carnation has very little place in English ceremony now, though in southern Europe it has played a flamboyant role in rituals and can match the rose as far as symbolism is concerned. It is viewed as a bloom of immense sexual promise; in Andalusia, Spain, it is synonymous with a woman. Quite often at *Feria* (festivals) Spanish women would wear red carnations. The full frilled dress worn by a female flamenco dancer was said to be like the petals of a full carnation; a woman attending a bullfight would wear a red carnation behind her ear – on the left if she were looking for a suitor, on the right if she were not. After the bull-fight the woman would throw the carnation into the ring, as a challenge, a statement or a symbol of her feminine power – her power to give herself to the one she chooses.

In other cultures red carnations were the traditional blooms for suitors to give their sweethearts. In folklore the carnation was said to have the ability to preserve the human body and to keep nightmares at bay. For the Koreans the carnation was a divination flower: a stem of *Dianthus* with three blooms would be worn in the hair – if the top bloom died first then the last years of the wearer's life would be arduous; if the bottom bloom were to fade first the early years would be hardest; if all three blooms died together then the wearer's troubles would last throughout her lifetime.

HEALTH AND WELL-BEING

For a flower that has such an ancient pedigree and history the carnation plays only a small role in healing. This is not the case in the Far East, however, where *D. chinensis* and *D. superbus* are called *qumai* and are used in Traditional Chinese Medicine.

D. caryophyllus was once used as a tonic and in cordials. In 1653 it was one of the ingredients for a very popular beverage of the Countess of Kent, who recommended red wine and claret mixed with sugared petals. After the petals or flower heads had been soaked long enough they could then be added to salads. The Countess of Dorset, for her part, made a sweet water from lavender, marjoram, bay leaves and pinks; she decanted this concoction and gave it to her lovers to 'spice up' their love life.

A sweet pickle can be made by soaking gilly flower (*D. caryophyllus*) petals in wine and sugar. This has to be done during the month of July. The Tudors, who created this recipe, also recommended a conserve of gilly flowers and sugar that would bring comfort to the eater and stimulate affairs of the heart, as the flowers were thought to cure melancholy they were in great demand as a tonic.

The carnation was very important as a flavouring during the Tudor, Elizabethan and Stuart ages. Cloves were an expensive commodity; the aromatic carnation species were used to flavour wine instead. Gerard says in his *Herbal*, 'these plants are not used in mete or medicine but esteemed for their beauty, to deck up gardens and the bosoms of the beautiful'.

The carnation has also had a place in healing as a stimulant and to treat fevers. The sweet william (*D. barbatus*) can be used to cure mouth problems. The juice of a sweet william would be mixed with vinegar and held in the mouth (for a considerable length of time), to cure toothache and also 'slimie flegm'. *D. chinensis* has been used for digestive and urinary problems; it can also be used on bacterial infections, skin problems, swelling and inflammation, and (taken internally) to lower blood pressure.

OBSERVATIONS

For my part, as a thing to keep, and not to sell; as a thing, the possession of which is to give me pleasure, I hesitate not a moment to prefer the plant of a fine carnation to a gold watch set with diamonds.

WILLIAM COBBETT, *THE AMATEUR GARDNER*

Cobbett was not writing about the modern ornate multi-petalled carnation that we see today in greenhouses and florists' shops, but instead the original *D. caryophyllus*, either in its native state or in a slightly fuller version. There's little doubt, however, that in this original species the perfume would have been exquisite.

Sadly, in the pursuit of 'perfection' something of the magic of a flower is often lost. Straighter stems, longer-lasting blooms and perfection of colour (with varieties of every conceivable hue) are desired, or so we are told, and in the process part of the plant's original magic and beauty is inevitably lost. The first thing that seems to go in the hybridization process is the perfume. What a pity, as losing touch with the perfume of a bloom is the first step towards denying its importance.

The carnation also suffers from that dreadful word, 'trend'. Once a popular gentleman's button hole, today it has been supplanted by ever more exotic blooms, the poor carnation being dismissed as too boring and unoriginal. Florists encourage designer button holes, yet if they were more conversant with the history of the carnation they would know it epitomizes love, sexual vibrancy and eroticism.

PRIMROSE

Primula vulgaris

BOTANICAL

Three very interesting and important flowers belong to the *Primula* genus: *Primula vulgaris* (also known as *P. acaulis;* the primrose), *Primula veris* (the cowslip) and *P. auricula* (the auricula).

The *Primula* genus belongs to the *Primulaceae* family. In general terms it is a genus of about 400 species, some of which hybridize very easily. They are deciduous winter-green plants, some of which are only half-hardy. All are perennial and produce flowers (often on long stems, sometimes on short ones) from central rosettes of low basal leaves.

PRIMROSE
The primrose (the Latin name *P. vulgaris* means 'common'; sometimes this species is called *P. acaulis,* meaning 'with stem') is one of the first spring flowers to bloom, and is a plant that is found throughout Europe. It is a native perennial in Britain, found in woods, grassy areas and hedge banks.

The word 'primrose' has several origins: *primus* means 'first', though the word 'rose' is a misnomer, as the primrose has nothing at all to do with the rose. It is thought the name is a corruption of *primeverole* in French or *primeverola* in Italian – in Latin it is referred to as *prima vera*, meaning the first spring flower.

A primrose hybridizes easily and quickly with *P. veris* (the cowslip) in the wild, to produce the oxslip, a plant with primrose flowers on cowslip-length stems. Primrose flowers can have two different kinds of stamens and style. The first type has blooms with short stamens and a long style, the second has a short style and long stamens. Despite the primrose's sweet perfume, honey bees very rarely use the bloom because the nectar lies too deep for their reach. The seeds are more often than not distributed by small insects, ants being the most common means of transport.

COWSLIP

Primula veris is found on most continents, in quantities throughout western Europe and south towards the Mediterranean, as well as in Asia. It is native to the northern hemisphere and has been introduced into other parts of the world as well, and as cultivars into gardens. It is a native perennial in meadows and on banks, but is becoming more and more rare. It can still be found growing wild in Ireland, Wales and England.

P. veris was once referred to as *P. officinalis;* in 19th-century gardening books it is sometimes (incorrectly) referred to as an auricula. The word 'cowslip' comes from the Anglo Saxon 'cu slyppe', meaning cow dung – a reference to the fact that it could be found in meadows used by domesticated animals. It carries orange spots upon the petals which act as a 'homing device' for bees in search of nectar. Like its cousin the primrose, the bloom boasts two different styles and stamens. The first variety has short stamens and a long style (the stalk that joins the stigma and ovary of a female flower), and is known as 'pin-eyed'. 'Thrum-eyed' flowers, for their part, have long stamens and short styles.

In the Americas the word 'cowslip' denotes a flower that is completely different to the European cowslip, though both belong to the *Primulaceae* family. American cowslips, sometimes called shooting stars, belong to the *Dodecatheum* genus; they are found in some European gardens.

AURICULA

Again, like the primrose and cowslip, the
auricula is a species of the *Primula* genus.
Found in the European Alps and developed into a cultivar to produce show
blooms of many colours, it is native to
the mountains of Central Europe – thus
one of its vernacular names, 'precipice
plant'. It is also called 'bear's ears' – the
name *auricula* comes from *auriculus*, meaning 'a little ear', a reference to the shape of
the leaves.

Auriculas are actually divided into
three groups: Alpine, Border, and Show
(Show being the most popular). Show
plants have a single stem with a white
centre (referred to as the 'paste'); the outer
ring is often a contrasting colour and is edged.
Sometimes a 'farina', or waxy white powder,
covers the blooms.

Primula veris, the Cowslip

ORIGINS

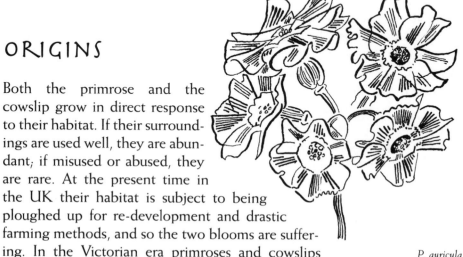

Both the primrose and the
cowslip grow in direct response
to their habitat. If their surroundings are used well, they are abun-
dant; if misused or abused, they
are rare. At the present time in
the UK their habitat is subject to being
ploughed up for re-development and drastic
farming methods, and so the two blooms are suffering. In the Victorian era primroses and cowslips

P. auricula

suffered from over-picking, as organized railway 'primrose specials' brought travellers who, with no notion of conservation, would dig the plants up haphazardly.

The ancients called the flowers 'small mulleins' or 'verbasculi'; 17th-century gardens often featured varieties called double, hose-in-hose and other strange forms. The Dutch botanist Crispijn van de Pas illustrated the double variety in his *Florilegium Hortus Floridus*.

The first primrose, so legend has it, was given in memoriam to a youth called Paralysus, son of Priapus and Flora. When the love of his life, Melicentra, died he followed her soon after, out of grief. His distraught parents gave the primrose to the earth in an act of remembrance, the first tender flower of the spring acting as a reminder of their cherished son.

Primroses in the wild grow in profusion and have over the centuries been heavily cropped and picked, sometimes for their beauty and perfume, but also to use in drinks, conserves and cosmetics. In medieval days primroses were popular in flowery meads, while the cowslip was much in demand for wines, meads, cordials, syrups, vinegars, pickles and conserves, cheese-making, cakes, tarts, creams and puddings.

The cowslip has had a host of names over the centuries, such as the 'double paigle', 'pena', 'pena hortensis', 'anglica omnium maxima' and 'serotina floribus plenis' – the serotina floribus plenis being 'the greatest English garden cowslip with double yellow flowers'. No doubt this refers to one of the double blooms featured in the Dutch *Florilegium Hortus Floridus*.

Some believe that the origin of the cowslip dates back to the time of St Peter, the flowers first growing from the ground where St Peter dropped his key to heaven (St Peter of course being the guardian to the gates of heaven). Its vernacular names included 'Keys of Heaven', 'Herb Peter', 'Peterwort' and 'Peterkin'. Similarly the French called the bloom *Clef de Saint Pierre*, the Germans *Schlusselblumen*. As with so many flowers, for every Christian 'origin' there is a pre-Christian one. In ancient Norse mythology Freya, ruler of fate, the stars and heavens, held the keys to the treasures in her possession. The Virgin Mary was also associated with the cowslip, which was called 'Our Lady's Keys' because Mary was credited as keeper of the keys to heaven.

From the 17th to 19th centuries the cowslip suffered from enormous culling, both physically and linguistically. Because the name 'cowslip' had originated from 'cow slop' or 'cow dung', the Victorians actually banned it, favouring instead the old name 'paigle'.

The *auricula* arrived in Britain in 1575, brought over by Flemish weavers. They settled in Ipswich, Norwich and Rochdale, and soon became fanatical in growing varieties such as 'Blue Velvet', 'Osborne Green' and 'Old Suffolk Bronze', all of which were very popular. This plant, which had originated in the Alps, spread to the gardens of the rich throughout the 16th century. Many hybrids were raised, collected and sought after, a few varieties 'escaping' to normal gardeners rather than show growers. During the British Civil War, Sir Thomas Hamner was said to have 40 varieties growing in his Welsh garden. During the 17th century, striped and double-striped blooms became popular, changing hands for vast sums of money. Many members of the European aristocracy sponsored and collected *auriculas* themselves. It appeared largely as a florists' flower in the 17th and 18th centuries, where it was considered a perfect example of nature under control. During the 18th century an edged bloom was produced, and it was during these years that the bloom developed as a result of constant breeding and experimentation. *Auricula* 'theatres' were created, with pots displayed on a 'stage' of slanted shelving, draped by curtains.

These brilliant hues are all distinct and clean,
no kindred tints, no blending streaks between,
this is no shaded, run off, pin-eyed thing:
The King of flowers, a flower for England's King.
GEORGE CRABBE

In England during the 19th century there existed many groups of *auricula* growers. Winning plants would be given grand names associated with the puissance of Victorian Britain, such as 'Glory of England', 'Privateer', 'Empress of Russia', 'George Lightbody' and 'Lancashire Hero'.

PLANT LORE AND HISTORY

For such small and delightful spring flowers, the plant lore and history surrounding the primrose and cowslip are vast. Yellow flowers have long been associated with superstitions about hens, ducks, geese and any other domestic laying fowl, and the primrose (*P. vulgaris*) is no exception. The number of primroses picked was said to influence the number of eggs that would hatch in a clutch (traditionally, 13 was said to be the size of a standard clutch). So if a bunch of primroses was brought into the house it was vital that no fewer than 13 blooms be brought in. Anything above 13 was ideal. Anything less in the bunch meant that that many eggs would not hatch. This same superstition was associated with daffodils.

Having just one primrose in the house was a grave error, meaning first of all that only one egg from a day's 'clutch' would hatch and also portending the death of one member of the family. If one bloom were accidentally brought into the house, then someone in the house would have to dance three times around the bloom to avert any ill luck. In the case of the primrose lucky 13 was the guide; quite often people would count the number of blooms growing in clumps in the garden to make sure there were 13 or more growing in each clump.

It was also considered bad luck to see one primrose flowering out of season. It was, however, good luck to pick a primrose with six leaves, as this would help affairs of the heart:

> *The Primrose, when with six leaves gotten grace*
> *Maids, as a true love in their bosom place.*

The primrose was also associated with safety – posies of the bloom would be left on doorsteps to encourage the fairies to bless the house and anyone living in it. Bunches of the blooms would be left in cowsheds as well, to convince the fairies not to steal the milk. Should you wish to see a fairy, you would eat the blooms. If this didn't work you might at least be granted the other benefit of the primrose – it was considered the key to secret treasure chests of the world.

The cowslip (*P. veris*), for its part, was very much associated with positive thought. Saxon women would make a love potion from cowslips, collecting them when the dew was still on the petals, soaking the blooms in rain water and leaving the mixture in the sun for a whole day. They would then take the potion and sprinkle it on the pillow of the person whose heart they wanted to melt – this person would be theirs within the month.

It was a bloom used widely by courting couples to improve the intensity of their love. Vast quantities of the bloom were sold in London streets to lovesick maids, but also as good-luck tokens. Blooms formed into garlands were also hung around cows' necks to increase their milk yield. Many folk believed tales that a plentiful field or pasture of cowslips meant that a nightingale lived nearby, as it was said that this bird would inhabit only places where the cowslip had chosen to grow.

The cowslip was indeed associated with good husbandry; in Aelfric's book or glossary the bloom was referred to as *cusloppe* and connected with good farming methods – perhaps because the bloom was believed to protect cattle. The Saxons spelled the bloom's name *Cuslippe*, meaning 'cow breath', thus linking the delicate perfume of the bloom with the rather sweet milky smell of a cow's breath. Other people felt that it was not cow's breath that the bloom's scent resembled, but baby's breath.

Some tales linked the cowslip with the Crucifixion:

> *Mark the five small spots of red,*
> *in the golden chalice shed*

The five small spots of red on the bloom were thought to represent Christ's blood. Still others felt that these five spots of red were rubies or fairies' favours.

Pervo-Tzuet was the Russian name for the cowslip, translated as 'the first flower of spring'. Children and young maids throughout Europe greeted the bloom with great joy, because for them much sport, fun and divination could now begin. In England masses of blooms were picked and constructed with twine into balls sometimes called Tissty Tossties,

Paigle balls or sometimes Titsy Totsy; the balls were then thrown as a game at the same time that a rhyme was chanted:

Titsy totsy cowslip ball, tell me true whom shall I be married to

– a series of suitors' names would then be called out, and the name on a girl's lips as the ball hit the ground would be destined for her. Sometimes suitors' professions would be guessed in the same manner, while children too young for courtship would use the game to try and work out what age they would grow to.

This game had many variations. Often the ball would be hung on a length of twine, with a young girl at each end. Again the rhyme would be chanted and the names called out, but this time the ball would be made to travel from one end of the twine to the other. The name spoken as the ball reached one end would be the suitor destined for the girl at that end.

Sometimes the ball would be strung between windows across a street. John Clare uses this image in his poem, *Cowslips*:

> *For they want some for tea and some for wine*
> *And some to make a 'Cuckaball',*
> *To throw across the garlands' silken line*
> *That reaches o'er the street from wall to wall.*

During May Day celebrations when the new period of Beltane began, yellow blooms were very important. Bunches of primroses and cowslips would be strewn across thresholds to welcome May Day, and carried by country folk to deter witches from spoiling any of the village festivities.

During the Elizabethan era the primrose (*P. vulgaris*) was plentiful in gardens. Gerard in his *Herbal* mentions the double primrose, a white one called 'Alba Plena' and another variety called 'Quaker's Bonnets'. The Elizabethans also had a popular variety, 'Jack in the Green', which was a single-flowering bloom with a Tudor-like ruff of greenery. A duplex form – that is, with one flower growing from another – was called 'Hose in Hose' after the Elizabethan style of wearing one stocking pulled up to the thigh and a second over it, turned down to the knees. The bloom was also a great inspiration to poets, who were inspired by its fragility and its charm (often associated with women). Chaucer in *The Miller's Tale* refers to a fair lady as a 'prime-robe', Spenser and Herrick also refer to the primrose in their works. Shakespeare uses the paleness of the bloom as a metaphor for the tenderness of spring.

Shakespeare also used the cowslip, more often in fact than he used the primrose, in his writings. Ariel, the fairy of his play *The Tempest*, was often to be found lying in a cowslip's bell (V.I.88):

> *Where the bee sucks, there suck I.*
> *In a cowslip's bell I lie.*
> *There I couch when owl's do cry.*
> *On the bat's back I do fly*
> *after summer merrily.*

And in *A Midsummer Night's Dream* (II.i.10), Shakespeare writes:

> *The cowslips tall her pensioners be;*
> *In their gold coats spots you see;*
> *Those be rubies, fairy favours,*
> *In those freckles live their savours.*
> *I must go seek some dewdrops here,*
> *And hang a pearl in every cowslip's ear.*

In 1883 Lady Randolph Churchill founded the Primrose League. Primarily the purpose of this organization was to promote Conservatism, but it was also to commemorate Disraeli, Prime Minister of Great Britain in 1868 and from 1874–80. The Primrose League was formed in 1883, and on Primrose Day, which commemorated Disraeli's death (the 19th of April) primroses would be worn in his honour. The bloom had been one of his favourites and was presented to him on every birthday by Queen Victoria. He would thank her wryly for giving him 'gold, not honours'.

In the language of flowers the primrose (*P. vulgaris*) symbolized eternal youth, birth, progeny, sweetness, tenderness and chaste behaviour. It also symbolized sadness and was the traditional bloom for planting on the graves of young children. This explains why many country church-yards in Britain contain vast numbers of the bloom, some of which are the palest pink.

In the language of flowers the cowslip (*P. veris*) symbolized winning grace and pensiveness, whereas the American cowslip (*Dodecatheon* spp.) symbolized 'you are my Divinity'.

A strange tale held that if cowslips were planted upside down they would become red or even turn into primroses, and if primroses were planted in cow dung they would turn pink. Quite often in its native habitat changes in the bloom did occur, due to cross-fertilization from garden varieties that became known as *polyanthus*.

Whilst the auricula (*P. auricula*) was in existence in certain parts of the world for quite some time, no folklore or superstitions have grown up about it, perhaps because of its exclusivity – it was the prerogative of growers and florists rather than the average person. In the Victorian language of flowers the *auricula* symbolized a painting – perhaps the perfection of the colours prompted this.

HEALTH AND WELL-BEING

Both the primrose and cowslip have been used in medicine throughout the ages, sometimes together, sometimes separately. The roots of both plants produce a high amount of saponins (chemicals with expectorant qualities) and salicylates (which have similar characteristics to aspirin).

The primrose (*P. vulgaris*) is certainly a flower to be called a 'kitchen and still room bloom' because it was used extensively in foods and healing. Primrose tea was a popular treatment, said to relieve insomnia and create good and pleasing dreams, and improve memory. Gerard in his *Herbal* suggests that any person who has fallen under a 'phrensie' should take primrose tea; he provides this delightful recipe:

> Take the leaves and floures of primrose, boile them a little in fountaine water, and in some Rose and Betony waters, adding thereto sugar, pepper, salt and butter, which being strained, to drink first and last.

Like Gerard, Culpeper used the primrose extensively, recommending a drachm and a half of dried root taken regularly in the autumn as an emetic. He also recommends making the primrose into a salve. These salves were often referred to as Spring Salves and were made of either the leaves, the blooms, or both:

> Of the leaves of primroses is made as fine a salve to heal wounds as any that I know; you shall be taught to make salves of any herb ... make this as you are taught and ... do not (you that have any ingenuity in you) see your poor neighbours go with wounded limbs when a half penny cost will heal them.

These salves were believed to cure skin blemishes or any other wound upon the skin. Quite often the leaves, as well as being put in salads for the relief of arthritis, were used to rub on the cheeks and create a reddening effect similar to rouge. The fresh leaves were also made into ointments to cure burns and ulcerated wounds, and as a flavouring for custard!

Thomas Tusser (1527–1580), an East Anglian farmer and author of *Five Hundred Points of Good Husbandrie* (1562), recommends the primrose as an important herb for the kitchen, to be used for food and healing in one go. In the *Family Herbal* of 1812, Sir John Hill recommends that the juice of the primrose should be inhaled on 'occasions of sneezing', adding that it 'is a good remedy against headaches'. In ancient healing the roots were believed to prevent paralysis and gout, and were used in medicines for coughs and bronchitis.

The cowslip (*P. veris*) also has a varied medical history. According to the Doctrine of Signatures the nodding heads of the bloom indicated that it should be used in healing for shaking and trembling problems with the head, and so over the course of history it has been used to cure shaking palsy, migraines and amnesia.

The Greeks called the bloom *paralysis* because they believed it strengthened the nerves and fortified the brain. They recommended that if it was taken with nutmeg each morning it would negate any internal diseases and problems; used externally and mixed with hog grease it would cure and heal wounds. The cowslip was also believed to be a form of sedative; a glass of cowslip wine taken one hour before bedtime would ensure excellent sleep. It could also be boiled in ale with lavender to produce a similar sleeping potion. Cowslip wine, like primrose wine, could be used as a beverage or as a healing agent; because of its bright yellow colour this wine was thought to cure jaundice (but also measles).

From medieval times through to the 19th century, cowslip wine was very popular, requiring thousands of gallons of 'pecks' (the nickname for cowslip flowers). A typical recipe for cowslip wine included loaf sugar (three pounds to every gallon of water), to be boiled for half an hour, any scum being removed. When cooled, a crust of toast spread with yeast would be added and the liquid allowed to ferment for 36 hours, then casked. Two lemons and the rind of a third, together with the rind and peel of Seville orange and a gallon of cowslip pecks would be added to every gallon of this liquid, which would then be stirred daily for a week. Finally, a pint of brandy would be added for every three gallons of the liquid, the cask closed and left to stand for six weeks. After this, the wine was considered ready for bottling.

Culpeper prescribed the cowslip as a treatment for spots and blemishes. The plant was also used to treat scalds and burns. An unguent made with cowslip juice and linseed oil was recommended by Gerard, again for the treatment of burns and marks upon the skin. A slightly less pleasant application for the plant was as a cure for fainting and dizzy spells – this treatment involved sniffing the juice of the plant through a quill!

As ancient as these healing remedies are, so too are the varied recipes for eating and preparing cowslips as food. They could be used in green salads and, brushed or dipped in gum Arabic and sprinkled with sugar, were used as crystallized flowers on puddings and other sweet desserts. The blooms could be candied or pickled into sweetmeats and preserves for the long winter months. Britain's King Charles II was particularly keen on cowslip tart; the recipe is found in *The Complete Court Book*, created for the King by his head cook, an Irishman named Patrick Lambe: A handful of cowslip flowers has to be pounded in a mortar and added to a pint of cream, then boiled, cooled and mixed with six beaten eggs. The mixture is then sprinkled with sugar and rose water, poured into a pastry case and baked.

Today both the root and the blooms of the cowslip and primrose are used for healing. The root can be used to treat coughs and bronchitis and other problems of the respiratory tract. It is a stimulant and adds warmth to the lungs. It makes an effective cough syrup.

The flowers do not contain the saponins or salicylates of the root, but have astringent qualities and bring about sweating, and will treat headaches and nasal problems.

Both the root and the flowers of the cowslip gain their perfume from anethol, an aniseed-like chemical. In homoeopathic medicine the cowslip can be used to cure anxiety, vertigo, headaches, neuralgia, eczema, palpitations, cystitis and stomach problems.

The handsome auricula featured in medicine for only a short length of time during the Tudor period, when it was used to cure headaches – it is possible, however, that this was only as a 'back up' to the cowslip and primrose.

OBSERVATIONS

These three species from such a beautiful genus have played an important role in history, healing and folklore, and yet the delicate blooms of the primrose and cowslip remain subject to the whims of modern farming methods. Expanding towns and business parks, out-of-town shopping complexes and other forms of 'progress' have robbed the countryside of valuable land. Thus many ancient cowslip meadows and primrose banks have been lost.

Auricula has occupied a slightly more favourable position because florists' societies and breeders have been keen to promote and protect the flower.

It is heartening that such an ancient bloom should still be used today to cure the same health problems as it did thousands of years ago. These lovely flowers, reminiscent of the sun, can grant relief to those who suffer during the winter months and pine for the return of the sun.

TULIP

Rembrandt variety

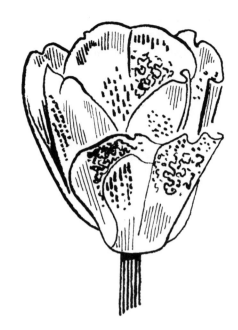

BOTANICAL

Tulips have been popular for over 300 years, providing a mass of colour in gardens.

The tulip belongs to the *Lilaceae* family, and is a genus (*Tulipa*) of over 100 species of bulbs. All the bulbs are either ovoid or round, usually producing one bloom on a stem, though in some cases three or more blooms. All the blooms have six petals, and their leaves are nearer to the ground than to the bloom.

The tulip was introduced from Turkey into European gardens in the form of previously hybridized or cultivated bulbs. Earlier, botanists and horticulturists regarded these introduced bulbs as true species, but these early introduced forms are now referred to as neo-tulipae.

Growers and horticulturists have over the ages spent much time in creating new varieties, while plant collectors continued to seek original forms from their native habitat, which covers Europe to the Himalayas and slightly beyond.

The word 'tulip' has evolved from the Persian word for 'turban' (*tulipant, tolibum* or *thoulyban*), which the bloom resembles in shape. Due to constant commercial experimentation, tulips fall easily to disease and pest problems. These diseases have created over the centuries the strange colour patternings which are often seen in some Dutch Masters' paintings, where can be seen tulips with vivid patches of odd broken colours. This 'breaking' can change a plain bloom to one with stripes and flames of colour; the infection that causes this is called 'the breaking virus' and is commonly thought to have been spread by aphids. It is important that blooms affected by this infection be kept away from other tulips.

The change from the naturalized tulip to the garden tulip that we are familiar with today has such long-ranging effects that no original 'father' remains of the garden tulip we know today, although there exist at least 100 natural species spreading through Europe, Western and Central Asia and Northern Africa. It is believed that so many have been collected from the wild that their original ancestor is now extinct.

Hybridized blooms are popular and include Cottage tulips such as 'Mrs John Scheepers', Rembrandt blooms such as 'May Blossom', Darwin tulips such as 'La Tulipe Noire', the Parrot variety as in 'Estella Rynveld', and Lily-flowered tulips such as 'Inimitable'.

Wild tulips include such species as *Tulipa maximoviczii, T. fosterana, T. whittallii, T. clusiana, T. kaufmanniana* and *T. kolpakowskiana.*

Some time ago all tulips were sectioned into divisions. These divisions firstly numbered 23 but were later reduced to 15. The Royal General Dutch Bulb Growers Society and the UK's Royal Horticultural Society were responsible for these divisions.

Division 1	Single early: cup-shaped single blooms
Division 2	Double early: double blooms
Division 3	Triumph: strong stemmed conical single blooms
Division 4	Darwin hybrids: large single blooms of differing shapes on strong stems
Division 5	Single late: single blooms, usually squarish or ovoid with pointed petals

Division 6   Lily-flowered: strong stemmed single blooms with
                pointed petals, narrow waists and sometimes reflexed tips
Division 7   Fringed: as for Division 6, but the petal tips are fringed
Division 8   Viridiflora: differing shapes of single blooms with petals
                showing green traits
Division 9   Rembrandt: old cultivars, similar to Division 6 but with
                'broken colours' creating feathered and striped viral
                patterns
Division 10   Parrot: single blooms, large and variable in shape, petals
                often twisted or fringed
Division 11   Double late or Peony-flowered: double, boldly shaped
                blooms
Division 12   Kaufmanniana hybrids: single bi-coloured blooms, often
                opening flat
Division 13   Fosterana hybrids: single blooms, often large, leaves
                striped or marked in a mottled fashion
Division 14   Greigii hybrids: as for Division 13 but with an undulating
                leaf edge
Division 15   Miscellaneous: all other hybrids, species and varieties

Vast quantities of tulip species are found growing wild in
central Asia, including:

T. DASYSTEMON   this has hairy stamens

T. DUBIA

T. FERGANICA

T. FOSTERANA

T. GREIGII   named after M G Greig, an
                   ardent supporter and patron of the
                   botanical world

T. HETEROPHYLLA

T. KOLPAKOWSKIANA

T. MAXIMOVICZII

T. PRAESTANS   meaning excellent, outstanding

T. TARDA

Single common garden variety

198

Other species are found in a larger and wider area than central Asia:

T. BIFLORA	from the Crimea, Caucasus, eastern Turkey, northern Iran to Afghanistan and Siberia, the two-flowered tulip
T. CLUSIANA	from Iran, named after the botanist Clusius
T. CRETICA	from the mountains of Crete
T. HUMILIS	from northern Iraq, northwestern Iran and eastern Turkey
T. JULIA	from western Iran and eastern Turkey
T. KAUFMANNIANA	from southeast Russia and central Asia, named after the Russian botanist Kaufmann
T. KURDICA	from northeast Iraq
T. ORPHANIDEA	from Greece, Crete, western Turkey and Bulgaria, the Orphanidean Tulip
T. SAXATILIS	from Crete
T. SOSNOWSKYI	from Armenia
T. SYLVESTRIS	from Italy, Sicily, Sardinia and northern Europe (including Holland and England), its name means 'wild and found in the woods'
T. SYSTOLA	from western Iran and northern Iraq
T. TURKESTANICA	from northwest China and central Asia

ORIGINS

Some people consider that the origins of the tulip lie in the short period 1634–37, a time known or referred to as the period of 'Tulipomania'. During that time tulip bulbs were exchanged for incredibly vast amounts of money and even goods. The bulb business was unpredictable, giving rise to the nickname 'The Wind Trade' for the practice of buying and selling bulbs. Their prices and popularity were as unpredictable as the weather.

One of the earliest tales about the tulip concerns a Dalmatian girl turned into a tulip so that she could escape the unwanted attentions of the Roman god Veruminus. One of the earliest illustrations of a tulip lies in a 12th-century bible, where the bloom is used in a typical floral illumination of a capital letter.

The tulip originated in Turkey and was exported to Vienna in 1554. The Turks grew and improved tulips right up to the end of the 18th century, long after Tulipomania had had its day. In fact, along with the carnation it was one of the first plants to be given a cultivar name. Because of the bloom's origins in Turkey it spread throughout Persia to the Holy Land, hence the theory that it is the true source of 'the Rose of Sharon' mentioned in the Bible's Song of Solomon (2:1). The word 'rose' comes from the Hebrew word meaning 'bulb'. There are three tulip species found in the Holy Land: *sharonensis*, a bright red bloom, *montana*, found in the mountains and *amplyophilla*, found in the desert areas near the Negu mountains.

Persian poets such as Hafiz and Omar Khayyam refer to the tulip a great deal in their writings, although again it is unclear whether they mean the wild or cultivated bloom. By the mid-16th century the Ottoman Empire had cultivated over 13,000 tulip varieties, and by the early 16th century Sultan Ahmed the 3rd had to set a fee on tulip bulbs to prevent a mania breaking out similar to the Tulipomania that occurred later in this century in the Netherlands.

Before this, in 1554, the Imperial Ambassador at the Sublime Porte was Ghiselm de Busbecq, during the time when Suleman the Magnificent was Sultan. Busbecq brought tulips through Adrianople to Constantinople and thence to Fuggers, the Augsburg Bankers, where the flowers were reared in their gardens. They were seen here by the Swiss botanist Conrad Gesner, who was fascinated by them; Linnaeus named the species *T. gesneriana* after him.

In 1559, the botanist Clusius also saw the bloom (sent to him by de Busbecq), and brought it to England. Clusius was also known as M Carolus Clusius. In 1582 the British geographer Richard Hakluyt said 'within these four years there have been brought to England from Vienna in Austria divers kinds of flowers ... Tulipes ... procured a little before from Constantinople by an excellent man called M Carolus Clusius'. Clusius, who at the time was professor of botany at the University of Leiden, grew tulips himself with great success, but this very success meant people wanted to buy his bulbs. As he had become very attached to them, he set a price far above anyone's bid – this strategy backfired, however, when the majority of his tulips were stolen and the seeds distributed.

While Tulipomania lasted only a short time, its intensity was extreme. In 1630, 5,000 Dutch florins and a coach and pair were exchanged for one bulb of the variety 'Semper Augustus'. A single bulb named 'Mariage de Ma Fille' was given as an entire marriage dowry, and an ebony sideboard inlaid and decorated with mirrors was exchanged for a yellow crown tulip. The highest price paid was for the variety 'Viceroy', which changed hands for:

> 2 loads of wheat, 4 rye, 4 fat oxen, 8 fat pigs, 12 sheep, 2 barrels of butter, 1,000 pounds of cheese, 2 hogsheads of wine, 4 barrels of special beer, a silver beaker, a suit and 1 bed.

There is also one story of a poor unfortunate who lost his entire fortune when he mistook his precious tulip bulbs for onions, and ate them!

Gambling played its part in the mania as well, with the colour of pending blooms wagered upon. Finally in 1637 any form of speculation on any part of the tulip plant or bulb was banned. This ban was spurred on by the 'market crash' of 1637, when the bottom fell out of tulip trading and the market was flooded with all forms of varieties.

The 17th-century species and hybrids included:

Tulipa clusiana
T. gesneriana
T. schrenkii
'Amiral de Constantinople'
'Columbus'
'Duc van Tol'
'Insurlinde'
'Lac van Rijn'
'Lutea Major'
'Perfecta'

'Paragon Everwijn'
'Zomerschoon'

In Turkey (where the tulip originated) the broken-coloured hybrids were not favoured, though they were preferred in England for quite some time. The tulips of the 16th and 17th centuries were very different from today's varieties. At that time there were three sorts of tulips: roses, bybloemens and bizarres. The roses had a white background with pink, crimson or scarlet patterns. Bybloemens also had a white background with purple/mauve and black patterns, whilst Bizarres had a yellow background with brown, maroon, red and orange patterns. The breeder tulip for all these was often plain, although occasionally one bulb would throw up a feathered or flaked bloom (that is, a plain flower with a contrasting colour); this bulb would then go on for its life producing this variety of bloom, the coloration of which depended upon a virus. Such a plant had to be kept away from all pure breeders.

As the 18th century neared, tulip shows began to be popular in British towns, and the Tulip Society was created. Interested amateurs produced yet more varieties.

European and British explorers and settlers brought tulip bulbs to the New World. Peter Stuyvesant, a Dutchman, grew tulips in New York (then called New Amsterdam), and nurseries sprang up throughout the colonies, where the bulbs were referred to as 'Tulip Roots'. President Thomas Jefferson used them in his garden, as did George Washington, and many grand gardens set in formal styles featured the tulip, which looked well in mass plantings.

PLANT LORE AND HISTORY

It is easy to think of the tulip as a typically European flower, due to its popularity and ubiquity, but its history lies far away, in Persia. Rich Ottoman Viziers used the tulip extensively, and the richest among them would make sure that the bloom took pride of place in their palaces and gardens. 'Lâlizari' was the nickname given to one Grand Vizier of the 18th century, a name that means 'Lover of Tulips' (the Turkish word for tulip being *Lâle*, also used as a girl's name) – it was said that his gardens hosted over 500,000 tulips.

Persian literature frequently makes reference to the bloom. For the Muslims it was a bloom that gave credence to the divinity of flowers, and in Ottoman temples and mosques tiles were illustrated with vast tulip gardens. In time the bloom became the flower of Islam, and mystics linked it to Allah. The tulip also came to symbolize the death of martyrs.

In the Victorian language of flowers the tulip meant fame, a red tulip the declaration of love and a variegated bloom beautiful eyes, while the symbolism of the yellow tulip was hopeless love.

As Tulipomania was evolving in Holland in the horticultural world, the art world was not left behind. As bulbs went for vast prices, so flower paintings became more valued. Artists such as Jan Breughel and Ambrosrus Bosschaert created grand flower paintings. As popular as these paintings were, however, their price remained carefully controlled, unlike that of the tulip bulbs themselves, as we have seen. By today's prices, one tulip bulb could command £150,000.

Very little folklore has survived regarding the tulip, which has almost since its origins been more highly prized by horticulturists and financiers than by ordinary folk. For many centuries it had no place in the garden of the common man; he was more likely to use it for healing. The bloom nevertheless had its place in the language. An 18th-century proverb warns that it never does to 'number the streaks of a tulip', a metaphor for paying too much attention to detail (a bit like missing the wood for the trees).

HEALTH AND WELL-BEING

There is little or nothing in ancient writings connecting the tulip with healing. Gerard's *Herbal* states, 'there hath not been anything set downe of the ancient or later Writers, as touching the Nature or Vertues of the Tulipa, but they are esteemed specially for the beauty of their Floures'.

Gerard does go on to point out that the roots can be carefully preserved and, mixed with sugar, eaten to provide a good and nourishing meal. In the 1600s, the famed botanist John Parkinson, author of *Paradisus Terrestris* (1629) and *Theatrum Botanicum* (1640, the largest herbal in English), considered it a medicinal plant and recommended mixing it with red wine to cure neck pain and strains.

OBSERVATIONS

Anyone seeing a tulip moving gently in a breeze has been touched by its simplicity and beauty. It has sometimes been an emblem of beauty or love. In *Travels in Persia* (1686), Sir John Chardin wrote:

> When a young man presents a tulip to his mistress he gives her to understand, by the general colour of the flower, that he is on fire with her beauty, and by the black base of it his heart is burnt to a coal.

It is man's sometimes reckless and greedy desire that led to Tulipomania, although this is no fault of the tulip's. The monetary value of the tulip was vast, yet can a price be put on its beauty?

We shall leave the final word to the poet Abraham Cowley (1618–67):

TULIPS

Let tulips trust not the warm vernal rain,
but dread the frosts and still their blooms restrain;
so when bright Phoebus smiles with kindly care
the moon not sullied by a lowering air,
early the beauteous race your wandering sea,
ranged in the beds, a numerous progeny:
the tulip with her painted charms display
through the mild air, and make the garden gay;
the tulip which with gaudy colours stained,

the name of beauty to her race has gained,
for whether she in scarlet does delight,
chequered and streaked with lines of glittering white,
or sprinkled o'er with purple charms our sight;
or widow-like beneath a sable veil,
her purest lawn does artfully conceal
or emulate, the varied agates' veins,
from every flower the beauty's prize obtained.

ROSE

Rosa canina, the dog rose

BOTANICAL

The rose belongs to the *Rosaceae* family, and the genus goes by the Latin name *Rosa*. Some feel that the origin of this name comes from the Celtic *rhod*, meaning 'red'. Roses grow in the northern hemisphere, where over 100 wild species grow. Other species are found further south, and some of the wild species have found their way into gardens. Today there are over 250 definite species as well as the many wild and natural plants.

Throughout civilization the rose has been grown, interbred and selected. For over 200 years gardeners have produced new varieties; before that time new varieties were the product of natural and accidental cross-pollination. Natural hybrids of existing wild roses have been found for over 2,000 years. These natural varieties from wild species were referred to as mutants or sports, and they provided the parentage for many gardener-reared varieties.

Rosa chinensis, the China Rose, was used from the late 1700s to produce new species. As China opened its doors to the West, so many plants were produced and seized upon by botanists and horticulturists. Four or five true species were used to produce the then-popular hybrids, from 1792 onwards *R. chinensis* became the breeding rose. When it was crossed with many of the European hybrids it produced what are now referred to as the Perpetuals – bushes producing larger blooms. Earlier roses were flatter with multiple petals and strong scents. The newly hybridized roses maintained the scent and multiple petals, but were more tulip-like in shape.

Up until the late 1700s the old European roses such as *R. gallica, R. alba, R. damascena* (the Damask Rose) and *R. moschata* (the Musk

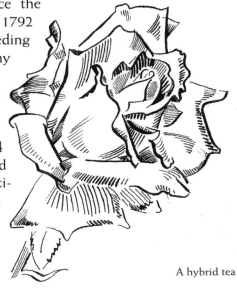

A hybrid tea

Rose) had been popular. Purposeful cross-pollination in the early 1800s produced new blooms, and France and England alike experimented, with 'Rose du Roi' being produced in 1861 as the first hybrid Perpetual. The Bourbon rose also appeared in the 1800s, a natural hybrid produced by crossing the China and Damask roses (*R. chinensis* and *damascena*). The modern hybrid tea rose became, from 1867 onwards, the favoured plant among rose-growers.

Roses, as with many large genus, have been divided into seven main groups and various subdivisions according to their individual appearance or characteristics:

SPECIES ROSES
Sometimes referred to as wild or species hybrids, some occur naturally and some are man-made. They are the 'parents' of modern roses. A single flower of five petals is produced. They are hardy and deciduous, some producing large red hips.

ROSA ALBA	The white rose of York, an ancient product of crossing *R. gallica* and *R. canina*
R. BANKSIAE	Banks's Rose, from central and western China
R. CALIFORNICA	from the western United States
R. CANINA	the Dog Rose, sometimes called the Briar Rose, found naturally in woods, hedgelands and scrub areas of Britain, native to Europe, northern Africa and western Asia. Varieties produce more than 50 differing flower forms.
R. CENTIFOLIA	the Cabbage or Provence Rose
R. CHINENSIS	the China Rose, sometimes referred to as *R. indica*, from central China
R. DAMASCENA	the Damask Rose from western Asia
R. EGLANTERIA	the Sweet Briar or Eglantine, sometimes called *R. rubiginosa*, from Europe and western Asia
R. FILIPES	from western China, a climber
R. GALLICA	the French Rose, from southern Europe and western Asia, the main native parent of old shrub roses – *officinalis* (a variety from *gallica*), sometimes called the Apothecary's Rose or the Rose of Lancaster; Versicolor/Rosamundi is a 'sport' (see below) from *officinalis*.
R. MOSCHATA	the Musk Rose
R. RUGOSA	the Japanese or Turkestan Rose, from eastern Asia
R. WILLMOTTIAE	from western China

OLD GARDEN ROSES

These deciduous plants are 'sports' or hybrids of species roses, and were produced before hybrid tea roses. These shrub roses are often divided into separate sections dependent on parentage. The list includes:

ALBAS	hardy plants with semi-double to double blooms. All originate from *Rosa alba*.
BOURBONS	descending from *R. odorata* and *R. damascena*, with heavily petalled blooms
DAMASKS	hardy shrubs from *R. damascena*, with highly perfumed blooms in clusters

GALLICAS	the largest of the old shrub rose groups and nearest to the wild *R. gallica*, with single blooms on dense branches
HYBRID PERPETUALS	popular with the Victorians and the forerunner of hybrid teas
HYBRID SWEET BRIARS	sometimes called Penzance Briars due to the fact that they were created by Lord Penzance in the late 1800s
MOSS ROSES	hardy shrubs closely related to Provence or Cabbage Roses, sports of *R. centifolia*, all blooms are double or semi-double
NOISETTES	climbing roses with clusters of double blooms
PORTLAND ROSES	early survivors from breeding with *R. chinensis*, with Damask-type blooms
PROVENCE OR CABBAGE ROSES	descendants of *R. centifolia* with double blooms and a strong fragrance
SCOTCH ROSES	used to produce shrub hybrids
TEA ROSES	shrubs and climbers producing semi- and double blooms

HYBRID TEA ROSES

These came after Hybrid Perpetuals, and are a well-loved popular variety. They are used as cut flowers as well as in the garden.

FLORIBUNDA ROSES

This is a modern group originating from Dwarf Polyanthus and early Hybrid Tea Roses. Blooms can be single, semi-double or double.

MODERN SHRUB ROSES

These are hybrids, all of which are deciduous and are derivatives of Species and Old Roses. Most are single or small clusters of blooms that are repeat flowering.

CLIMBERS AND RAMBLERS
Their growth habit is self-explanatory. Some have originated from native climbing plants while others are sports. (A sport or mutant is a plant that has been a result of a spontaneous action. It is always a deviation from the parent. It can also take the form of a shoot that is then propagated by cutting.)

MINIATURE ROSES
The true miniatures are from *R. chinensis minima*, found in Switzerland. Some climbing miniature varieties are available.

In Britain there are four native roses:

ROSA ARVENSIS	The Field Rose, a native shrub found in southern and central England, Wales and Ireland. It was introduced into Scotland. It is smaller than the Dog Rose.
R. CANINA	The Dog Rose, a native shrub found in hedgerows and woods which exists in over 50 forms, with blooms ranging from pink to white throughout the various forms.
R. PIMPINELLIFOLIA	The Burnet Rose, a native shrub found in coastal areas, rarely found inland. The stems carry dense prickles and creamy-to-white blooms.
R. RUBIGINOSA	The Sweet Briar or Eglantine, a native shrub found in hedgerows and scrub throughout Britain. The Sweet Briar is less common than other native roses. It has dark pink petals and small rounded leaves.

ORIGINS

The rose is the honour and beauty of floures,
The rose in the care and love of the Spring:
The Rose is the pleasure of th'heavenly Pow'r's.
The Boy of faire Venus, Cythera's Darling,

Doth wrap his head round with garlands of rose,
When to the dances of the Graces he goes.

ANACREON THIUS

This quotation from an ancient Greek poet tells us much about the importance of the rose. It has throughout history taken pride of place and has often been used in garlands, chaplets and crowns for royalty and other notables. Its bloom is the perfection of nature, the form of the petals and the shape of the head have perfect symmetry and harmony. It is the queen of flowers. As such it has represented or symbolized many important women throughout history. Ishtar, Astarte, Semiramis, Isis, Venus/Aphrodite and the Virgin Mary have all been worshipped and venerated with this bloom.

The rose has been cultivated for at least 5,000 years. In 2600 BC King Saragon of Egypt cultivated it, as borne out by excavations in Ur and Akkad. Further excavations at the palace of Knossos in Crete provide us with evidence that from about 2000 BC an Attar of Roses was created, possibly from the Damask rose. The great Chinese philosopher Confucius (551–479 BC) mentions roses growing in the Imperial Gardens at Peking. Babylonian paintings attest to the existence of the bloom in 540 BC. The ancient Persians called the rose *gul*, a word with links to both their word for 'flower' and for 'spirit' – this may well be the origin of the belief that the rose embodies the spirit and soul of a woman. Ancient folktales describe the belief that when the soul or spirit passes from the human world to the next world it can only ever be accompanied by a single red rose.

The Attar of Roses was very important in the ancient Eastern world. The Persians discovered rose oil. It was said that a princess at her wedding feast noticed that the mass of rose petals floating in a pool of water began to leave an oily residue as the heat of the sun made the water evaporate. This oily deposit was culled to make rose oil, which became very popular, as did rose water. Persia became a major producer and trader of both commodities, although as the popularity of rose oil and rose water spread, so countries such as India, Bulgaria and Turkey began to produce them. *R. damascena* was the rose most often used for the oil and the waters, though in Morocco *R. gallica* was the preferred bloom, and in France *R. centifolia*. Sixty thousand roses were required to produce just a single ounce of rose oil – a high price indeed, and yet the oil was so exquisite that roses were produced in profusion to meet demand.

Many of the myths surrounding the rose come from the East, as befits a flower with origins in this part of the world. It was believed that the first rays of the newly-born sun gave birth to the first rose which flowered in the great garden of Persia. Another Persian legend tells of a nightingale who sang in honour of the beauty and perfection of the rose, inhaling the heavy perfume of the bloom as it sang. The nightingale then fell to the ground, wounding itself; its blood spilled upon the white roses, turning them red – thus the origin of the red rose.

In many cultures there exists the belief that the first roses were all white, only becoming coloured as a result of a miracle, accident or blood-letting. In Greek myth the god Jupiter saw Venus bathing, and she was so embarrassed that she blushed and the white roses nearby turned red in sympathy. Another myth says that the rose became red because Venus cut her finger on one of its thorns while picking it, and still another that the rose became red when Cupid spilled red wine upon it. Numerous stories abound attributing the change in hue to the spilling of the blood (or in some instances, the sweat) of Christ, Venus and Adonis or Mohammed.

In Judeo-Christian mythology it was said that the red rose originated from the burned remains of a virgin martyr. Sir John Mandeville recounts the Hebrew tale of a young girl from Bethlehem called Zilla. A local leader who was rather undesirable and cruel was said to be besotted with her, however Zilla rejected his love and so the brute sought revenge, spreading stories about the young girl being in league with a demon. Zilla was duly arrested, tried and burned at the stake, but God stopped the flames. Buds formed upon the charred wood and both white and red roses sprang up from it. These were said to be the first roses since the time of Adam and Eve's banishment from the Garden of Eden to appear on the Earth.

One of the most endearing tales of the origin of the rose deals with Chloris, Greek Goddess of Flowers. One day she found a forlorn and weakened nymph; wishing to restore him to health, she asked the three Graces for help. The Graces granted him the gifts of joy, brightness and charm. Chloris did not stop there, but appealed to the other gods for assistance. Aphrodite gave him beauty, Dionysus nectar and Zephyr (the West Wind) blew the clouds away, allowing the sun to shine on him. Miraculously, he was thus transformed into a beautiful bloom, which Chloris christened the rose.

Statues of Aphrodite would be covered in rose garlands. It was said that the Earth created the rose in homage to Aphrodite, and that the red rose sprang from her blood, shed as she ran towards the dying Adonis and cut her feet upon the thorns, changing them from white to red.

Many women have been associated with the rose, its sensuousness and tenacity reflecting, to some minds, female characteristics. The Bishop Noyon of France (475–545 AD) established the tradition of offering a reward of 20 gold coins and a crown of roses to the most virtuous maid in the area. In Christian iconography the Virgin Mary became referred to as the Mystic Rose.

The Egyptians, Greeks and Romans had thriving rose-growing industries, producing cargoes of blooms to be shipped across the seas. Visitors entering Greek and Roman cities would be greeted with rose petals, thrown at their chariot wheels as they arrived. Wreaths and garlands were made in profusion. The Egyptians had a long tradition of decorating tombs and other sacred buildings with roses, the Christian equivalent being to decorate the tombs and memorials of martyrs with the blooms.

Children were left bequests of rose bushes in their parents' wills, to ensure they would continue to plant them. Roman soldiers also put by part of their wages to buy rose bushes to be planted upon their return from arduous and dangerous battle campaigns. The production of rose bushes was such that at one stage they were scarce along the banks of the Nile, where once they had been profuse.

At one stage, however, Christian writers banned references to the rose because of its associations with Greek and Roman 'debauchery'. The voluptuousness of the bloom and its links with the Greeks and Romans lost it favour despite the fact that it had been a popular flower, it became an unnatural luxury. These early Christian scribes were aware that the rose had been the flower of Aphrodite, Goddess of Love. During the period 150–211, Clement of Alexandria dictated that the rose should not be used in crowns for Christian ceremonies, and so the rose saw a partial eclipse in Rome.

For other early Christians the rose was regarded as a heavenly spirit of the highest degree and various mystics and wise men associated the bloom with Jesus Christ.

In 428 BC Herodes is credited with finding a bloom with 60 petals – not to be outdone, in 286 BC Theophrastus found a *R. canina* with 100 petals.

By 6 AD, rose gardens had been established, first of all in France. The rose garden reached a height of popularity in Europe just after *R. chinensis* was introduced to the continent in the 18th century. In China roses were planted, grown and sold in pots, so they were easily transported by plant-hunters and travellers alike. Roof gardens were created in medieval manors, fortresses and monasteries, as places of quiet meditation – the higher it grew, the closer the bloom was to its 'home' in paradise.

The physical appearance of these 18th-century roses was vastly different from the roses we know today. *Rosa provincialis*, often called The Provins Rose, is possibly the oldest cultivated rose, brought back to Provins in Champagne by Thibaut the 4th on his return from the Crusades in about 1239/40. It was then brought to England by Edmund of Lancaster in 1279, for his personal use. It thus became the Red Rose of the Lancastrians (the white rose of the Yorkists was of course *R. alba*). The so-called Tudor Rose was created by crossing the roses of York and Lancaster, to celebrate the marriage of Henry VII (a Lancastrian) and Elizabeth of York. In the 1st century AD Pliny christened the British Isles as 'Albion' because of the predominance of white roses.

During the 15th century the Rosicrucians took the bloom as their symbol. Dante wrote of the bloom being the centre of the spheres of the universe:

Brighter than a million suns, immaculate, inaccessible, vast, fiery, and with magnificence, and surrounding God as if with a million veils.

Indeed, the rose was viewed by many as the mystic centre of the universe; many philosophers and alchemists saw it as being an important central point of learning. The spiritual and mystical symbolism of the rose was seized upon in the 17th century by the alchemists, who quite often in illustrations to their work would use two roses – one red and one white – to symbolize the red king and white queen.

The Dog Rose (*R. canina*) was so-named as a derogatory term, because it was so widespread or 'common'. In the Middle Ages the root of *R. canina* was used to cure rabies – this is the plant's only link with dogs.

The Eglantine Rose (*R. eglanteria*) was named from the medieval Latin word *aculentus*, meaning 'thorny' – the stems certainly live up to this name.

The Bourbon Rose (a descendant of *R. odorata* and *R. damascena*) was named after the island in the Indian Ocean (now known as Reunion Island) on which it was found, in 1822. A sport of the Gallica Rose called 'Rosamundi' was said to have been named after Rosamund Clifford, a much-beloved mistress of King Henry II.

R. indica, the Chinese Rose, was sometimes referred to as 'Hume's Blush Tea-scented China', as it was taken from Canton by Sir Abraham Hume in about 1809 to England's Chelsea and Colvilles nursery, where it was grown. The Napoleonic Wars were then in progress, but this did not stop samples of this variety being sent to Empress Josephine's gardens at Mal Maison. The Empress Josephine was a keen rose collector and had a vast assortment of different varieties. She encouraged the breeding of these varieties, and employed the artist Pierre-Joseph Redoute to paint her prize blooms. His works of art were published in the book *Les Roses* between 1817 and 1824.

The 19th century saw the rose become an extremely popular flower for decorative purposes. New varieties with more frequent and longer flowering periods were being introduced. In the 1660s there had been 21 listed rose varieties; by 1836 there were many, many more:

ALBAS	25 varieties
BOURBONS	38 varieties
CHINA ROSES	70 varieties

CLIMBERS	53 varieties
DAMASKS	19 varieties
GALLICAS	99 varieties
HYBRID CHINA ROSES	89 varieties
MINI CHINA ROSES	16 varieties
MOSS ROSES	24 varieties
MUSKS	10 varieties
NOISETTES	66 varieties
PERPETUALS	50 varieties
PROVENCE/CABBAGE ROSES	25 varieties
OTHER SPECIES AND UNCLASSIFIED VARIETIES	54

PLANT LORE AND HISTORY

Damask

What's in a name?
That which we call a rose,
By any other name
Would smell as sweet.
WILLIAM SHAKESPEARE, *ROMEO
AND JULIET* II.II.43

The perfume of the rose is known and recognized world-wide; as a genus the rose belongs to Group 9 of the scent groups. This Group includes all plants whose essential oil is *geraniol*, the same essential oil found in the rose-scented geranium. It is *geraniol* that is used so much in the rose oil industry.

It may well have been the rose's beautiful perfume as well as its fascinating shape that drew the Reverend Reynolds Hole to the plant in the Victorian era. This cleric became fascinated with the plant and recognized its importance in history and folklore. He spent all his spare time campaigning for greater recognition of the rose – together with his wife he created rose shows, wrote books and, in 1876, formed the Rose Society.

Among the stories in folklore which intrigued the Reverend were many linked with divination. Over the centuries the rose and its leaves have been used to foretell the future and to find out the names and even the physical characteristics of one's future marriage partner. It was said that if a woman entered a garden backwards, without speaking, on midsummer's eve she would begin the process of finding her future husband. She had to pick a rose and wrap it in clean paper without looking at it, then leave this wrapped safely until Christmas Day. On unwrapping it she would find it fresh as the day it was picked, and would put it into the bodice of her dress, as close to her bosom as possible. It was said that the man intended as her husband would be the one to take it out. Unfortunately no mention is made of how long she has to go around with this rose in her bodice! Some versions, however, hold that her future husband would arrive next morning, but warns that if when she opens it on Christmas Day it has faded, her intended is unfaithful:

> The moss rose that, at fall of dew,
> 'ere eve its duskier curtain drew,
> was freshly gathered from its stem,
> she values as the ruby gem;
> and, guarded from the piercing air,
> with all an anxious lover's care,
> she bids it, for her shepherd's sake,
> awake the new year's frolic wake:
> when faded in its altered hue,
> she reads — the rustic is untrue!
> but if its leaves the crimson paint,
> her sickening hopes no longer faint;
> the rose upon her bosom worn,
> she meets him at the peak of morn.

The rose could also foretell the strength of one's bond with another: If two lovers snapped a rose stem, the louder the snap, the stronger their love. Another tale concerns the scattering of petals and, again, midsummer's eve: To find the man of her dreams, a woman had only to scatter red rose petals while reciting this rhyme:

217

*Rose petal, rose petal, rose petal I strew,
he that will love me come to me soon.*

Other superstitions surrounding the rose included the belief that dreaming of a white rose bush meant that there would be a death in the nearest neighbouring house. Dreaming of roses set out in a garden was a much better prospect, however, foretelling success. It was also considered vital that any plans or hopes for the future be discussed out of 'earshot' of any rose bushes. Doing so would blight these plans.

Traditionally it is held that roses start to fade on the Feast of St Mary Magdelene (July 20th). Today with so many long-lasting modern varieties this is of course no longer the case.

Anyone picking a rose and holding it would do so with great care because it was said that if any petals fell it was a bad omen, perhaps signalling the person's death. It was also considered a great misfortune to throw a rose into a grave; in spite of this, roses and rose petals have long been thrown on the graves of the dead. Rose bushes blooming beyond their natural season were said to foretell a death, as it was believed the roses were 'waiting' to be picked to be thrown upon a grave.

Roses were a vital part of any housewife's Still Room and kitchen. In 1594 Sir Hugh Platt wrote *Delights for Ladies,* and nearly a century later Mary Doggett produced a book of rose recipes – both were Still Room books filled with information about how to pick roses, dry them and preserve their beauty and perfume for the long and miserable winter months ahead.

The beauty, form and mystery of roses have long been associated with women. It was said that Cleopatra used roses to lure Mark Anthony, and that she seduced him in a room filled to knee height with rose petals. The Italian version of the Cinderella story is called 'Rosina' or 'little rose', while the Hungarian variation on this theme has a golden rose, rather than a glass slipper, as the means through which the Prince identifies his love.

In ancient times rose water and rose oil were used to purify unholy or disease-ridden places; it was also employed in the art of wooing. It was said that when a woman received a rose from a man, a powerful magic would be exchanged, with origins so primitive and ancient that they transcended understanding.

In medieval times knights would refer to their women as 'roses', as the perfection, tenderness and softness of the rose was seen to personify woman. Christianity associates the rose with honour and virtue, and so by extension with the Virgin Mary. In the 12th century a monk called Josbert was said to recite five psalms in honour of the Blessed Virgin Mary, the first letters of these psalms spelling out the name Maria. It was said that on one occasion he failed to turn up to prayer; his fellow brethren later found him dead in his cell, with a rose in his mouth, two in his ears and two in his eyes – the five roses symbolic of his piety.

Vishnu was said to have made his bride Lakshmi from 108 large rose petals and 1,008 smaller ones. In some countries of the world the vernacular name for the rose is the same as the word for woman. This is true in Malaya, where, as elsewhere around the globe, the rose is seen as the perfect gift for one's love. Chaucer is reputed to have said that a woman in love smells as delicious as the Eglantine Rose.

There is one rose from the alba group called 'Maiden's Blush', in French called 'Cuisse de Nymphe', or nymph's thigh – quite a different thing entirely from a maiden's blush!

The Latin phrase *sub rosa* ('under the rose') comes to us from mythology. Cupid gave Hippocrates a rose to ensure the latter's discretion after Hippocrates had discovered Cupid and Venus meeting secretly. From about 479 BC the white rose in particular has been associated with silence. In Greek and Roman society any people wishing to discuss something and ensure its confidentiality would meet beneath hanging white roses, and many establishments where confidences were exchanged had ceilings adorned with bunches of roses. From about 1526, confessionals used the white rose as a symbol for confidentiality and silence, and the robes of early church officials included a rosette made of ribbon, worn in the centre of their hat bands. This indicated their religious vow of confidentiality.

The ribbon rosette went on to be used in prize-givings, with different colours denoting different levels of honour. And so the rose became associated with power. Throughout the Middle Ages nobility were known to have rose chaplets, and it also became a bloom common in Middle Age heraldry, symbolizing authority and prestige.

A red rose with a crown, short stalks and 12 leaves became the badge of England and the official bloom to celebrate the patron saint of England, St George, whose feast day is April 23rd. A further link with power is evident in the phrase 'a bed of roses' – at the height of the Greek and Roman Empires, rich women slept on mattresses stuffed with rose petals. Several centuries later in Britain, 'rose rents' were put in force for people wishing to build bridges or buildings in public areas. Payment was demanded in the form of an annual rent of a rose.

In Elizabethan times, it seems that the fashion was to have a rose stuck in your ear! As bizarre as this sounds, certain Elizabethans chose to be painted in such a manner, the rose in the ear indicating their blue blood and birthright.

Religions throughout the world have been associated with the rose. The Christian Church has long revered the bloom, despite its suspect links with pre-Christian celebrations. The seven-petalled bloom was said to symbolize the seven degrees of absolute perfection, while the eight-petalled bloom represented regeneration or resurrection and rebirth. The Damask rose was sometimes referred to as the holy rose, symbolizing God's love for the world and it was this bloom that often appeared in religious paintings and was grown in the rose gardens of religious establishments. Many religious communities grew roses to be used in the production of rose oil. A by-product would be a large quantity of crushed rose petals – these would be rolled and then squeezed into small beads with a hole in the centre; when dried they were threaded upon a twine. The necklaces made in this way were used as an aid to prayer, and given the name Rosaries.

The five-petalled wild rose was said to symbolize Christ on earth, the five petals creating the shape of Christ outspread on the Crucifix. The flower was Christ's divine love, the thorns his suffering.

Many Christian saints have the rose as their emblem. Saint Dorothea, patron of gardeners and an early Christian martyr, is often depicted with a rose branch in her hand, a wreath of the blooms around her head and roses and fruit growing at her side. Saint Valentine has a more tenuous link with the bloom, in spite of the fact that more roses are exchanged on his feast day than on any other. St Alban was an early English martyr, his day falls on the 22nd of June and traditionally on the Sunday nearest that day red roses are put upon his shrine, red being the traditional colour for saints' days.

The Christian Church dedicates the fourth Sunday in Lent to the rose. On this day the Pope blesses the Golden Rose, dips it in balsam, sprinkles it with holy water and then burns it. In certain Catholic ceremonies, rose petals are strewn along the path of high-ranking clergy or processions of penitents carrying statues. Many churches have their 'rose windows', the circular shape echoing that of the rose. The Unitarian Church uses the rose in their equivalent of a Baptism, the naming ceremony, as for them the rose symbolizes beauty and, in its thorns, the sense that life is never perfect and much is learned through hardship.

During the Victorian era the rose was a popular button-hole flower, often seen as accentuating male sexual prowess and force. The red rose has long been associated with 'profane' love and sexual power. The white rose, for its part, has symbolized virginity.

In the Victorian language of flowers many, many roses are listed:

RED ROSES	passion, love
THE CABBAGE ROSE	ambassador of love
CHINA ROSE	new beauty
DAMASK ROSE	brilliant complexion
'MAIDEN'S BLUSH' ROSE	if you love me you will find it out
MUSK ROSE	capricious beauty
DOG ROSE	pleasure and pain
WHITE ROSES, FRESH	I am worthy of you; also, generally, pure love, virginity, love for mankind
WHITE ROSES, WITHERED	transient impressions
YELLOW ROSE	jealousy
MOSS ROSE	confession of Love

HEALTH AND WELL-BEING

Needless to say the rose takes a prominent place in healing. Interestingly enough for a flower that is associated so much with sexuality and love, it was discovered that some parts of the rose could be used to cure male impotence, and other parts to help a women's reproductive system function and flow fully. Right up to the 1930s the rose was listed in the *British Pharmacopoeia*, and was a popular and well-recommended medicine. A tincture made from the Apothecary's Rose (*R. gallica* var *officinalis*) would be used for sore throats.

In ancient Greece and Rome, the rose was used to cure many medical problems and disorders. In AD 77 Pliny quoted over 32 conditions that could be cured with the rose, including sea sickness, toothache, insomnia and any problems to do with the eyes, ears, mouth or stomach. He also stated that the rose could be used to purify the mind.

In the 3rd century AD *R. laevigata* was used extensively in healing. Brought to the US by the East India Company in 1759, it became known as the Cherokee Rose and was adopted by the state of Georgia as its state flower. *Jin Ying Zi* was the name given by Traditional Chinese Medicine to the hips of the Cherokee Rose. These were used to balance out urinary dysfunction.

During the Ming Dynasty (1368–1544), the Japanese rose, *R. rugosa*, was used in healing. The flowers of this species were the prime source of rose water, first distilled by Avicenna, the Persian physician, in the 1st century AD. *R. rugosa* has thus long been known as a tonic which can stimulate the digestive system and increase the appetite. In Chinese medicine the flowers are referred to as *Mei Gui Hua*.

During the Middle Ages, monastic gardens would certainly have included *R. gallica officinalis*, the Apothecary's Rose, used to cure colds, gastric problems, depression, eye and skin complaints and sore throats. It was said that if a barren woman swallowed a petal of this rose, she would become fertile.

The majority of well-known old roses are still used in healing. The Dog Rose (*R. canina*) provides blooms, hips and leaves for medicine. It was believed that a poultice made from the leaves of the Dog Rose bush could be used to cure dog bites. From the 10th century onwards rose water from this variety was used to cure skin sores, dryness and other skin irritations, while a syrup made from the plant was used to treat colds and flu. Even the galls on the plant (a gall is a growth formed on a rose bush or tree by the hostile action of insects, fungus or other forms of bacteria) were used, as a diuretic and (if worn around the neck) to cure toothache and insomnia. Over the centuries the Dog Rose has been used to create tonics, laxatives and astringents. During the Second World War in Great Britain, the hips from the Dog Rose were used a source of vitamin C.

R. damascena is a nervine and has often been used to lift depression and acute anxiety. It was a popular tonic taken by people who needed to instil more love and meaning within their lives. *R. centifolia*, on the other hand, was reputed to be a powerful aphrodisiac if taken in the form of a rose oil.

R. rubiginosa (The Sweet Briar or Eglantine Rose) was used as an astringent and a good and successful cure for diarrhoea and colic. More recently it has been used in the treatment of burns, scars and wrinkles.

As would be expected, the rose genus has also provided the ingredients of many folk remedies. Rose oil has always been considered the least toxic of all natural oils and the most antiseptic. It is said to soothe nerves and lift depression and to tone various body systems. In 1550, one Anthony Askham used a potion of honey and red roses to comfort and cleanse. He noted that if the potion was used through the winter and summer it would cure melancholy and cholera.

The red rose has often been likened to a woman's rosy cheeks, and dark red rose petals used to ensure a woman maintained a good rosy glow. The darker the red, the more it was likened to blood, and any woman wanting rosy cheeks was advised to spill spots of her own blood under a rose bush, to ensure rosy cheeks in the months to come. Because of the colour of the dark red rose it was also believed to be a charm against haemorrhaging. During the 18th century Englishwomen would wear bags of roses round their necks to ensure continued and bountiful fertility.

Culpeper was a great believer in the rose, and quotes that the Damask Rose (*R. damascena*) is under the aegis of Venus and could be used as a purgative for children and a digestive aid to adults if made into a syrup. He recommended the red rose for fluxes (the 'morbid discharge of blood, excrement', etc.) and to strengthen the stomach to prevent vomiting and coughing. A conserve of red rosebuds could be given to consumptive patients. The white rose, he suggests, being under the dominion of the moon, could be used to cool, dry and bind together.

The rose has also been used in food preparation. Gerard recommends distilled rose water to lift the heart and spirits, but also as an ingredient in cakes, sauces and junkets. Rosebuds can be pickled and used in salads, or rendered down to use in jams, sweetmeats and conserves. The buds (or individual petals) can also be crystallized.

Throughout the centuries rose hips have been used in jellies to accompany meats and tarts, while the Tudors used them in an invigorating mead. The simple rosehip tea, still popular today, provides ample amounts of vitamin C.

OBSERVATIONS

THE ROSE
Oh rose, thou flower of flowers, thou fragrant
    wonder,
Who shall describe thee in thy ruddy prime,
Thy perfect fullness in the summer time,
When the pale leaves blushingly part asunder
And show the warm red heart lies glowing under?
Thou shouldst bloom surely in some sunny clime,
Untouched by blights and chilly winter's rime,
Where lightnings never flash nor peals the thunder.
And yet in happier spheres they cannot need thee
So much as we do with our weight of woe;
Perhaps they would not tend, perhaps not heed thee,
And thou wouldst lonely and neglected grow;
And He who is all wise, He hath decreed thee
To gladden earth and cheer all hearts below.
CHRISTINA ROSSETTI

A flower to gladden the heart, to heighten the senses and to bring beauty to our sometimes harsh reality – the rose symbolizes the balance of pleasure and pain. The beauty of the bloom sometimes takes our breath away, making us forget the thorns beneath it.

The tale of Sleeping Beauty conceals a fierce morality. It was often believed that the bush that grew up around her castle was the Eglantine rose, a barrier symbolic of the hurdles we find between this life and the next, which must be experienced before we can reach our heart's desire. Quite often in life the battle to the goal teaches us much along the way.

During the 19th century the writer Oscar Wilde retold an ancient tale based on Persian myth:

A young student studied hard every day. As he studied he became aware of the presence of a very beautiful woman, who became his sweetheart. The student, madly in love with the woman, wished her to dance for him, but she replied that she would do so only if he could give her a red rose. The student at first felt this would be an easy task, until he discovered that no red roses could be found in the garden.

The student had at an earlier time been kind to a nightingale, who in return wished to repay the student's kindness, and so said that she would find a red rose among the many other coloured roses in the garden. However, when the nightingale led the student to a red rose bush, they found that the blooms had been frosted. The nightingale pleaded with the bush for one red rose. The bush replied that there was only one way a red rose could be taken – that the rose had to be 'built out of music by moonlight and stained with your own heart's blood'. The rose bush then added that the nightingale had to sing all night long to it, whilst leaning against its thorns. This would mean the end of the bird's life. The nightingale nevertheless made the decision to help the student create the red rose, because 'love is better than life'. The nightingale sang, sacrificing her life to create the rose for the student. The student picked the rose and eagerly gave it to his sweetheart, who tossed the bloom away, saying that she preferred jewels to flowers.

One moral of this story would be, in the words of the nightingale herself, that love is better than life – that is, that it is better to die for love than to live without love. It is also, of course, a tale of selfishness and vanity: the student does not appreciate the nightingale's sacrifice, while his beloved is vain and foolish. This tale of the red rose and its power forces us to consider again the balance of life, and the necessity of experiencing both the good and the bad to find your own true measure and your own inner worth and strength.

CONCLUSION

Go, little book, and speak my heart,
by every precious flower;
say that it loves, and will love on,
while it has the vital power!

ANON

So what are flowers, and what have we learned from reading about them?

Flowers are universal acceptance and love, they are givers to all aspects of life, and they fill our lives from the cradle to the grave. When we are born our parents are often given gifts of flowers. As children we run through meadows picking buttercups and daisies – if we are mischievous, we may well take prize blooms from others' gardens in our innocent desire to collect these wonderful creations. Our youth may well bring us gifts of roses from loved ones, bridal bouquets and romantic dinners where flowers form the centrepiece. As we mature gardens become more therapeutic, places of pleasure to stroll and chat in, places to sit and reflect. Milestone birthdays are celebrated with bunches of florists' blooms and gifts of small flowers from our grandchildren and even great-grandchildren. And then we face our end, a return to the earth, to the womb of nature. And our death is marked with more flowers, to observe and honour our passing.

Flowers are observers of our lives here on earth and they reflect ourselves – they too have their springs, summers, autumns and winters.

Of all the plants upon this planet, at least 80 per cent are flowering. The magic of the flower is its transience and ephemeral beauty; their benefits are long-lasting, however, as they give us so much beauty, healing and well-being.

Each era of the world's history has close associations with plants. Climate, political intrigues and the differing peoples of the world all seem to make a difference as to the usage or misuage of plants and flowers.

Tales exist in all cultures about important women who are linked with the moon, flowers, trees and the earth and all its natural beings. Rhiannon in Welsh tales, Cybele, Diana, Juno and Hecate are all powerful female figures in history. Flora, Freya and Blodeuedd are all women who occur in the myths and tales of this earth; they are fruitful and feminine forms of great importance, the essence of which is sometimes believed to be found in the May Queen venerated on May 1st in folklore customs. Interestingly enough the first florists of the Greek and Roman civilizations were women, and flowers held a prominent place in everyday Greek and Roman life.

Throughout history flowers have been overused to some extent. During the Victorian era plant hunters were paid astronomical amounts of money to go to the far-flung ends of the earth to bring back prized blooms, tearing them from their native habitat. To some extent the Victorians did not honour the earthly values, as their language of flowers limited blooms to a particular meaning, denying their true variety, meanings and origins.

In nature flowers are so simple, but art and science have intervened. Sometimes this intervention has been benevolent, as in the discovery that many plants have medicinal uses. The oldest Herbal is *De Materia Medica* written by Pedanios Dioscorides of Anazarba, who was a Greek doctor employed by the Roman army. This Herbal was written in AD 512; for over 1,000 years it was the authoritative book on the medicinal use of plants in healing. By the time of the Elizabethans, *Florilegia* came into the frame. These were books full of drawings of flowers intended for study purposes. Then towards the beginning of the 18th century, plant-hunting and cultivation became the focus. *Flora* were books listing and illustrating native species of particular areas, of great scientific interest but serving no purpose so far as healing or ancient folklore were concerned. Nature began to be organized. Linnaeus classified plants, renaming many species so that they lost their old meanings and associations. Money began to be an important criteria. 'Designer' flowers began to take pride of place, based only on their value as a marketable commodity, all historical references, healing powers and associated traditions and folklore lost. Flowers were not now to heal with, but to emphasize their owners' position, wealth and power. The people who worked with flowers became known as florists and horticulturists, while herbalists fell into the background. New varieties were created just for the rich. Gardens were no longer places to grow food and herbs; the physic gardens that originated in the 1540s turned into private gardens for enjoyment and relaxation.

Today flowers are used by designers to create magnificent master-pieces of ingenuity. Floral design has become an art form with, sadly, scant regard for the importance and the mysticism behind each individual bloom. People have forgotten the importance of heeding Lord Tennyson's words:

> *Little flower – but if I could understand*
> *what you are, root and all, and all in all,*
> *I should know what God is and what man is.*

Flowers are more than just show-pieces. They are a form of therapy. They heal the soul with their perfume, their texture, their shape and their colour. And some have the power to heal the body as well. Yet their power can go unnoticed, even as they keep life going – along with the trees and other plants, they are the very essence of our being.

And what of flower wisdom? As we learn about the world of flowers, we learn about ourselves. Flowers are mirrors of ourselves and of a world that has gone by, a world that understood flowers' importance and their place in society. Flowers speak to us of a world that has many more facets than we ourselves have the power to understand. Their very presence on this planet is a joy and yet a mystery. Their link with the world that came before tells us that flowers possess the most vital of life-forces, a spirit and an energy that is receptive to much more than we can ever understand. Flowers touch the world of imagination and the world of reality.

There is now a battle being fought beneath our feet and in front of our very eyes. Land is disappearing in the course of 'progress'. New cities, shopping centres and leisure areas are being built to make the aesthetic environment of man more pleasing and his leisure time more profitable, yet those who try to point out that this sort of progress is not necessarily the way forward are flattened, their views regarded as anti-social and reactionary. Sadly those who appreciate the importance of nature and all that it implies are in the minority.

We all have the ability to access ourselves to the wonder of flowers, to their importance and their spirit and power, but sadly very few choose this path. Modern life does not give us time to stand and capture the ancient magic of the natural world. And although we have many advantages in this day and age, they bring with them certain disadvantages, as we move faster and faster away from the life-force of the earth. We are losing our senses, our ancient instincts. It is only after the moment has gone that we realize what we have lost. Flowers and all the natural world symbolize hope, a hope that life will be colourful, fruitful and pleasurable, full of positive and pleasant events and experiences. If paradise was a garden, then maybe we have to make our own paradise here upon this earth, our own private paradise so that we can ensure that the wisdom of the flowers is treasured and continues for the souls that will follow us and will need them as much as we do. As Ralph Waldo Emerson wrote

Though we travel the world over to find the beautiful, we must carry it with us, or find it not.

So much has been written about flowers in history, yet much lies unwritten, much lies unrecorded, and we must ensure that there will be much more yet to come. For the wisdom of the flowers is ours to find.

Katherine Charlotte Mary Kear, April 2000

INDEX